Discovering John

Discovering John

Essays by John Ashton

John Ashton

EDITED BY

Christopher Rowland and Catrin H. Williams

CASCADE *Books* · Eugene, Oregon

DISCOVERING JOHN
Essays by John Ashton

Cascade Books
An Imprint of Wipf and Stock Publishers
199 W. 8th Ave., Suite 3
Eugene, OR 97401

www.wipfandstock.com

PAPERBACK ISBN: 978-1-5326-3601-1
HARDCOVER ISBN: 978-1-5326-3603-5
EBOOK ISBN: 978-1-5326-3602-8

Cataloging-in-Publication data:

Names: Ashton, John, author. | Rowland, Christopher, editor | Williams, Catrin H., editor.

Title: Discovering John : essays by John Ashton / by John Ashton; edited by Christopher Rowland and Catrin H. Williams.

Description: Eugene, OR : Cascade Books, 2020 | Includes bibliographical references and index.

Identifiers: ISBN 978-1-5326-3601-1 (paperback) | ISBN 978-1-5326-3603-5 (hardcover) | ISBN 978-1-5326-3602-8 (ebook)

Subjects: LCSH: Bible. John—Criticism, interpretation, etc.

Classification: LCC BS2615.52 .A84 2020 (print) | LCC BS2615.52 (ebook)

Manufactured in the U.S.A.   APRIL 20, 2020

Contents

Introduction

John Ashton often spoke to his close friends about the reinvigoration or new lease of life he experienced after his retirement in 1996, when he began working again on the Gospel of John. During this time—over the course of nearly twenty years—he wrote a number of essays on a range of Johannine topics; he also worked on a second edition of his landmark study, *Understanding the Fourth Gospel* (2007), and, two years before his death in 2016, he published his final book entitled *The Gospel of John and Christian Origins*. John also discussed with both of us his plans to publish in a single collection many of the essays he wrote during this period, as he had done with other essays several years earlier in *Studying John: Approaches to the Fourth Gospel* (1994).

In the last months of his life John asked Chris whether he would be his literary executor. He was especially concerned that the collection of essays that he had by now submitted for publication, but without success, should reach a wider public. The collection that he contemplated, which is substantially what is contained in this volume but with the addition of the tribute given at John's funeral, is distinctive. It was John's intention to preface his later essays on the Gospel of John with an autobiographical essay setting the evolution of his interest in and understanding of the Gospel of John in the context of his life. It is a remarkable testimony not only to the origins of John's thinking but it helps us to "discover John" and the long journey that led to him to teaching at the University of Oxford—a journey that continued many years after his retirement. His preface to what is essentially an exegetical volume is a welcome offering, as it offers significant glimpses of the ways in which life and intellectual engagement overlap and interact with each other.

Of particular interest is what John wrote about what he learned from French biblical scholars and the ways in which those ideas inform his writing, from *Understanding the Fourth Gospel* to *The Gospel of John and Christian Origins*. But, as Chris wrote in a foreword to the second edition of *Understanding the Fourth Gospel*, the climax of John Ashton's book is his exposition of the theme of revelation, identified by Bultmann as the key idea of John's Gospel yet here located within a thoroughly Jewish milieu. John Ashton's original, and substantial, exposition of John's Gospel in the light of the apocalyptic tradition is masterful in its economy and profound in its insight. The phrase he used to describe John, "an apocalypse in reverse," is so fitting in its allusiveness and also its applicability to a narrative of the revelation of God in human form. The Apocalypse and the Gospel of John are very different texts. Both texts, however, offer in narrative and visionary form words which seek to bring about an epistemological and ethical transformation in readers/hearers in preparation for the eschatological meeting "face to face" either in the New Jerusalem (Rev 22:4) or in heaven with the exalted Christ (John 17:24).

Nearly a decade ago the two of us had the privilege of gathering together a group of scholars to explore several aspects of "Intimations of Apocalyptic," as had been deftly articulated by John in his *Understanding the Fourth Gospel*. On this occasion we are grateful to Cascade Books for working with us to bring John Ashton's final collection of essays to publication, thus fulfilling the end-of-journey wishes of this truly remarkable Johannine scholar and dear friend.

We gratefully acknowledge the permission granted by the following publishers to reproduce John's essays, which are placed in a largely thematic rather than strictly chronological order: Mohr Siebeck; Cambridge University Press; Westminster John Knox Press; SBL Press; and Bloomsbury Publishing.

— "Really a Prologue?" In *The Prologue of the Gospel of John: Its Literary, Theological, and Philosophical Contexts. Papers Read at the Colloquium Ioanneum 2013*, edited by Jan G. van der Watt et al., 27–44. WUNT 359. Tübingen: Mohr Siebeck, 2016.

— "John and the Johannine Literature: The Woman at the Well." In *The Cambridge Companion to Biblical Interpretation*, edited by John Barton, 259–75. Cambridge: Cambridge University Press, 1998.

— "Riddles and Mysteries: The Way, the Truth, and the Life." In *Jesus in Johannine Tradition*, edited by Robert T. Fortna and Tom Thatcher, 333–42. Louisville: Westminster John Knox Press, 2001.

— "'Mystery' in the Dead Sea Scrolls and the Fourth Gospel." In *John, Qumran, and the Dead Sea Scrolls: Sixty Years of Discovery and Debate*, edited by Mary L. Coloe and Tom Thatcher, 53–68. Early Judaism and Its Literature 32. Atlanta: Society of Biblical Literature, 2011.

— "The Johannine Son of Man: A New Proposal." *NTS* 57 (2011) 508–29.

— "Reflections on a Footnote." In *Engaging with C. H. Dodd on the Gospel of John: Sixty Years of Tradition and Interpretation*, edited by Tom Thatcher and Catrin H. Williams, 203–15. Cambridge: Cambridge University Press, 2013.

— "Browning on Feuerbach and Renan." In *Sense and Sensitivity: Essays on Reading the Bible in Memory of Robert Carroll*, edited by Alastair G. Hunter and Phillip R. Davies, 374–94. JSOTSup 348. Sheffield: Sheffield Academic Press, 2002.

Christopher Rowland and Catrin H. Williams

18 March 2019

1

Discovering the Gospel of John

A Fifty-Year Journey of Exploration

La rage de vouloir conclure est une des manies les plus funestes et les plus
stériles qui appartiennent à l'humanité.

—GUSTAVE FLAUBERT

I: The Early Years (1964–70)

THE FOLLOWING ESSAY IS autobiographical only insofar as events of my
own life have a bearing upon my study of the Gospel of John and the conclusions I have reached concerning its nature and significance. Looking
back now, in my eighties, I note that if the Gospel was composed during
the 80s of the first century CE (as it may well have been) its author, if he
too was in his eighties, could have been recollecting events that had occurred fifty years previously.

One main purpose of this essay is to summarize my own thinking as
it has developed over the years on a variety of topics related to the Gospel
of John. On some issues it has scarcely changed, and my comments on
these have come to seem wearisomely repetitive even to myself. But it
should nevertheless be possible, even so, to single out certain key points
or especially telling arguments. On other topics an initial insight has been
reinforced from time to time by ideas that seem to emerge from different
areas of thought, and I want to describe these as carefully as possible. On

one or two topics I have increased my knowledge, occasionally because new evidence, mostly from Qumran, has come to light, more often because my own reading has broadened. On others, looking at the evidence and the arguments afresh, I have become more critical and more cautious. On one particular topic my ideas have been in a constant state of flux, so that even now, so many years later, I cannot be sure that they will not change again.

If I were to discuss all these topics one after the other without interruption, the biographical element would be lost. Instead, I propose to intersperse them between snippets of biography. The order in which I treat them may seem random; but I will take them up as closely as I can to the point in my own story in which I began to give each careful attention.

Except for a few passages of personal reminiscence I leave aside those aspects of my life (several of them very important to me) that have nothing to do with scholarship. The biographical sections of the essay will be placed between summaries of my work on John, especially *Understanding the Fourth Gospel*.[1] But some of what I consider to be the most important ideas occurred outside the context of the composition of that book, and I will consider each of these in full, starting from the moment in which I began to give them serious consideration.

Understanding the Fourth Gospel, begun in 1980, took nearly ten years to write and has fourteen chapters. Four of these, written between 1980 and 1981, will be summarized in the fourth section of this essay, five more in the sixth, and the remaining five in the seventh. Shorter contributions, notably the articles contained in my collection *Studying John: Approaches to the Fourth Gospel* and the chapters added to the second edition of *Understanding the Fourth Gospel*, will be summarized at appropriate points. I will end with a résumé of the main conclusions of my recently published book, *The Gospel of John and Christian Origins*. Not all readers of this essay, of course, will wish or need to be reminded of the substance of my work on the Gospel: warned in advance, they are invited to skip paragraphs that do not interest them. But a main part of my purpose here is to repeat in shortened form the work of the last fifty years. I will also note briefly issues on which I have changed my mind.

In 1949, at the age of eighteen, I joined the Society of Jesus (usually known as the Jesuits, or the Jesuit Order), accustomed to providing a very full education for those of its members thought likely to benefit from it.

---

1. Ashton, *Understanding the Fourth Gospel*, 1st edition, 1991; 2nd edition, 2007.

After three years studying scholastic philosophy, plus a fourth learning how to be a schoolteacher, I was sent to Campion Hall, Oxford (to this day still run by the Jesuits) in order to pursue the four-year course of classical literature, philosophy, and history known as Greats. Both the scholastic philosophy I had been taught earlier and the mixture of modern (analytic) and classical philosophy (Plato and Aristotle) that I learned in Oxford have influenced my thinking ever since. But the journey I am about to describe had not yet begun, for it was not until 1964—the third year out of the four that I spent studying theology at a Jesuit seminary in France—that I was stimulated to think seriously about the Gospel of John.

The so-called Séminaire des Missions, high up on the Montée de Fourvière, was housed in a large building (now a musical conservatory) that overlooks the old quarter of the city of Lyons; and it was there, listening to the lectures of Xavier Léon-Dufour, that it first dawned on me that there is more to John's Gospel than meets the eye. The insight that most impressed me (as, looking back, I came to realize) was based on an article he had written many years earlier on the story of the cleansing of the temple in John 2 and Jesus's subsequent prophecy of his own death and resurrection. Dufour had stressed the distinction implicit in this story between the partial comprehension of those listening to Jesus's words *within the story* and the fuller understanding to be expected of *readers of the Gospel* (who, of course, already knew the outcome).[2] He summed up this insight in the phrase *deux temps de l'intelligence*. The evangelist was not just telling a story, the story of Jesus's life and death, but underlining its significance for his readers.

After acknowledging Léon-Dufour's insight that "les deux temps de l'intelligence" is one of the organizing principles of the Fourth Gospel, I went on to link it with the theory of "the two-level drama" outlined in J. Louis Martyn's little book, *History and Theology in the Fourth Gospel* (1968). Although Martyn nowhere refers to the temple episode that interested Léon-Dufour, what he calls "the two-level drama" represents an alternative way of highlighting the evangelist's steady insistence on the essential difference between how Jesus's words and deeds were understood before his death and how they were understood after. Both scholars, I believe, had laid their hands on an essential key to the comprehension of the Gospel, and it is illuminating to consider their approaches, however

2. Léon-Dufour, "Le signe du Temple selon saint Jean," 155–75.

different they may be, together. Yet here I want to consider certain weaknesses in each of them that I detected only later.

In the first place, for Léon-Dufour the fundamental distinction was between what he called *the time of Jesus's hearers*, and *the time of John's readers*. True, he refers occasionally to the *milieu historique* in which John was written, but the thrust of his article was to distinguish between Jesus's actual hearers (both Jews and disciples) and the Christian readers of the Gospel (among whom he obviously numbers himself). Léon-Dufour was certainly correct to point to the gap between the universal misunderstanding that preceded Jesus's death and resurrection and the illumination that succeeded it. But he fails to observe that the most important lesson of this episode concerns the disciples' failure to grasp Jesus's meaning when he prophesied his own resurrection whilst standing on the temple site, measured against their full understanding later. Martyn's contribution at this point was to stress that the disciples play a double part in the Gospel: on the story level as those whom Jesus called to follow him, and on the higher level of understanding as those for whom the evangelist is actually writing his Gospel. (Martyn's name for these is *the Johannine community*, an important topic which I will treat below.) It follows that some knowledge of their situation at the time of the Gospel's composition is required if we are to gain a proper understanding of it.

In the second place, Léon-Dufour specifically rejects the suggestion that in speaking of the destruction and resurrection of "this temple" to refer to his own body, Jesus was employing the same kind of riddling expression found later in the Gospel to mean one thing to his interlocutors within the story and quite another to those reading it in the light of the resurrection. Yet this is the one riddle in John whose significance is clearly spelt out: "he spoke of the temple of his body" (2:21); "when therefore he was raised from the dead, his disciples remembered that he had said this; and they remembered the scripture and the word which Jesus had spoken" (2:22). Moreover, although Léon-Dufour begins his article by quoting two relevant passages in the Farewell Discourse that highlight this gap, he does not see that in the first of these (14:25), the phrase "bring to your remembrance all that I have said to you" must surely be linked with the observation concerning the memory of the disciples that concludes the temple episode (2:22). In citing this and other passages from the Farewell Discourse towards the end of his book, Martyn, though without insisting upon the reminding role of the Paraclete, succeeds in showing his true significance as an interpretative key to the Gospel. Indeed, in stressing that Jesus returns to continue his work on earth in the person of the Paraclete, he is able to conclude that "*it is precisely the Paraclete who creates the two-level drama*"[3]—and also, evidently, the two times of understanding illustrated most clearly in the temple episode.

Whilst reflecting on the related insights of these two scholars, I managed to collate, as it were, the passages in which the evangelist himself informs his readers of the key principle that guided his composition. Taken together, the two times—or levels—of understanding, the device of riddling terms or expressions, the passages concerning the Paraclete (especially in his role of teaching or reminding the disciples after Jesus's death), show a clear and profound conception of how Jesus continued to be present in the life of the Johannine community.

The notion of the Johannine Community, strongly urged not only by Martyn but, soon afterwards, by Raymond Brown and Wayne Meeks, has been challenged headlong by Richard Bauckham,[4] and although it was much further in my journey through John that I found myself having to meet this challenge, I will anticipate it here because of its connection with another key point of disagreement between scholars: whether the Gospel was written at a stretch from start to finish, or whether its composition was interrupted from time to time, so as to justify the idea that it went through several stages before completion. So there are two additional ideas to be discussed here: first the question of a hearing or reading audience, and secondly the question of whether or not the Gospel should be read as an integrated whole.

I was equally impressed by the lectures of Paul Lamarche, who also taught at Fourvière. Among other things he convinced me that the opening verses of John's Gospel were not about creation, as is widely assumed, but about God's plan for humankind, and that this was the true meaning of the Greek Logos, always misleadingly translated as *Word*. He defended this view in an article published in 1964,[5] the year I heard the lectures on which the article was based. Long afterwards I was to uphold Lamarche's view in the first of many articles of my own on the Fourth Gospel; and in my most recent book—fifty years after listening to Lamarche—I have backed it up with additional arguments.[6]

3. Martyn, *History and Theology*, 1st edition, 140; emphasis in the original.

4. Bauckham, *Gospel for All Christians*.

5. Lamarche, "Le Prologue de Jean," 529–32.

6. Ashton, *Gospel of John and Christian Origins*.

The journey begun at Fourvière has been interrupted, more than once, for years at a time. If I accept my friends' assurances that some account of this journey (which I now think of, tentatively, as approaching its end) is likely to be of interest to others, this is largely because of my own awareness of its many twists and turns. Of the many great scholars who have influenced my own thinking most have stuck undeviatingly to their own path. Here I need only mention the greatest of them all, Rudolf Bultmann, who outlined his ideas on the Gospel very clearly in two brilliant articles in the 1920s[7] and incorporated them later in his incomparable commentary, first published in 1941.[8] Although he subsequently acknowledged the importance of the Dead Sea Scrolls, still hidden at the time, and first disclosed to an astonished world in 1947, they did not cause him to alter his considered opinion that the primary influence upon the Fourth Evangelist was the writings of the obscure sect known as the Mandaeans.

Ordained priest in 1964, along with about twenty others, in the Cathédrale de Saint Jean in Lyons, I stayed a further year at Fourvière before returning to England. In the following summer (1966) I visited Jerusalem, where I spent some months at an Ulpan (a crash course mainly designed for Jewish immigrants) in a vain attempt to learn modern Hebrew. It was the last summer in which it was possible to pass through the Mandelbaum Gate into the eastern part of the city, still at that time part of Jordan, as were the town of Jericho, the caves of Qumran (which I visited then for the first and only time), and the Dead Sea. After a mere fortnight in Jordan and a brief holiday in Greece with a friend, who was himself about to embark on a course of study at the École Biblique in Jerusalem, I went to Rome for further study at the Pontificio Istituto Biblico, located in the Piazza della Pilotta, at the very heart of the city. This school of biblical learning, like the Gregorian University opposite, is run by the Jesuits. A short distance away is the bustling Piazza Venezia, with the vast Vittorio Emmanuele monument at its center (which, every time I passed, made me think of an old-fashioned Underwood typewriter).

The teachers of the Biblical Institute lectured twice a week in hour-long sessions (the sole form of instruction except for those studying for

---

7. Bultmann, "Der religionsgeschichtliche Hintergrund des Prologs zum Johannesevangeliums," 3–26; Bultmann, "Die Bedeutung," 100–46. See also Bultmann, "Die Eschatologie des Johannesevangeliums," 4–22.

8. Bultmann, *Das Evangelium des Johannes*, translated as *The Gospel of John: A Commentary* (1971).

doctorates). I remember two series in particular, first those of Norbert Lohfink, struggling with some success to convey his very considerable insights on the book of Deuteronomy in German-accented Latin, and secondly the exciting tale of the avatars of one of the oldest complete Greek manuscripts of the Bible, the Codex Vaticanus (Codex B), a tale told in flawless Latin by Carlo Martini, Rector of the Institute in my second year there and later to become Cardinal Archbishop of Milan.[9] I had less appreciation of Ignace de la Potterie's fifty-or-so lectures on John 9 and 10, which formed his entire course on the Fourth Gospel during the two years I spent in Rome. During much of the time I should have been attending these lectures I was poring over Rudolf Bultmann's magisterial commentary, *Das Johannesevangelium*, not yet translated into English. I have my copy still, with highlights and pencilled annotations on almost every page. Yet I have to admit that I owe to de la Potterie (though not from those lectures) a detailed and convincing refutation of Bultmann's view of the meaning of the word *truth* in the Gospel;[10] and when, many years later, I was searching for articles to put in a collection of essays on the Gospel called *The Interpretation of John*,[11] I was pleased to find in a short article of his, written in Italian,[12] a distillation of a much longer piece entitled "L'arrière-fond du thème johannique de vérité dans saint Jean."[13] Yet this disagreement scarcely diminished my great admiration for Bultmann's work.

After I had left Rome and returned to England two more years passed before I began to think seriously again about the Gospel of John. The first of these years was spent in rural Oxfordshire, in a grand Victorian mansion called Heythrop College, where the Jesuit scholastics, who had been there for many years attending lectures on philosophy and theology, had recently been joined by members of the secular clergy

9. Martini was one of the editors of each of the four editions of *The Greek New Testament* (1966–83) published jointly by the Deutsche Bibelgesellschaft and the United Bible Societies.

10. The Johannine usage of the word ἀλήθεια, says Bultmann, is based on the meaning of "divine reality" that it has in Hellenism, "with the connotation that this divine reality reveals itself" (*Gospel of John*, 74n2; see too 53n1, 434). Similarly Dodd: "the use of the term ἀλήθεια in this gospel rests upon common Hellenistic usage in which it hovers between the meanings of 'reality,' or 'the ultimately real,' and 'knowledge of the real'" (*Interpretation of the Fourth Gospel*, 177).

11. Ashton, *Interpretation of John*.

12. de la Potterie, "De sensu vocis 'emet in Vetere Testamento," 336–54.

13. de la Potterie, "L'arrière-fond du thème johannique," 277–94.

and other religious orders studying for the priesthood. Yet I scarcely had time to settle down to teaching there, before it was decided that I should begin doctoral studies in the University of Cambridge. Although one of the great biblical scholars of the twentieth century, Ernst Bammel, was a fellow of St Edmund's House, my new home, the real expertise of the scholar appointed to supervise my work, Geoffrey Lampe, was in Patristics. My year in Cambridge was a lazy one, in which I learned little, and I was relieved rather than disappointed when the unexpected departure of John Bligh from the Jesuit order (a scholar still remembered for his brilliant, if eccentric, commentary on Paul's letter to the Galatians) led to a request that I should abandon my doctoral studies in order to take up a post at the new Heythrop College, which, retaining its name, had just been transferred to London (Cavendish Square), with an affiliation to the university. This was in 1970; and I taught there for eight years.

Since the primary purpose of this essay is to record notable moments in my study of John, I should perhaps add that whilst at Cambridge I had developed an interest in the poetry of Wallace Stevens. One of Stevens's favorite themes is the role of imagination in transforming the world around us (the real, all that is) into poetry; and this idea, I had observed, is analogous to the emphasis placed in John's Gospel on the transformative power of faith. Whilst in Cambridge I regularly attended the weekly meetings of the D Society, presided over by Professor Donald MacKinnon in his rooms in Corpus Christi College; and when he invited me to read a paper at one of these meetings, the subject I chose was "Wallace Stevens and the Gospel of John." Twenty years later, composing my book on John, I was able to compress the argument of this paper into less than a page:

> [Stevens] was aware that "to be at the end of fact is not to be at the beginning of imagination but to be at the end of both." Equally, however, to attempt to extract the fact from the poem is to be at the end of both fact and imagination—at the end of poetry. The absence of any fruitful interaction between the imagination and reality was for him a grim and intolerable poverty of spirit.
>
> Stevens saw imagination as having virtually ousted faith from its throne: imagination was now what he called "the reigning prince." In his work the transforming power of the imagination has seized and irradiated reality in such a way as to make it irrecoverable in the form in which the poet found it. Similarly the visionary glow of the Johannine prophet has welded tradition and belief into the shining affirmation of the finished

Gospel. If the result appears new and extraordinary this is because his religious genius impelled him to disclose more and
more of what he called "the truth," that is to say, the revelation
of Jesus. What he saw and what he inherited are now contained
in the book he wrote.[14]

It remains to add that faith (by which I mean the full acceptance
of the revelation of Jesus) is always accompanied in John's Gospel by an
awareness of the presence of the Risen Jesus independent of actual sight.
Faith is neither a belief in a series of propositions that can be outlined in
a catechism, nor, as Bultmann held, a positive response to an existential
challenge held out to all mankind. Rather, like the imagination for Stevens, it functions as an *illumination* of the truth—in John's case the truth
that is Jesus—which otherwise remains veiled in darkness.

II: Teaching at Heythrop (1970–78)

When I took up my demanding new post in London, the Gospel of John
was one of many New Testament writings that I had to teach from the
outset, and I realized straightaway that I had much to catch up on. First
on my book list was the outstanding commentary of Raymond Brown.
(The second volume had only just been published, but the first had appeared in 1966, shortly after my arrival in Rome.) Three features above
all of this large and remarkably comprehensive work left a lasting impression on me: 1) Brown's rapid assimilation of the Dead Sea Scrolls, which
had enabled him to argue convincingly that, whether or not John had any
direct debt to these, it is in relation to Second Temple Judaism, not Gnosticism (Bultmann) or the Hellenistic Hermetica (Dodd) that his Gospel
must be understood.[15] 2) Brown realized that the Gospel as we have it is
the product of several years' work, and suggested that it went through at
least five stages. Most strikingly he thought of the second stage as "lasting

14. Ashton, *Understanding the Fourth Gospel*, 1st edition, 434. Quotations are
taken, respectively, from Stevens, *Opus Posthumous*, 175; and Stevens, *Necessary Angel*,
171.

15. Bultmann could scarcely be blamed for his ignorance, because his commentary
had been published in 1941, six years before the discovery of the Scrolls; but Dodd's
Interpretation came out six years later, in 1953, a long time after other scholars—notably Kuhn, "Die in Palästina gefundenen hebräischen Texte," 192–211—had begun to
make tentative comparisons between the Scrolls and the Fourth Gospel.

perhaps several decades."[16] He also followed Bultmann in attributing a considerable amount of the finished Gospel to a final redactor.[17] These were bold ideas, some of them perhaps too bold; but Brown put forward strong reasons for advancing a full theory of composition, and I have never changed the view I formed on first reading his book that he was working along the right lines. The hypothesis that the Gospel underwent a number of changes before reaching its final form is shared by a number of scholars (including, I was surprised to learn much later, Martin Hengel).[18] *As one of the crucial points of disagreement, even today, between interpreters of the Fourth Gospel, the importance of this hypothesis cannot be over-emphasized.* 3) A third point of interest was Brown's introduction of the idea of a Johannine community,[19] and a fourth his suggestion that the Gospel was written as a response to the expulsion of Christians from the synagogue occasioned by the publication of the Twelfth Benediction of the *Shemoneh Esreh*.[20]

The bulk of Brown's commentary, like most biblical commentaries, is designed to be consulted rather than to be read, and I cannot claim to have gone through it all with the same assiduity with which I perused the long introduction (over a hundred pages). My attention was soon drawn, however, to a much shorter and very different book that also made a profound impression on me, which has already been mentioned, namely, J. Louis Martyn's *History and Theology in the Fourth Gospel*,[21] a book with which I have been engaging off and on ever since. Martyn was by no means the first scholar to point to the conflict between Jews and Christians as the most likely historical background of the composition

---

16. Brown, *Gospel According to John*, xxxiv.

17. Brown, *Gospel According to John*, xxxvi–xxxix.

18. Hengel, *Johannine Question*, 94–95. "The different 'strata,' breaks, supposed 'contradictions,' inconsistencies and explanatory glosses," he says, "are best explained as a result of this slow growth of the Gospel." The much larger German version of this book was published in 1993, under the title of *Die johanneische Frage*; see especially page 264.

19. He was to pursue this idea some ten years after the completion of his commentary in a new book: Brown, *Community of the Beloved Disciple*.

20. Brown, *Gospel According to John*, lxxiv–lxxv.

21. Martyn, *History and Theology*, 1st edition, New York: Harper & Row, 1968; 2nd edition, revised and enlarged, Nashville: Abingdon, 1979; 3rd edition (unaltered), Louisville: Westminster John Knox, 2003. Thus Martyn's book was published two years before the second volume of Brown's commentary.

of John's Gospel.[22] Where he advanced upon all his predecessors was in his specificity. "Our first task," he says, "is to say something as specific as possible about the actual circumstances in which John wrote his Gospel. How are we to picture daily life in John's church? Have elements of its peculiar daily experiences left their stamp on the Gospel penned by one of its members?"[23] I now think that he was over-ambitious in hoping to learn anything significant from the Gospel about the daily life and the daily experiences of the community. Nevertheless, his careful study of John 9 and 5 under the heading "A Synagogue-Church Drama" (a study taking up over half the book) made exciting reading for someone already fascinated by what Adolf Harnack, as far back as the end of the nineteenth century, had called "the greatest puzzle [or riddle, *Rätsel*] presented by the earliest history of Christianity," namely the origin of John's Gospel.[24] By quoting this dictum on the preceding page Martyn showed his awareness that he was taking it up and formulating it afresh—for what interested him was not just the early history of Christianity in general, but the moment at which a group of practicing Jews, having just been expelled from the synagogue, became from that moment no longer Jews in the religious sense of the word, but Christians.

There is one other scholar whose name I must mention in the same context: Barnabas Lindars—first for his stimulating little book, *Behind the Fourth Gospel* (1971), and secondly for his admirable commentary, *The Gospel of John* (1972), both published in time for me to be able to study them alongside the work of Brown and Martyn. All three had worked along similar lines, and all three were especially interested in the composition of the Gospel and the nature of the Johannine community.

22. This had been already anticipated by Karl Gottlieb Bretschneider (*Probabilia de evangelii et epistularum Joannis apostoli*) and Moritz von Aberle ("Über den Zweck des Johannesevangelium") in the nineteenth century, the latter being the first to propose that the row between the Christians of the Gospel and their Jewish contemporaries focused on what is called the *Birkath ha-Minim*—the revised Twelfth Blessing (really a curse) of the Eighteen Blessings of the *Shemoneh Esreh*. At the beginning of the twentieth century, William Wrede argued robustly that the Gospel was "a writing born out of and written for conflict (*Kampf*)" (*Charakter und Tendenz des Johannesevangelium*, 40); and similar suggestions were later put forward by Bultmann, Barrett, Brown, and many others. On this question, see my discussion in pages 85–95 of *The Gospel of John and Christian Origins*; and for a list of less well-known scholars who have also related the term ἀποσυνάγωγος (John 16:2) to the *Birkath ha-Minim*, see D. Moody Smith's essay, "Contribution of J. Louis Martyn," 292 n14.

23. Martyn, *History and Theology*, 1st edition, xviii.

24. Harnack, *Lehrbuch der Dogmengeschichte*, 1:108.

Martyn and Lindars (Brown less so) were also interested in a rather different problem posed by the Gospel: the problem of sources. Martyn was inclined to favor a rather speculative solution to one aspect of this problem, set out by his doctoral student Robert Fortna in a book with a self-explanatory title, *The Gospel of Signs: A Reconstruction of the Narrative Source Underlying the Fourth Gospel.*[25] This book was partly based on the exceedingly complex solution proposed by Bultmann that had governed the equally complex structure of his commentary, where he attempted to set out the Gospel in the order in which he thought—and argued—it had been composed.[26] This is not the place to enter into this question in any detail (though it should be added that Lindars was much more skeptical than Martyn).[27] I mention it here because it is one of the problems that I dealt with in my lectures at Heythrop during the years in which I taught there.

One thing that strikes me now about this period of my life is my lack of scholarly ambition. At the age of thirty-seven Raymond Brown had published a collection of *New Testament Essays* and had almost completed his massive two-volume commentary, while C. K. Barrett too (born in 1917) had published the first edition of his large commentary on John at the age of thirty-eight. Apart from a number of articles written for the Jesuit periodical *The Way* (of which I was an assistant editor), my single scholarly publication (at the age of forty-two) was a book of less than a hundred pages entitled *Why Were the Gospels Written?* (1973). Yet on reading this little book now, more than forty years after it was published, I am gratified to think that were it still in print I could recommend it to undergraduates and sixth-formers as a good introduction to the Gospels. Indeed there is very little in it that I would want to alter today.

By now I had become convinced that one crucially important feature of the Gospel had never been properly recognized. This was its affinity with apocalyptic literature. Eventually I developed this idea, which has remained central in my own thinking, in a chapter of *Understanding the*

25. See Martyn's stimulating essay, "Source Criticism and *Religionsgeschichte* in the Fourth Gospel," 247–73, quoting Fortna's *Gospel of Signs*, which had appeared earlier in the same year.

26. One of the many great services of Dwight Moody Smith to Johannine scholarship is his careful and critical study of this aspect of Bultmann's work: *The Composition and Order of the Fourth Gospel.*

27. Anyone interested can find a summary of my conclusions in *Understanding the Fourth Gospel*, 1st edition, 76–90.

Fourth Gospel entitled "Intimations of Apocalyptic." Here I quote from the little book in which it was first expressed. After a paragraph summarizing Léon-Dufour's insight concerning two levels of understanding (outlined above), I continued:

> The idea of a two-tier revelation was a familiar theme of contemporary Jewish apocalyptic. John's adaptation of this idea is strikingly original, but the idea itself was widespread and crops up in one form or another throughout the New Testament. In apocalyptic literature there is first of all a distinction between two types of revelation, one obscure and original, given in a vision or a dream, the other clear and explicit, usually consisting of an interpretation of the mysterious vision or dream. The Book of Daniel is full of examples of visions or dreams whose significance is only dimly perceived by the person to whom they are vouchsafed and has to be explained subsequently by a prophet or seer. [I had not yet noticed the presence of the interpreting angel, whose role I would later compare with that of the Paraclete.][28]

The second distinction that can be drawn concerns not two *types* but two *times* of revelation and consequently two sets of people to whom the revelation is granted. Very often, this distinction between two times is sharpened to a point where it becomes necessary to speak of two epochs or *ages*. In the first epoch there is a revelation which is reserved to a few just men, such as prophets or visionaries especially favored by God. During this time the world as a whole remains in the dark, and the mystery disclosed to a few continues to be hidden from the rest of humankind. In the apocalyptic tradition itself, this distinction between the few and the many is a feature of the present age. Only in the age to come, *ha'olam habba'*, will the mystery be made manifest to all. A good example of this belief is to be found at Qumran, where the community, convinced that it had been privileged to receive the revelation of the New Covenant, apparently made no attempt to communicate the revelation to those outside.

The Christian adaptation of this distinction between the two ages is marked by a conviction that the world to come is with us now, that the kingdom of God has arrived and is among us. A particularly striking example occurs at the end of Saint Paul's letter to the Romans: "Now to him who is able to strengthen you according to the revelation of the mystery which was kept secret for long ages but which is now disclosed

---

28. Ashton, *Why Were the Gospels Written?*, 80.

and through the prophetic writings is made known to all nations, according to the command of the eternal God, to bring about obedience to the
faith—to the only wise God be glory for evermore through Jesus Christ!
Amen" (Rom 16:25–27). The Markan "messianic secret," implying as it
does that during Jesus's lifetime much must remain hidden and that the
time of full revelation will come only after his death, harnesses the distinction to the gospel form. The reasons for Jesus's extreme and rather
puzzling discretion within John's Gospel are to be sought not only in the
bitter opposition of the Pharisees, which certainly invited prudence, and
in Jesus's reluctance to see a false interpretation put on his claim, but
above all in the incapacity of Jesus's hearers to grasp the real meaning
of the events they were witnessing until their minds and hearts were so
flooded with the light of the resurrection (or, alternatively and equiva-
lently, the light of the Spirit) they could not reach an understanding of
who Jesus was.

It is left to John to work out the divine logic of this revelation of
the Spirit: "If anyone is thirsty, let him come to me; and let him who
believes in me drink. As the Scripture says, out of his belly shall flow
rivers of living water" (John 7:39). This solemn proclamation is interpreted as referring to "the Spirit which those who were to believe in him
were to receive; for there was as yet no Spirit, because Jesus was not yet
glorified" (7:40)—that is, according to the early theology of Acts 2:33, the
Spirit had not yet been received by Jesus for pouring out on others. So on
the first level of understanding the water is a metaphor for the *word*, the
revelation of Jesus (as it is in the conversation of Jesus with the Samaritan
woman in chapter 4). Jesus invites his hearers to come and drink from
the fountain of the living word. On the second level of understanding, the
one to which the evangelist draws attention, the word and the Spirit are
inseparable. In accepting the word of Jesus in faith, the believer receives
the Spirit, and conversely it is the function of the Spirit to teach and remind the disciples of the message of Jesus.

> "These things I have spoken to you while I am still with you. But
> the Paraclete, the Holy Spirit, whom the Father will send in my
> name, he will teach you (i.e. explain to you) all things, and bring
> to your remembrance all that I have said to you" (Jn 14:25–6).
> "Bring to remembrance"—not to add anything new, but to re-
> call. But remembrance is not simply a question of flashing a re-
> corded image onto an inner screen. Suddenly, one remembers,
> and in remembering grasps the full significance of the event or

remark for the first time: "Ah, now I understand what he meant when he said . . ."[29]

Then, a few pages later, some further conclusions:

> In John's theology of revelation, hints and guesses scattered throughout the other three gospels come to fruition. The synoptic gospels make it plain that the main burden of Jesus' own preaching was the kingdom of God. Tentatively identified by Mark with the person of Jesus and by Matthew with his ethical teaching, this notion gives way in the fourth gospel to the mystery of revelation itself. And the revelation is simply Christ and his own essential being, which is to be the Son of the Father, sent into the world to bear witness of the truth. Consequently, this truth is none other than Christ itself. The real irony of Pilate's famous question is that truth in person stood before him as he wondered. Jesus is himself the revealer par excellence and the object of his own revelation.[30]

According to Bultmann, the revelation of Christ in the Fourth Gospel is restricted to the fact that he is the Revealer.[31] With a truly Kantian repugnance for the messy, uncontrollable data of the phenomenal (i.e., historical) world and a longing for a direct communication with the Revealer that does not need to be channeled through a heteronomous magisterium, Bultmann envisages faith as the term of an encounter with an exiguous Christ, pared down to the ultimate essence of a word. So in some respects Bultmann's conception of the word of God is the antithesis of John's. Where Bultmann narrows, John enlarges, so as to embrace the whole of the life and teaching of Jesus.

The images and symbols employed by John exhibit both manner and meaning of Jesus's message. He is the light shining in the darkness, the path to the Father, the shepherd and the vine. Man's necessities as well as God's goodness become plain, since all the symbols are comprehensible

---

29. Ashton, *Why Were the Gospels Written?*, 80–82. One reason why this idea had not occurred to earlier students of the Gospel was the mistaken notion that the main characteristic of Jewish apocalypses more or less contemporary with the Fourth Gospel was a futuristic eschatology totally at odds with the so-called realized eschatology of the Fourth Gospel—so much so that in many quarters the word *apocalyptic* had come to mean nothing more than "prophetic of disaster or of the end of the world." (Indeed, this is the dictionary definition!) This mistaken notion was not fully dispelled until the publication of Christopher Rowland's *The Open Heaven* in 1982.

30. Ashton, *Why Were the Gospels Written?*, 84.

31. Bultmann, *Theologie des Neuen Testaments*, 419.

only in a human context. The cripple, the blind man groping in the dark, the lifeless corpse, images of the human condition without God, they are the almost-necessary correlatives of the way, the light, and the life. They enrich the message without distracting from it. It is the truth (or the word) that looses the bonds of sin, so that one can walk again: "the truth will set you free" (John 8:32); "You are already made clean by the word which I have spoken to you" (15:3). It is the truth that opens the eyes, so that one can distinguish between the right and the wrong, the ugly and the beautiful, and go through life without stumbling incessantly: "For judgment I came into the world, that those who do not see may see" (9:39). It is the truth, finally, that gives life, a special form of life no doubt, but one in which all the qualities of life—energy, movement, vigorous activity, and social communication—play their part: "Truly, truly, I say to you, he who hears my word and believes him who sent me, has eternal life" (5:24).

III: Emerging from Depression (1978–80)

Up to this point I have been writing about the life of the mind, and about a single topic. No one lives solely a life of the mind or thinks solely about a single topic. Although throughout this essay I am chiefly concerned with the Gospel of John, I cannot avoid saying something about a long period in which an overwhelming depression made it impossible for me to do any work at all.

As early as the summer of 1974, halfway through my eight-year teaching stint at Heythrop, I decided that I could no longer remain a Jesuit priest. Not only had I ceased to believe that the Pope had any right to determine what I should think, especially on moral issues, but I had even begun to wonder about God. Who is this God to decide my moral views for me? Kant, I concluded, was right to put this question, and to answer it as he did. Again, largely because of my scriptural studies I had also ceased to believe in the Virgin Birth and in the physical resurrection of Jesus. I would soon be puzzled by Raymond Brown's dogged defense of doctrines which, to me, had long become incredible in the true sense of this over-used word; though I suspect that my disagreement on these issues with Brown and my fellow Jesuit Joseph Fitzmyer would not of itself have been enough to compel me to leave the priesthood. Much more seriously, I had also become convinced that there is no life after death, and after some time I came to acknowledge to myself that I no longer believed in God. These were matters of a different order of gravity. I knew of one or two Christian theologians who could proclaim out loud their disbelief, even their disbelief in God, and yet remain clergymen in their own church with no apparent embarrassment. For me, though, this was not an option. I had come to think that as long as I remained respected, indeed venerated, simply for being a priest, I was in effect living a lie. A public renunciation of my priesthood (for I did not feel under any moral obligation to broadcast my loss of faith) would—for me—mean nothing less than a restoration of my personal integrity. In this sense, if in no other, I came to sympathize unreservedly with Luther's famous statement: "Hier stehe ich: ich kann nicht anders."

Something else in my life was also instrumental in my decision to leave the priesthood. In the course of the preceding ten years I had fallen in love, not once, but three times. This was a period when Jesuit priests, and also younger Jesuits, not yet ordained, were leaving in increasing numbers to get married. Many of these were close friends of mine, and some still are. I guess that if marriage with any of the three women whom I loved had been possible I might have left for that reason. But I was not so fortunate. Better to have loved and lost, wrote Tennyson, than never to have loved at all. I think he was right. But when you have taken a vow of chastity, falling in love cannot be an unalloyed joy. The joy I found in each of my love affairs, great as it was, was marred by guilt. As long as they lasted I was living a lie. I am clear that my reason for leaving the priesthood was a loss of faith. But if things had worked out differently I might have felt obliged to leave for other reasons.

Long afterwards, having just retired, at the age of sixty-five, from my teaching post at the University of Oxford, I was clearing my desk in the Theology Faculty Centre in St Giles's when I came across a diary I had not looked at for years. This gave a day-by-day account of an eight-day retreat I had made in the summer of 1974 at Ampleforth, the well-known Benedictine Monastery in Yorkshire, whose Abbot at the time was Basil Hume, later to become Cardinal Archbishop of Westminster. I was shocked to read the stark conclusion of this personal diary: "I must leave: I cannot stay." Shocked, and somewhat ashamed, because I had forgotten that it had taken me all of four years, from 1974 until 1978, to summon up the courage to carry out the most important decision of my life since my entry into the Society nearly thirty years earlier.

As I write now, June 2015, I have just read Anthony Kenny's review of an edition of the tenth volume of Newman's letters, published in 2006. "It is impossible not to feel," writes Kenny, "that Newman took an extraordinarily long time to take leave of a Church which he had believed, ever since 1839, to be in schism." Nevertheless, he continues,

> if Newman's position between 1840 and 1845 is difficult to vindicate either theologically or logically, it is surely psychologically easily comprehensible. He was drawn to the Roman Church not by any ambition or by any affection for its rituals or its adherents. His letters make clear that his conversion was based entirely on religious and intellectual grounds. But in the lives of many besides Newman, the intellectual conviction of a duty to say farewell to the ambitions, affections and familiarities of a lifetime has often taken periods of years to take effect. In the life of St Augustine, for instance, five years elapsed between his disillusionment with Manicheism and his baptism as a Christian. . . Indeed, anyone who has resigned from office, changed profession or decided on divorce is familiar with that painful period between a life-altering decision and its execution.[32]

Yes indeed!

Why, though, could I not simply abandon the priesthood and apply for dispensation from my vows whilst continuing my work of teaching and research at Heythrop? First, because it would have entailed great difficulties for the College, which had only recently had considerable problems with the Catholic hierarchy because of the obduracy of another ex-priest (not a Jesuit) who had left to get married and yet refused to give up his job. (Why should he? It was his livelihood.) But for me it was different. To insist on staying would have been a betrayal of trust. I had no quarrel with the Society of Jesus, which had been my home and my family for the greater part of my life. What is more, in a state of confusion approaching despair, I had no wish at that time to carry on teaching, and I doubt if I would have had the strength to do so.

After a delay of four years, then, in the summer of 1978, I resigned from my teaching post at Heythrop and began to negotiate my departure from the Society of Jesus and from the priesthood. (Like a divorce, this process takes time.) Well over thirty years later I find it hard to write about this period of my life; but living through it was very much harder; for in less than a week I had given up my job, my home, and what had

32. Kenny, *Christianity in Review*, 130–31.

been my family for nearly thirty years. In fact I had pretty well given up my identity.

So I found myself at the end of that summer living in a crummy little bed-sitter halfway up Albany Street, London NW1, looking out upon a military barracks. I stayed there for three years, for almost half that time doing virtually nothing except playing patience and reading trashy novels. It must be hard for people who have never experienced depression to empathize with those who have. I learned afterwards that I could have been helped by anti-depressant drugs. But since I knew perfectly well that I had good reasons for being depressed, it never occurred to me to seek help either from counsellors or from doctors. I had the support of three Jesuit friends. The first of these was Robert Murray, grandson of James Murray of dictionary fame, my closest colleague at Heythrop, and a brilliant scholar. Both of the other two, Maurice Keane and Robert Butterworth, subsequently left the Society and married. I was fortunate also in having other deeply sympathetic friends, one of whom, James Bradley, I had got to know during the year when we were both living in St Stephen's House (as it then was), Cambridge. Jim's grandmother, as it happens, was a good friend of my own mother, but besides that we shared many interests and opinions. Ten years later Jim was still living in Cambridge, and when I visited him there, as I did quite often, he kept urging me to start writing. Otherwise I shrank from the company of people I did not know, dreading to be asked, "And what do *you* do?" Throughout this period I was applying for a variety of jobs, without much prospect of getting any of them. One that would have interested me was a post teaching French and German at Westminster School. Another, where my French would also have been useful, involved visiting France as the representative of a wine firm. A third was for a job in the manuscript department of the British Museum. My failure to get any of these jobs deepened my gloom. Yet depressed as I was, with no foreseeable end to my misery, I never for a moment regretted my decision to leave.

After more than a year of this experience, not of living but of partly living, at a speed somewhere between dead slow and stop, like a hibernating hedgehog, I received a call from another ex-Jesuit friend, who was teaching religious studies at a sixth form college called Price's, in Fareham, Hampshire. At very short notice he was about to move north to take up another job but had agreed to help the college to find a temporary replacement for the summer term. Would I be interested? The short answer was yes, and within a week or two I found myself confronting a group of bright and lively sixth-formers whom it was easy to interest in questions like the existence of God and the problem of evil.

Well received by both students and staff, I soon became aware that I was beginning, both mentally and spiritually, to thaw out: looking back, I realize that it was my time at Price's that made it possible for me to rejoin the human race. I would have continued to teach there had the permanent job been offered to me, but was quite clear, when it was not, that I had to do something with my life. But what? As a middle-aged out-of-work academic I had little inclination for the kind of study that would be involved in working for a doctorate—such as crawling for months on end over some relatively green patch of one of the books of the Bible. Perhaps, though, I could still find something of interest to say on the Gospel of John. With this thought I retrieved my books from the dungeon basement to which I had consigned them, and set to work. This was in the last few months of 1980.

IV: Beginning *Understanding the Fourth Gospel* (1980–81)

I soon realized that I had first of all to come to terms with the work of Rudolf Bultmann. His outstanding commentary had been available in an excellent English translation since 1971, but I knew I had to reach further back. The first few pages of a major article published in 1925 gave me the clue I needed.[33] Here Bultmann identifies the two great puzzles (or riddles, *Rätsel*) that his future commentary was designed to solve. Both in the book I was about to embark upon, as I now see, and in much of the work that followed it, I too have felt impelled over and over again to find answers to these questions. Bultmann found his solution to the first of them, *the riddle of where John's Gospel stands in relation to the development of early Christianity,* in the newly discovered Mandaean and Manichean sources of the article's title. Two pages further on he spelled out his second great riddle: *what is its central insight, its basic conception?* "Doubtless," he answered, "it must lie in the constantly repeated proposition that Jesus is the emissary of God (e.g., 17:3, 23, 25) who brings revelation through [his] words and deeds."[34] In chapter 2 of the first edi-

33. Bultmann, "Die Bedeutung," 100–146. As far as I know no English translation of this article has ever been published.

34. Bultmann, "Die Bedeutung," 102.

tion of *Understanding the Fourth Gospel* I analyzed and reflected upon this answer.

Bultmann addressed a third important question in his commentary, which I dealt with under the heading "Literary Questions,"[35] conscious that in doing so I was returning to one of the topics of the course on John I gave at Heythrop in the early 1970s. In this section I summarized Bultmann's explanation of the problem-spots of the Gospel (the rough sutures that disfigure the apparently seamless garment the Gospel was held to be by David Friedrich Strauss), and offered reasons for rejecting it.

All three of Bultmann's problems (historical, exegetical, literary) had cropped up before, and would crop up again; so in the first chapter of part I ("Before Bultmann"), I discussed the earliest appearances of these questions, and in the third ("After Bultmann"), the most recent discussions of them, up to 1979. But there is a fourth question too, the question of the Gospel's intended readership, which Bultmann dodged—or at least deliberately set aside: "Unlike the prophets' words," he declares, à propos of the Gospel, "Jesus' words do not thrust the concrete historical situation of the People into the light of God's demand with its promise or threat: they do not open men's eyes to what some present moment demands. Rather, the encounter with Jesus' words and person casts man into decision in his bare, undifferentiated situation of being human."[36] From this clumsily translated passage we can see that Bultmann's existential interpretation of the challenge presented by John's Gospel to its readers dispensed him from the need to enquire into the particular situation in which it was composed, or into the nature of the Johannine community—a phrase he never used.

Accordingly, in chapter 2 of *Understanding the Fourth Gospel*, which was devoted to Bultmann, I say nothing about the intended readership of John's Gospel. In chapter 1 the section on this topic comes first, under the heading "Aims and Audience";[37] in chapter 3, which focuses on the contributions of J. Louis Martyn and Wayne Meeks, it comes last, under the heading "Audience: Situation and Circumstances."[38] (Part 1 of the book, omitted from the second edition, was planned as a gigantic chiasm.)

35. Ashton, *Understanding the Fourth Gospel*, 1st edition, 45–50.

36. Bultmann, *Theology of the New Testament*, 2: 62–63 (quoted in *Understanding the Fourth Gospel*, 1st edition, 102).

37. Ashton, *Understanding the Fourth Gospel*, 1st edition, 9–15.

38. Ashton, *Understanding the Fourth Gospel*, 101–11.

My original intention was to preface the body of the book with a full introduction summarizing earlier scholarship; but it was rapidly borne in on me that I had assembled far too much material to squeeze into a single chapter, so some expansion was unavoidable. It involved a great deal of research. Who else would bother hunting up the aggressive little diatribe of Karl Gottlieb Bretschneider (1820), composed in Latin so as to restrict his readership to the *eruditi* to whom it was addressed? Scarcely anyone nowadays pays any attention to the partitionist theories so common in the nineteenth century, or to the curious view of the Dutch scholar W. C. van Unnik that the Gospel was intended to persuade the congregation of a synagogue in the diaspora that Jesus was the Messiah.[39] But all these theories, however bizarre they seem today, have their place in the history of research, if only to show how easy it is to go wrong, sometimes wildly wrong.

Although I worked quite hard during the twelve months following my term's teaching in Hampshire, I managed to get just four chapters written of a book that would eventually comprise fourteen. The fourth was not the chapter 4 of the published book ("Religious Dissent") but what was to become chapter 7 ("Messiah").[40] By the middle of 1981, however, I knew that I would soon have to defer any further work on the book for quite some time—for a reason I need to explain. In April or May of that year (I can't remember which) I received a telephone call from a friend at the University of St Andrews, whom I knew well—we had entered the novitiate on the same day in 1949. He had rung to suggest that I apply for a temporary lectureship in the School of Divinity, advertised so as to allow each of the two New Testament teachers in the faculty to take some sabbatical leave. Naturally, I was delighted with what looked like the chance to resume an academic career. So I went up to Scotland for an interview, was appointed to the job, and a few months later found myself driving up to St Andrews, for the start of the new academic year. Another friend had offered to store what I called my fun books (literature, philosophy, art) in her big house in Ealing until I was in a position to shelve them myself. All the rest of my worldly possessions—clothes, notes, study books, the lot—I crammed into a hired Ford Escort car, and, shaking the dust of Albany Street off my heels forever, set off excitedly for Scotland.

39. van Unnik, "Purpose of St. John's Gospel," 382–411.
40. Ashton, *Understanding the Fourth Gospel*, 1st edition, 238–79.

Meanwhile I had to decide what to do with my unfinished manuscript. I believed I had done enough to persuade a publisher to give me a contract, and decided to try SCM Press. So I put together what was already quite a bulky package, carried it in person to the SCM offices in Bloomsbury, and left it on the receptionist's desk, with a covering note to the editor. The next day I drove to Scotland.

V: Teaching in Scotland (1981–83)

Whilst unloading my books, the following day, in the quadrangle of St Mary's College, and carrying them up to the office that had been assigned to me, I was greeted by Professor Wilson, who had given me the job a few months earlier. "Come up and have a word," he said. Robin Wilson was one of the kindest men I have ever met. He was also undoubtedly the slowest. So when he began to tell me in minute detail how to get to Dundee, which was where I had to deliver the car that morning, I sensed that his instructions might take almost as long as the drive itself. Disengaging myself as politely as I could, I drove to Dundee, delivered the car, and returned to St Andrews. There were others to thank for their assistance, including Bill Shaw and Peter Coxon, both of whom taught at St Mary's.

Within a week or two of my arrival in St Andrews I received a letter from John Bowden, the editor at SCM Press, offering a contract for *Understanding the Fourth Gospel*. It was a risk, he wrote, "but I have been long enough in theological publishing to know a great book when I see one." Not surprisingly, I was anxious to spend as much time as possible working on this book (which I agreed to complete by the end of 1983), but decided to write a chapter on the prologue first. This project occupied all of my spare time in my year at St Andrews, but when it was finished, realizing that its arguments were too detailed and intricate to justify including it as a chapter in the book I was writing, I submitted it to *New Testament Studies*, where it was published three years later, in 1986.[41] What surprises me now, long after, is that its most important conclusion has been pretty well ignored. Following a suggestion of T. E. Pollard that had been taken up by my old Jesuit teachers, Paul Lamarche and Ignace de la

---

41. Ashton, "Transformation of Wisdom," 161–86 (reprinted with minor corrections in Ashton, *Studying John*, 5–35).

Potterie,[42] I added a number of additional arguments to show that what the term *Logos* signifies in the prologue is *God's plan for the world*, that is to say for humankind. To understand the Logos simply as the agent of creation is wrong. Why, then, am I (to the best of my knowledge) one of only three scholars (two Jesuits and one ex-Jesuit—myself) to have seen that Pollard's original suggestion can be backed up by cogent arguments of several different kinds? Why is it that commentators on John's Gospel have failed to admit that the πάντα of John 1:3 does not mean the created universe (the Greek for which is τὰ πάντα), that the verb γίνεσθαι does not mean *to be made*, but *to happen* or *to come to pass*, and consequently that the translation of πάντα ἐγένετο as "all things were made" is not only erroneous but thoroughly misleading? The evangelist John was not the original author of the prologue, but in adopting it as the preface to his Gospel he was effectively acknowledging that *the story of Jesus he had just told was God's plan for humankind*. Should not this conclusion have been welcomed by exegetes, rather than dismissed out of hand in favor of a traditional but impoverished reading of a passage all agree to be crucial for the understanding of the Gospel?

Lamarche had based one of his arguments on a passage from a gnostic sermon known as *The Gospel of Truth* (written in Greek but now only extant in a Coptic translation), which contains numerous allusions to John's Gospel. Knowing no Coptic, and confronted by alternative English renderings of the passage in question, I went to consult Professor Wilson, an acknowledged expert in that language. Half an hour later I left his room none the wiser, with no clear idea which alternative he preferred. I had more luck with Robin Salters, particularly interested in the wisdom writings of the Old Testament, who had no hesitation in confirming that the Greek translator of Qohelet ("Vanity of vanities, all is vanity," 1:2)—who renders the "all" as τὰ πάντα—worked independently of the translators of the remainder of the Septuagint, and that his idiosyncratic Greek is quite untypical of the Septuagint as a whole.

In the summer of 1982 another job came up, this time at New College, Edinburgh, where a temporary replacement was being sought to allow two professors, one of the Old Testament, the other of the New (both called Anderson), to take half a year's leave of absence. One thing I remember from the interview was the embarrassment of John Gibson, then in charge of the Old Testament department, at his inability to offer

42. Pollard, "Cosmology and the Prologue," 147–53; Lamarche, "Le Prologue de Jean," 497–537; de la Potterie, *La vérité dans saint Jean*, 162–66.

me more than £6000 for a year's work. Little did he know how relieved I was still to have gainful employment, however low the salary. Although in some respects this was a strenuous year, because for the first and only time in my life I had to teach Hebrew, I enjoyed my time there, and felt especially privileged in having been able to form two new friendships, that of Douglas Templeton, along with his wife Elizabeth and their three young children, and secondly that of the Old Testament scholar, Graeme Auld, and his wife Sylvia. But by the summer of 1983 I was once again out of a job.

VI: Getting On with the Book (1983–84)

One advantage, I reflected, of being both unattached and unemployed, was that I could choose where to live. I quickly decided upon Oxford, partly because it would give me the opportunity of seeing more of my mother, who was then living in my brother's house in Cheltenham, but also for the sake of getting access once again to the Bodleian Library. Moreover, I still had friends in Oxford, especially Peter Hebblethwaite, who had left the Jesuits shortly before I did, and who now had a wife, Margaret, and three children, whom I soon got to know. Another friendship I was glad to renew was that of John Hyman, whose parents I had become friendly with in London in the seventies. Aged eleven when I first met him, John was about to be examined for a postgraduate philosophy degree at St John's. Within another couple of years he had become a fellow of Queen's.

That was the year in which the English politician Norman Tebbit uttered the famous words "On your bike!" and in which I was in fact climbing onto my bike every fortnight to cycle down past the police station, over Folly Bridge, to the offices of the Department of Social Security, where I would sit patiently waiting my turn to be summoned to the counter to receive the check on which I relied to keep me out of debt for the next couple of weeks. (Having had paid employment for the past two years, I was entitled to housing benefit.) On one occasion I informed the girl behind the counter that I would be unable to come the next time because I was to be interviewed for a job in Scotland on the date in question. She asked me to sign a form stating that I was going on holiday. When I pointed out that a job interview was not the same as a holiday she sheepishly admitted that she did not have the right form. So much,

I thought, for the advice of Norman Tebbit. Only too willing to take his advice to travel, I applied for jobs during that year at the universities of Bristol, Exeter, Nottingham, Glasgow, Cambridge, and Oxford. Short-listed for them all, I was exceptionally lucky at the age of fifty-three to be appointed to a lectureship at the last of them, Oxford, where I became a fellow of Wolfson College, and taught New Testament in the Theology Faculty for the next twelve years.

Meanwhile, although jobless once again, I was no longer despondent. On the contrary, I was eager to get on with the book I had left unfinished two years previously. I began by taking another long hard look at Bultmann's two great puzzles, the first historical, the second exegetical. The first of these, as I have already observed, was to locate the position of the Gospel in early Christian thought. He summed up his answer to the second, what was the *Grundkonzeption* of the Gospel, in a single word, *revelation*. It was obvious to me that I could not tackle both of these questions together. And being in basic agreement with Bultmann's answer to the second question, I decided to make a start with the first.

Having been persuaded long ago by Raymond Brown, J. L. Martyn, and others (above all Wayne Meeks) that Bultmann was wrong to ignore the Jewish context of the Gospel,[43] and convinced, like them, that no proper understanding of a work of literature can be reached without some knowledge of its historical context, I realized that my first task was to deepen my knowledge of Second Temple Judaism. Two books published about this time were immensely helpful in this project: Christopher Rowland's *The Open Heaven*, which I had bought as soon as it was available in 1982, and the massive two-volume edition of *The Old Testament Pseudepigrapha*, edited by James Charlesworth. I went through the first volume (*Apocalyptic Literature and Related Works*) with some eagerness, though I cannot pretend to have studied it all with the same care. Two writings in particular, however, caught my eye at this time. The first of these was *The Apocalypse of Abraham* (extant only in Old Slavonic), where the angel Yaoel, on whom God had bestowed his name, plays a role

---

43. In the light of the Dead Sea Scrolls, Bultmann came to acknowledge the existence of "a pre-Christian gnosticizing Judaism." This, he implies, could have been the matrix of John's Gospel. See the footnote in his *Theology of the New Testament*, 2:13: "While a pre-Christian gnosticizing Judaism could hitherto only be deduced out of later sources, the existence of such is now testified by the manuscripts recently discovered in Palestine." Yet he saw no reason to alter his earlier views.

resembling that of Jesus in the Gospel of John. The second, for reasons I will explain later, was the *Testament* (or *Assumption*) *of Moses*.

I also want to highlight two features of the chapter entitled "Religious Dissent" in *Understanding the Fourth Gospel* (the fourth in the first edition, the first in the second). It had long been recognized that, as C. K. Barrett put it, "John is both Jewish and anti-Jewish"[44]—Jewish in the sense that the Gospel is permeated through and through with Jewish customs, traditions, and ways of thought; anti-Jewish in the sense that the term "Jews" in the Gospel is used typically of those who reject the message of Jesus. My attempt to resolve this puzzle (first published in *Novum Testamentum* in 1985) was later expanded in the chapter entitled "The Jews in John" in *Studying John*.[45]

The long section headed "Family Quarrels" is one for which I claim some originality.[46] In three chapters in the Gospel (5, 8, and 10) "the Jews" make an attempt on Jesus's life because something he has just said seems to them to merit death. In each case they think he is claiming equality with God, but in none of the three is this claim immediately perspicuous, and the exegesis is tricky. In my study of John 5 ("equal with God"), drawing upon the idiosyncratic commentary of Hugo Odeberg,[47] who cites a number of rabbinical texts, I pointed out that "the dispute is conducted close to the borders of a shared faith in which both parties had laid claim to the exclusive possession of the truth."[48] With regard to John 8:58–59 ("Before Abraham was, I am"), I believe I was the first scholar to appeal to *The Apocalypse of Abraham*. In the case of John 10:34–36 ("I am the Son of God") the key is to be sought, I argued, in two passages from the Dead Sea Scrolls discussed in an article by J. A. Emerton.[49] I do not pretend that the texts I cited are the only ones relevant to the passages in question, only that it is in these various Jewish writings that the deepest explanations of Jesus's frequent altercations with "the Jews" are to be found. "Only by abstracting altogether from the circumstances of the Gospel's composition," I concluded, "and treating it as nothing but a repository of revealed truths or as a timeless call to faith . . . can one fail

---

44. Barrett, *Gospel of John and Judaism*, 71.

45. Ashton, *Studying John*, 36–70.

46. Ashton, *Understanding the Fourth Gospel*, 1st edition, 137–51.

47. Odeberg, *Fourth Gospel*.

48. Ashton, *Understanding the Fourth Gospel*, 1st edition, 140.

49. Emerton, "Melchizedek and the Gods," 399–401.

to recognize in these hot-tempered exchanges the type of family row in which the participants face one another across the room of a house which all have shared and all call home."[50]

In the chapter entitled "The Community and its Book,"[51] which zooms in from the broad study of the Gospel's Jewish background conducted in the previous chapter to focus on the immediate circumstances of the Johannine community, I was fortunate in being able to draw upon the work of Brown, Martyn, and Lindars, who had all suggested how the gradual progress of the Gospel might be conceived, from the first through subsequent editions. My own theory is a sort of pick-and-mix version of theirs. Of the three, only Martyn had been bold enough to search within the pages of the Gospel for evidence of the activity of the Johannine community. Pointing out, in his introduction, that the famous saying "You shall know the truth, and the truth shall make you free" occurs in the midst of a sharp and decidedly unpleasant exchange between Jesus and a group of Jews,[52] he goes on to argue that chapters 5 and 9 contain remnants of actual controversies between the supporters of Jesus in the synagogue and those who, according to the Gospel, declare themselves to be "disciples of Moses" (9:28).

Taking a step further than Martyn, who had restricted himself to the controversy material, I extended his insight to cover two other literary genres representing different features of the community's activity:

> Altogether three aspects of the life and teaching of the Johannine group will be considered: universalism, particularism, and polemicism. To these correspond three different literary styles or modes of discourse: revelation, riddle, and debate. If we wish to avoid taking a one-sided view of the gospel and do justice to all its rich variety, we should begin by recognizing that the community looks both outwards and inwards, sometimes addressing itself to the world which God loves and wishes to save (3:16f.), at others hiding itself away from a world it has come to regard as alien and threatening.[53]

The evangelist uses riddles in two ways, first to emphasize the privileged position of the followers of Jesus vis-à-vis "the Jews" in their knowledge of the truth, secondly to point out the essential difference

50. Ashton, *Understanding the Fourth Gospel*, 1st edition, 151.

51. Ashton, *Understanding the Fourth Gospel*, 1st edition, 160–98.

52. Martyn, *History and Theology*, 1st edition, xvi.

53. Ashton, *Understanding the Fourth Gospel*, 1st edition, 174.

between the disciples' understanding of Jesus's message before his death and resurrection and after (when their knowledge was passed on to the community). Revelation was communicated through prophecy. Like Paul's Corinthians, this was a prophetic community, and in the proper setting its members spoke out—notably but not exclusively in the I-am sayings—in the name of Jesus.

After completing these two chapters, which represented my solution to Bultmann's first puzzle, I added a further chapter on Dualism.[54] Since a chapter on the title of Messiah was already included in the manuscript I had carried three years earlier to SCM Press, I then turned to the other two titles given to Jesus in John's Gospel, Son of God and Son of Man (chapters 8 and 9).[55] Altogether, the five new chapters were to occupy some two hundred pages of the finished book.

So far, however, none of my work had been published, and this lack of published work was a serious obstacle standing in the way of my getting a permanent academic job. When applying for university posts I always offered to send as much as had been completed of the book I was working on, but only two universities took up this offer: one was Cambridge, the other Oxford. I learned later that two old Jesuit friends had written to the Chairman of the Faculty in Oxford urging him to give some consideration to my application; and I am confident that an appreciation of what I had written in my unpublished manuscript was an important factor in my being given the appointment.

VII: Teaching in Oxford: the First Years (1984–91)

At the end of September 1984, about to start work as lecturer in New Testament studies, I moved from my comfortable rented room in the Banbury Road to one of the so-called penthouse flats in Wolfson College, built in the 1960s on the bank of the river Cherwell. At last I had enough space to retrieve the rest of my books and to place them on the shelves of my new flat, where I would live for the next twelve years.

Thus far my journey of discovery of the Gospel of John had lasted twenty years. I could not know then that it would continue for another thirty.

---

54. Ashton, *Understanding the Fourth Gospel*, 1st edition, 205–37.
55. Ashton, *Understanding the Fourth Gospel*, 1st edition, 292–329, 337–73.

Although there are only eight weeks in the Oxford term, so that less than half the year is taken up with actual teaching, the amount of free time I now had was limited. Lectures, tutorials, and committee responsibilities meant that there was no time at all for other work during term, and quite often there were examining duties too. One further responsibility I undertook was that of honorary faculty librarian. At that time the theology library was housed in rooms belonging to Pusey House.

During the 1980s and early 1990s the faculty of theology could still afford to defray the expenses of those of its members who wished to travel abroad in order to attend meetings of one or other learned society—which for me meant the annual meeting of the Society of New Testament Studies. Among the many seminar groups that were arranged every year there was always one dedicated to the study of different aspects of the Johannine writings. But since I already had a very clear idea of the direction my own book was taking, I always chose instead a seminar on the Dead Sea Scrolls or on the apocryphal writings of the Old Testament. That way, I thought, I would always learn something new. Unfortunately this did not always happen, and my choice had the disadvantage that it never brought me into contact with other Johannine scholars from all over the world, something I came rather to regret.

Meanwhile I was busy writing. Professor James Barr, who had chaired the committee that interviewed me, was interested in the progress of the book, and asked me from time to time when it was likely to appear. All I could do was to assure him that I was getting on with it steadily, but that there was still some work to be done. In fact it took me nearly five more years to complete the five chapters that remained to be written.

One reason why it took me so long was that I had taken on an extra commitment. My closest colleague, Robert Morgan, immediately supportive in all sorts of ways, had been impressed by what he had seen of my book, and asked me to select a number of essays on John's Gospel to form one of a series of small books he was editing under the general title of *Issues in Religion and Theology*. I was able to include in this little volume (published in 1986 as *The Interpretation of John*) not only a shortened version of Bultmann's important article on the prologue, but also essays by two of my own early Jesuit teachers, and contributions by five outstanding Johannine scholars: Nils Dahl, Ernst Käsemann, Peder Borgen, J. Louis Martyn, and Wayne Meeks.

The preparation of this little book, however, including my own introductory essay, was hardly a distraction from my main concern, which was simply to finish the book that I had been contracted to submit to the publisher the year before by adding a third part to the two I had already written. The title I gave to this part, "Revelation," reflects my agreement with Bultmann that this was the *Grundkonzeption* of the Gospel. Whereas I had approached the Gospel as a historian in part II ("Genesis"), I took on the role of an exegete in part III. The essence of my ideas about the meaning of the Gospel, many of which had come to me years earlier, is contained in these chapters; and since I still subscribe to most of them I will conclude this major section of this introductory essay by summarizing what I wrote during this time.

The slant I put upon the theme of revelation is discernible chiefly in the chapter entitled "Intimations of Apocalyptic,"[56] in which I expanded upon insights I had had many years earlier, and in another chapter, "The Gospel Genre,"[57] where I argued that the evangelist was consciously drawing out and reflecting upon the implications of the gospel form. (Just how greatly John was indebted to Mark is even today a matter of scholarly debate. I myself am inclined to think that he did not consciously use or cite Mark's Gospel, but knew it in some form or other, and liked the format—stories and sayings preceding a long passion and resurrection narrative—enough to adopt it for his own work.) But these are only two of the five chapters that make up part II of *Understanding the Fourth Gospel*, and this is the appropriate point to reflect upon all five.

In the chapter on the gospel genre I cited and expanded upon Hans Conzelmann's dictum that "the secrecy theory is the hermeneutical presupposition of the genre 'gospel,'"[58] pointing out too that the "identity-in-difference" between the human earthly Jesus and the Risen Lord "constitutes the basic structure of both creed and Gospel."[59] At first sight the article of the creed that asserts belief "in Jesus Christ our Lord" poses no problem. "Only when it is fleshed out in a story does it seem strangely paradoxical, even though the paradox is implicit in the creed as well. For on the face of it this story is recounting the events of Jesus' earthly life whilst urging on every page that this same Jesus is the object of Christian worship. He is not yet risen: but he is, so the writer implies and expects

56. Ashton, *Understanding the Fourth Gospel*, 1st edition, 383–406.

57. Ashton, *Understanding the Fourth Gospel*, 1st edition, 407–42.

58. Conzelmann, "Present and Future," 26–44, here 43.

59. Ashton, *Understanding the Fourth Gospel*, 1st edition, 409.

his readers to believe, our Risen Lord."[60] The same point is made in different ways in all four Gospels—by Mark, very obviously, through the secrecy theory first detected by William Wrede,[61] by Matthew repeatedly in the course of his Gospel but especially in the climactic utterance at the end where, after an initial hesitation on the part of some of the disciples, Jesus's pronouncement that he will be with them to the end of the world (perhaps recalling the name of Emmanuel he was given before his birth) amounts to a declaration that the Christ of Christian worship is no other than the Jesus of Nazareth whose story he has just told. Luke makes the same claim through the Emmaus story, when the two disciples suddenly realize who their traveling companion really is, and John uses the story of doubting Thomas, no less vividly, to reinforce the much-more systematic distinction he has already made by insisting that no proper understanding of Jesus's true identity is possible before his death and resurrection—the Easter event.

How much feebler is the very different view that once the Gospels are ranged, as they should be, on the same shelf as the lives of great men composed before and after the turn of the era by Greek and Roman authors (*bioi* and *vitae*), no more need be said about the gospel genre. The advocates of this view are deaf to the proclamatory note that runs through all the Gospels and blind to the challenging paradox that, as a consequence, confronts the Christian theologian. Insofar as this view is wedded to any particular theological position, it must be that of liberal theologians like Harnack, at the beginning of the twentieth century, content to base their Christian belief on ramshackle and unreliable historical reconstructions of the story of Jesus. Bolder theologians, such as Rudolf Bultmann, facing the paradox unflinchingly, demand the unequivocal answer of a faith commitment. (Bultmann's view is surprisingly close to that of Ludwig Wittgenstein, who declared that Christianity is not based upon historical truth: "rather it offers us a (historical) narrative and says, now believe! But not, believe this narrative with the belief appropriate to a historical narrative, rather: believe through thick and thin."[62]) Søren Kierkegaard, confronting what Lessing called "*der garstige breite Graben* (the bloody great ditch)" separating "accidental truths of history" from "necessary truths of reason," thinks that the right response is to be found

---

60. *Understanding the Fourth Gospel*, 410.

61. *Das Messiasgehemnis in den Evangelien*.

62. *Culture and Value*, 32e.

in the moral drawn from the story of doubting Thomas: "The thought that it is profitable for the disciple that the God should leave the earth . . . is found in the Gospel of John." Kierkegaard says that "the fact" (by which he means the truth of Christianity) is not a simple historical fact (if it was, then contemporaneity would be a desideratum), nor an eternal (i.e., nonhistorical) fact, but an absolute fact (which is also historical).[63] But one may well wonder whether, in propounding this solution, Kierkegaard actually succeeded in leaping over Lessing's ditch—he himself often speaks of the leap of faith—or whether it is rather the case that he refused the jump.

All these answers are basically solutions to the essential paradox of the gospel genre. If the paradox is not recognized, then of course no solution will be attempted, and the discussion of Christian belief, whatever form it takes, will be all the weaker.

The next chapter of my book, "Departure and Return,"[64] composed over four months in a long summer vacation, is one I particularly enjoyed writing. Yet now I admit to finding it somewhat turgid, so I will restrict myself here to its most important findings. It is really nothing more than an exegetical reading of John 14, the first version of what is now widely known as *the Farewell Discourse*. This had long been recognized as a *testament* (a form widely represented among the Old Testament Pseudepigrapha), in which a dying man addresses a final message to his son or heir. It had also been noticed that Jesus's action in handing over authority, on the eve of his death, to the Paraclete (a term that does not figure in the New Testament except in John and 1 John), was prefigured by Moses's transmission of his authority to Joshua. What had not previously been observed was that this transmission exemplifies another literary form too, that of the *commission* or *appointment in office*. Here I am pleased to acknowledge a debt to the outstanding scholar Norbert Lohfink (the best of my old teachers in Rome), who had studied the passages in the books of Deuteronomy and Joshua describing how the leadership of the people of Israel is handed over from Moses to Joshua.[65] Lohfink concludes his article by reflecting that the presence in the deuteronomical tradition of what he calls a theology of office or appointment (*Amt*) may have some importance for understanding this in the New Testament too. (Was he

63. Kierkegaard, *Philosophical Fragments*, 124–25.

64. Ashton, *Understanding the Fourth Gospel*, 1st edition, 443–78.

65. Lohfink, "Die deuteronomistische Darstellung," 32–44.

perhaps thinking particularly of the Gospel of John?) From Deuteronomy we learn how Moses, on the eve of his death, surveying at God's
command the land he himself was never to enter, entrusts Joshua with
the task of leading the people there. I believe that this account may have
been in the mind of the Fourth Evangelist as he tells of Jesus's promise to
his disciples, on the eve of his own death, that the Paraclete would lead
them into all truth.

I appended to this chapter a translation (with short notes) of a major
section of *The Testament of Moses*,[66] an apocryphal writing based upon
the conclusion of Deuteronomy that has some striking resemblances to
John 14. Then, with scarcely a break, I began work on the final chapter,
"The Medium and the Message."[67] Here my chief concern was to find a
convincing refutation of Rudolf Bultmann's notorious assertion that John,
in his gospel, "presents only the fact (*das Daß*) of Revelation, without illustrating its content (*ihr Was*)."[68] I concluded that Bultmann's mistake
lay in his determination to filter out the quintessence of Jesus's message
(that he was the Revealer) from all else that he says and is said about him
in the Gospel. It is true that he says nothing specific about "the heavenly
things" concerning which he claims authoritative knowledge. But God's
plan for mankind, the Logos, is revealed not in Jesus's words alone but in
the whole story of the Gospel that follows. "The medium," I concluded,
"is the message."[69]

The penultimate chapter, "Passion and Resurrection,"[70] was not part
of my original plan. But when I looked back on what I had written thus
far, it struck me that without some consideration of chapters 19 and 20,
which are, after all, the climactic conclusion of the Gospel, the claim implicit in the title of my book to offer a comprehensive reading of the whole
could scarcely be justified. Underlying and even controlling my observations on John's version of Jesus's passion and resurrection, so different
from that of the Synoptics, were, as I now realize, the contrasting views of
Rudolf Bultmann and his pupil Ernst Käsemann. Bultmann, convinced
that "the theme of the Gospel is stated in 'the Word was made flesh,'"[71]

66. Ashton, *Understanding the Fourth Gospel*, 1st edition, 479–84.

67. Ashton, *Understanding the Fourth Gospel*, 1st edition, 515–53.

68. Bultmann, *Theologie des Neuen Testaments*, 419.

69. Ashton, *Understanding the Fourth Gospel*, 1st edition, 553.

70. Ashton, *Understanding the Fourth Gospel*, 1st edition, 485–514.

71. Bultmann, *Gospel of John*, 64. He returns to this theme at several points in his
commentary: pp. 151, 468, 631, 632, 634, 659. (In fact, incarnation is never mentioned,

had no difficulty in fitting the passion account into his understanding of John's Jesus,[72] but found the resurrection stories a major stumbling block. Käsemann, by contrast, had no problem with the resurrection stories, but was unable to reconcile the passion account with his conviction that the key to the Gospel is to be found in the second half of John 1:14, "and we have seen his glory." To him the passion narrative seemed "a mere postscript." Most scholars nowadays pay little attention to Käsemann's view, because unlike him they are confident that the Jesus of the Gospel is fully human. My own view is that Käsemann's case for a docetic Christ (seemingly human, but really divine) is much stronger than most people are prepared to admit; so I was careful in this chapter to spell out exactly why I found it finally unconvincing. I prefaced my discussion of the resurrection stories in chapter 20 by illustrating the absurdities that arise from any attempt to read them as a continuous narrative, and continued by showing that each of them, taken on its own, has a particular point that would have made a convincing conclusion to the gospel story. I still believe that the idea of elevation and glorification is what gives John's passion narrative a bright epiphanic coloring absent from the other three; and I still believe that the resurrection stories make much more sense when each is considered singly than when they are taken together in an attempt to give them some sort of historical significance.

Although there remained a lot of checking and tidying-up to be done, by the middle of 1989, nine years after starting, I now had at last a first draft of a big book of well over 100,000 words, comprising fourteen chapters. Fully aware that it was long overdue, since the contract stipulated completion by the end of 1983, I wrote to SCM Press to explain why the book had taken so long to write, and apologizing for the delay. I received the reply that the delay was far too long, the contract had expired years ago, and that consequently the Press was no longer prepared to publish the book. Even so, confident of its quality, I wrote back requesting a further assessment on the basis of what was still, admittedly, a first draft; and when this was agreed I sent off what I had—a bulky, somewhat untidy parcel of papers—to the Press, fully expecting, in the light of the enthusiastic reception given to the opening chapters years before, to receive a positive reply. So I was surprised when I received

---

or even alluded to, in the body of the Gospel.)

72. "The passion," he says, "grows out of the work of Jesus as the necessary consequence of the struggle of the light against the darkness" (Bultmann, *Gospel of John*, 632).

another rejection, this time final. Although disappointed by the decision, I was not discouraged. My friend Bob Morgan, sharing my confidence, suggested that I submit the book instead to Oxford University Press— which is what I did. By the time the Syndics of the Press had registered their approval I had finished all the necessary revisions, and the book was duly published in April 1991, a publication that marked the end of the first phase of my exploration of the Gospel. The next phase would end three years later, in 1994, with the publication of a volume of collected essays, *Studying John*.

VIII: Up to Retirement (1991–96)

At the time of the publication of *Understanding the Fourth Gospel* I had no idea that I would carry on studying John's Gospel for more than twenty years. Yet it was clear that there was still a lot of work to be done. In fact, even before the book had gone to press I had become aware of a serious gap in my argument, a gap I attempted to fill in an essay entitled "Bridging Ambiguities," mostly written during a period of sabbatical leave in Cambridge, Massachusetts, that followed immediately after the publication of the book. I earned my keep by lecturing at Weston, a graduate divinity school run by the Jesuits, where I was welcomed by Dan Harrington, a fine scholar whom I had first got to know in Jerusalem some twenty years earlier. Published three years later in a collection entitled *Studying John*,[73] this essay was an attempt to answer a question raised by Wayne Meeks in a recent article. "As knowledgeable Jews themselves," he asked, "how could the shapers of the Johannine tradition have come to speak of Jesus in a way that the Jews took to be self-evidently blasphemous?"[74] (A more abstract way of putting the same basic question is this: how did the Johannine community progress from the low christology of the messianic sign source to the high christology that was to determine its break with the synagogue?)

Meeks answered his question by pointing to the glory of God seen by Isaiah (John 12:41) and the "day" of Jesus, seen by Abraham (8:56). My own solution focused rather on the ambiguity of certain biblical passages concerning the angel-messenger of God, where human interlocutors find it hard to know whether they are speaking with God himself

---

73. Ashton, "Bridging Ambiguities," 71–89.
74. Meeks, "Equal to God," 309–22 (here, 310).

or his angel-messenger. Of especial significance is a text concerning the angel-messenger appointed to guide Israel out of Egypt (Exod 23:20) that appeared to put in question the unique status of God himself as Israel's sole deliverer—so much so that numerous later authors felt impelled to remove or at least to disguise the equivocation: Numbers 20:16; Judges 2:1; the LXX translator of Exodus; the Mekilta of Rabbi Ishmael; the Passover Haggadah; and Leviticus Rabbah. Here, I argued, is the most likely source of John's provocatively ambiguous portrayal of Jesus's relationship with the God who sent him. The bridge between the biblical angel-messenger and the mission of Jesus in the Fourth Gospel, I concluded, is "probably connected with the more prominent bridge that leads back to the Danielic Son of Man."[75] But it was another twenty years before I felt able to cross that other bridge and thus round off my argument.

The theses of the first two essays in my collection *Studying John*,[76] published in 1994, had already been incorporated in an abbreviated form in *Understanding the Fourth Gospel*. I postpone until the conclusion of the present essay any discussion of the literary-critical questions that occupy two of the others (essays 6 and 8),[77] and I will treat the seventh essay ("The Discovery of Wisdom")[78] when dealing with the additions to the second edition of *Understanding the Fourth Gospel*. Leaving aside a rather dry methodological treatment of the signs-source theory,[79] I think that the remaining essay, "The Shepherd,"[80] an early example of a new style of Johannine criticism that later came to be called *relecture*, merits some discussion here. (The French word is now standard usage—probably because this was the term employed by its first advocate, the bilingual Swiss scholar, Jean Zumstein, even though he and most of the other practitioners of the method also often write in German.)

Any *relecture* (rereading) depends upon a recognition that the Gospel as we have it was composed over a long stretch of time, and that different parts of it reflect the Johannine community's responses to its changing situation, especially vis-à-vis those it calls *the Jews*. This approach was anticipated as early as 1977 in J. Louis Martyn's "Glimpses

75. Ashton, "Bridging Ambiguities," 89.

76. Ashton, *Studying John*, 5–70 .

77. Ashton, *Studying John*, 141–65, 184–208.

78. Ashton, *Studying John*, 166–83.

79. Ashton, *Studying John*, 90–113.

80. Ashton, *Studying John*, 114–40.

into the History of the Johannine Community."[81] Those who adopted it later, whether they realized it or not, were drawing upon the much earlier insights of scholars such as Eduard Schwartz and Julius Wellhausen, who had concluded from the Gospel's aporias that certain passages must have been composed later than others.[82]

Along with a number of other scholars I think that the story of the cure of the blind man in John 9 originally concluded with verses about a division (σχίσμα) between the Jews, verses that end with a clear reference to this episode: "Can a demon open the eyes of the blind?" (10:21). The events recorded in chapters 7–8 took place at the Feast of Tabernacles, which is an autumn feast, and the next indication of time (10:22), a refer-ence to Dedication, a winter festival, indicates a fresh start. In chapter 9 we had learned of the decision of the disciples of Moses to expel from the synagogue anyone who confessed Jesus to be the Messiah (9:22), thus making the refusal to confess the touchstone of loyalty to their cause. Now, in 10:24, this key issue is picked up again: "If you are the Messiah, tell us plainly." In his response Jesus asserts that the reason for the Jews' disbelief was that they did not belong among his sheep (10:26). This, I think, was the *first* occurrence, in the earliest version of the Gospel, of Jesus's claim to be the shepherd of his flock. The parables of the Good Shepherd and the door of the sheepfold (at the beginning of chapter 10) follow awkwardly upon the miracle story of chapter 9. The division or schism recorded in 10:19 (in which some accuse Jesus of having a de-mon, whereas others take his side) is a much more appropriate response to the rows following the cure of the blind man than the simple failure to understand that is recorded in 10:6. By the time 10:1–18 was added to the Gospel text (presumably in a later edition) the community had grown in cohesiveness and self-awareness, and their uneasy relationship with traditionalist Jews in their own synagogue had changed. The flock of sheep, which might originally have been pictured (as in Matthew and Luke) as grazing undisturbed on the hillside (10:26–29), has come to be thought of as confined in a fold or a pen with a gate and a gatekeeper, and menaced by dangerous enemies coming from without, a thief, a robber and a wolf, much more serious threats than before. In this rereading the image of the shepherd and the sheep, and the original promise that "no

81. In de Jonge, *L'Évangile de Jean*, 149–75.

82. Schwartz, "Aporien im vierten Evangelium"; Wellhausen, *Das Evangelium Johannis.*

one shall snatch them out of my hand" (10:28), have been expanded and given a new and greater significance.

Bultmann had recognized long ago that it makes no sense to see John 10:1–18 as a continuation of chapter 9. But I am convinced that my own diachronic reading, an example of *relecture* dating back to the 1990s, offers a richer as well as a much-less-strained interpretation than the dislocation theory on which Bultmann relied.

With the publication of *Studying John* I believed that I had come to the end of my work on the Fourth Gospel; but looking back now, twenty years later, I have to acknowledge that it is always a mistake to suppose that, however much work and effort one may have devoted to a particular topic or subject, there is nothing more to be learned or said about it.

In 1996, having taught in Oxford for twelve years, I reached the age of sixty-five, and according to the terms of my contract was compelled to retire. Though generally speaking enjoyable and satisfying, this time had been marked by three losses. My mother had died in 1987 in the Cheltenham nursing home where she had spent her last months. I loved her very much, and she still sometimes visits me, consolingly, in my dreams. Then, in 1994, came the death of my brilliant friend Peter Hebblethwaite. At the request of his wife Margaret, I wrote his obituary for *The Times*, which was published the day after he died. A year later came the premature death, from cancer, of my good friend Judy Ebbett, whose husband David asked me to speak at her funeral.

The very last seminar I attended as a New Testament lecturer, chaired by Christopher Rowland, took place on June 13, which, as it happened, was my birthday. Meanwhile Chris had prepared a surprise party. At the end of the seminar, after asking me to accompany him out of the building, he led me into a room where, to my confusion, I was greeted with what seemed to me like thunderous applause. When the applause died down he presented me with a Festschrift in my honor which he had secretly put together, with the help of several friends.[83] Eighteen years later I had the satisfaction of celebrating his own retirement with a similar gift.

---

83. Two years later this was published in book form: Rowland and Fletcher-Louis (eds.), *Understanding, Studying and Reading*.

IX: Diamond Court (1996–2004)

On leaving my job I was also obliged to quit my comfortable penthouse flat at Wolfson College, and to look for somewhere else to live. I had earned scarcely a penny until I was past fifty, and had no money except for what I had managed to save during my twelve years of employment (plus a sum bestowed by the Jesuits as a parting gift). So all I could afford (and this only with the aid of a generous interest-free loan from my friend John Hyman) was a two-bedroomed flat in a large sheltered-housing complex called Diamond Court on the edge of Summertown in Oxford. At the end of September 1996, with some help from the college, I moved into my new home, where I was to remain for the next eight years.

I would gladly have continued teaching if the opportunity had presented itself, and did what I could to obtain a lectureship at one of the Oxford colleges. (Despite its name, a college lectureship is simply an agreement to take on undergraduate tutorials: no lecturing is involved.) Unfortunately, no such post was available. So what was I to do? I had given up playing bridge and had never played golf, but I could still read and I could still write.

One area of the New Testament on which I thought I had something fresh to say was the writings of Paul. Whilst lecturing on his letter to the Romans both much earlier, at Heythrop, and quite recently, at Oxford, I had formed a number of theories about Paul that I wanted to develop and explore. The opportunity to do so came in the form of an annual series of lectures with the general title of *The Wilde Lectures in Natural and Comparative Religion*. The rubric of the first series of these lectures, in 1908, included an explanatory note: "Comparative Religion shall be taken to mean the modes of causation, rites, observances and other concepts involved in the higher historical religions, as distinguished from the naturalistic ideas and fetishisms of the lower races of mankind." The egregiously racist concluding clause ("as distinguished from . . .") remained in place until 1969, when it was quietly dropped by the electors. Nevertheless I was intrigued by the possibility of reviving the spirit of the original rubric by comparing Paul's religious experience with the surprisingly widespread phenomenon (widespread both in time and place) of shamanism. The eight lectures I delivered in 1998 were expanded into a book published in 2000 under the title *The Religion of Paul the Apostle*. Most reviewers, not surprisingly, were offended by the comparison with shamanism, and the book fell flat.[84] (My friend Chris Rowland, who had introduced each of the lectures, was confident that the book would have its day, "but maybe not in your lifetime, John.")

This is not the place to discuss this book in any detail, or the beautiful coffee-table book I set to work on immediately afterwards, along with my friend Tom Whyte (an ex-student). Tom had suggested the theme of *The Quest for Paradise*, and this is what we called the book that resulted from our joint efforts, published in 2001 with the subtitle *Visions of Heaven and Eternity in the World's Myths and Religions*. (One reviewer wrote of it as "a gorgeous book," and indeed it is, with pictures on every page.)

More relevant to the present essay is a chapter I wrote at the request of Professor John Barton for *The Cambridge Companion to Biblical Interpretation* (1998). The other chapters in the second part of this book, "Biblical Books in Modern Interpretation" (the first part was on "Lines of Approach"), simply summarized scholarship on broad swathes of the Bible, ranging from the Pentateuch, by Joseph Blenkinsopp, to apocalyptic literature by James C. VanderKam. But although my own contribution was given the grand heading "John and the Johannine Literature,"[85] I had insisted from the outset on being allowed to restrict my survey to the single episode in John 4 that tells the story of the woman at the well. Anything much more extensive, I thought, would make it impossible to focus on what seemed to me the most interesting aspect of such a survey: the differences between types or models of interpretation. What struck me most, upon perusing as many as I could find (more than thirty) of the multitude of books and essays devoted to this episode, was that with only a couple of exceptions they assumed that it was composed from start to finish in the form that it has come down to us—which is to say that almost all of them adopted a synchronic (smooth) approach to the text. Even so, many of the points on which they disagreed, such as whether the words "You have had five husbands" should be taken literally or symbolically, and what was the precise relevance of the *setting* of the story (Jacob's well), were intriguing proofs of how interpretative choices that are sometimes made quite unreflectively can result in widely divergent readings of the text.

84. For me, the one good consequence of the book took the form of an invitation from Harvard University to deliver the annual William James Memorial Lecture. I gave this lecture, "The Religious Experience of Jesus," in April 2003. The war in Iraq began the next day.

85. Ashton, "John and the Johannine Literature," 259–75.

Barton's was only the first of a series of invitations to contribute to a variety of different types of collections of essays on John. Though asked more than once, I never consented to write a commentary, which would have required more time than I was prepared to give; but I was pleased to receive a request to contribute to a memorial volume in honor of Robert Carroll, whom I had got to know, to like, and to admire whilst in Scotland in the early eighties. Besides being a careful and assiduous Old Testament scholar (witness his two-volume commentary on Jeremiah), Robert had as broad a range of intellectual interests as anyone I have ever known. His untimely death of a heart attack in May 2000 at the age of fifty-nine was a very great loss. The request gave me an opportunity to write about Robert Browning's meditative poem, "A Death in the Desert," centered upon John's dying words, above all the famous reflection on the Gospel, "What first were guessed as points, I now knew stars," words first quoted by Archbishop Westcott in his commentary of 1880, and very often since. A careful rereading of the poem convinced me that underlying its composition was a wish to respond to two nineteenth-century critics, Renan and Feuerbach; so I entitled my essay, "Browning on Renan and Feuerbach."[86]

A third essay published whilst I was living at Diamond Court was written in response to a request by Tom Thatcher to contribute to a volume he was editing entitled *Jesus in Johannine Tradition*.[87] (Tom is now a well-known Johannine scholar who, besides significant contributions of his own, has worked tirelessly in persuading others to write on different aspects of the Gospel and Letters of John.) I was somewhat hesitant at first, because I think that the suggestion of a tradition or traditions that the Fourth Evangelist "used to create the Gospel of John" conveys a misleading impression of how the Gospel came to be written. Eventually, however, I agreed to contribute a piece on the riddles of the Gospel.[88] My essay focused on the term ὑπάγω. Ordinarily this word means simply depart/go away, but in its esoteric meaning it refers to Jesus's return to the Father—the Easter event. In my discussion of 14:6 ("the way, the truth and the life") I argued that the motif of *the way* found in this verse is derived from Jewish wisdom literature, and that a knowledge of its provenance is required if we are to be in a position to assess the significance of the motif for the Fourth Gospel as a whole.

86. Ashton, "Browning on Renan and Feuerbach," 374–94.

87. Ashton, "Riddles and Mysteries," 333–42.

88. Ashton, "Riddles and Mysteries," 333–42.

Amongst the other contributors to this volume were Johannes Beutler, a Jesuit contemporary of mine at the Biblical Institute in Rome, Alan Culpepper, Robert Fortna, and Catrin Williams. I had first met Catrin some years earlier, when she invited me to act as external examiner of the doctoral thesis of Wendy North, another Johannine scholar, in the University of Bangor. At that time her own doctoral thesis had not been published. When it was, in 2000, I realized straightaway that she was the latest among a relatively short number of scholars (in a line that reaches at least as far back as Adolf Schlatter at the beginning of the twentieth century) who have fully recognized the relevance of the study of rabbinic tradition to the understanding of the Fourth Gospel. (The names of Hugo Odeberg, Wayne Meeks, Peder Borgen, Jan-Adolf Bühner, and, more recently, Loren Stuckenbruck, should also be mentioned in this connection.) Although Catrin did not specify the Gospel of John in the title of her thesis, *I Am He: The Interpretation of 'Anî Hû' in Jewish and Early Christian Literature*, that was its focus. At my suggestion Tom Thatcher agreed to invite Catrin to contribute to the collection he was editing, and she produced what is in effect a distillation of her thesis.[89] This and other articles along the same lines have put Catrin at the forefront of Johannine scholars in the twenty-first century. (I should add that my own most serious weakness in the realm of Johannine scholarship is an inability to do anything more than to assess and evaluate work that takes full account of the rabbinic tradition.)

X: Paris (2004–10)

In October 1998 I had taken on the post of senior tutor at Wolfson College (then still a part-time job), and so for the next three years, although no longer doing any teaching, I remained more or less in touch with university life. After 2001, however, beginning to feel cramped and confined in my Diamond Court flat, I found myself drifting apart both from the college and from the university. At some point, therefore, I began to investigate the possibility of moving back to France, with the result that in a rainy July in 2004 I rented a bed-sitter in Paris, a city I had always loved, and started to search for somewhere to live. After a busy, wet, and rather miserable fortnight I was directed to an apartment in the Marais, on the north bank of the Seine, which I immediately fell in love with. On

89. Williams, "'I Am' or 'I Am He'?," 343–52.

the fifth floor, with a hundred and two steps and no lift, it had a beautiful sitting room, a balcony overlooking the Rue du Temple, a well-equipped kitchen and an *en suite* second bedroom. Perfect! On the spot, with the telephoned approval of my friend John Hyman, who had been associated with this project from the start, I agreed to the asking price, and four months later, on October 16, 2004, I took the Eurostar to Paris. The two employees of the Oxford removal firm I had hired spent that night in their van, which they had parked in the Square du Temple, a couple of hundred yards up the road. Early the following morning I watched them wheel my clothes, my kitchen equipment, my heavy furniture, plus all my books and records (thousands of them, in about fifty cardboard cases) down the street and into the courtyard of the building. Then I climbed up to the flat and waited for them as they heaved the furniture and the boxes, one after the other, up the five flights of stairs. (I had earlier advised the firm's representative in Oxford of the need of a hoist, but he had simply responded, "Don't you worry about that, sir.") After toiling almost uninterruptedly the whole of the previous day and part of the next morning, the senior of the two removal men took me aside: "Should you ever think of returning to England, sir, remember that there are some very good removal firms in Paris."

Though it did not occur to me at the time, my move to Paris was made exactly forty years after my first flurry of excitement as I listened to lectures on the Gospel of John in the city of Lyons, some two hundred and fifty miles to the southeast of France. A contributory factor in my decision to move to Paris was a half-promise of a job at the Centre Sèvres, a teaching establishment run by the Jesuits in which lectures on philosophy and theology are offered to a discerning audience. I had come to know Jacques Trublet, one of the Scripture teachers there, as long ago as 1969, when we were both studying in Cambridge, and we had met occasionally since. Jacques thought that I could make a valuable contribution with a course on the Gospel of John. Unfortunately, however, this would have clashed with lectures already being given by one of the other professors; so nothing came of it. Had I got this job I would undoubtedly have had the opportunity of making acquaintances, perhaps friends, in the city, and my life there would have been fuller and more interesting than it turned out to be. I was too lazy to seek other opportunities, and was once more thrown back on my own devices.

As it happens, thanks once again to Tom Thatcher, I was spared the task of hunting around for further study projects. Already making plans for a special session in one of the annual meetings of the Society of Biblical Literature (SBL), Tom had emailed me even before I left Oxford with a request for an essay outlining any second thoughts I might have on the Fourth Gospel. He had conceived the idea of gathering together a number of senior scholars (whom he called, with some exaggeration, "living legends of a golden era of scholarship," and, in my own case, in a private communication, "undoubtedly one of the juggernauts of Johannine scholarship"), and asking each of them to read a short paper discussing "his or her journey with John." He further proposed that these papers should be followed by responses from younger scholars "who will carry the study of the Fourth Gospel into the next several decades." The book Tom compiled from the contributions he received contains eighteen substantial essays and the same number of shorter responses.[90]

Not all the contributors, unfortunately, were able to attend the meeting in San Diego in November 2007. I was particularly sorry to miss Marinus de Jonge, an exceptionally perceptive New Testament critic with whom I had become friendly in the 1980s, and the author of an influential collection of essays on John.[91] On the other hand, I was delighted to meet for the first time not only Tom Thatcher himself, but also two very distinguished American scholars, Dwight Moody Smith, the undisputed doyen of Johannine scholars in America, and (above all) J. Louis Martyn, whose little book, *History and Theology in the Fourth Gospel*, had so much impressed me when I first read it and had continued to influence my own thought.

2007 would be the sixtieth anniversary of the discovery of the Dead Sea Scrolls, and Tom Thatcher, seizing the opportunity of conducting a survey of the views of current Johannine scholars concerning possible links between the Scrolls and the Johannine writings, had organized a second session at the San Diego meeting for those interested in this question. Once written up, the papers read at this session appeared four years later in volume 32 of a series on *Early Judaism and its Literature* published by SBL.[92] Inspired chiefly by the work of Raymond Brown, I had long been interested in probing the relationship between the Gospel and some of the Scrolls, and in the first edition of *Understanding the Fourth Gospel*, basing my argument on the close resemblance between

90. Thatcher, *What We Have Heard from the Beginning.*
91. de Jonge, *Jesus.*
92. Coloe and Thatcher, *John, Qumran and the Dead Sea Scrolls.*

the dualism of the Gospel and that of the *Community Rule*, I had put forward the view that the evangelist was a converted Essene. A number of reviewers pointed out that dualistic ideas were quite widespread at the time, and that the confrontational tone of the Gospel could easily be accounted for by the social circumstances of John and his community. In the second edition, therefore, I withdrew this suggestion, but my views about the precise relationship between John and the Essenes have continued to fluctuate ever since, and I have never lost interest in the Scrolls.

In 1996 Dan Harrington had published an English translation of a number of Qumran documents in a book he called *Wisdom Texts from Qumran*. One of these that had caught my attention was a curious writing that was later to receive the title *4QInstruction*, and then, later still, *4QMysteries*. So when Tom Thatcher invited me to read a paper at the special session he had arranged at San Diego I had no hesitation in accepting. I focused my study on the key term רז נהיה (*raz nihyeh*). The readers of 4QInstruction were urged to "meditate day and night upon the *raz nihyeh* and study it always." This term, which had already been found in two other scrolls, had usually been thought to have a future meaning (*mystery of the future* or *mystery that is to come*). In the paper prepared for San Diego,[93] I argued that its meaning is present rather than future, *the mystery that is coming to pass*, and that it is rightly understood to refer to the unfolding mystery of God's plan for the world. Before reaching this conclusion I had spent many hours consulting the work of a dozen or more other scholars;[94] so it was with great satisfaction that I later discovered that this was the meaning proposed in the official edition of the Scrolls published by the Clarendon Press. "רז נהיה," the editors noted, "refers to the secret of that which is coming into being," and they pointed to Sirach 43:19 and 48:25, "where נהיות [plural of נהיה] is parallel to נסתרות, secrets."[95] Among other proposals in my own paper I remarked that the reference of the *raz nihyeh* is intriguingly close to that of the Johannine Logos—the mystery of God's plan for the world as, no longer hidden, it has finally been incarnated and revealed—pointing out too that the members of the Johannine community were said to have

93. A revised version of this was published as Ashton, "'Mystery' in the Dead Sea Scrolls," 53–68.

94. I did all this work in the excellent biblical library of the Paris Institut Catholique, in the Rue d'Assas, where all the relevant publications were ready to hand. If I had had to do the work in the Bodleian library in Oxford it would have taken much longer.

95. Fitzmyer, *Discoveries in the Judaean Desert*, 20:105.

gazed on or contemplated the Logos just as the members of the Qumran community were invited to meditate on the *raz nihyeh*. (When I read this paper at Yale University before taking it to San Diego, I was particularly pleased when a member of the audience who happened to be working on 4QInstruction for a doctoral thesis told me that he found my argument quite persuasive.) These two communities, though moving in opposite directions in their response to God's revelation to Moses—one group still eagerly accepting it, but alert to the possibility of further revelations, the other convinced that it had been totally superseded—were united in their prayerful contemplation of God's plan for humankind.

Returning now to Tom's request to think again about the Gospel as a whole, after giving it some thought I decided to undertake a complete revision of *Understanding the Fourth Gospel*, which had been published well over a decade earlier. After some hesitation the Clarendon Press gave this project the go-ahead, and I set to work. Tom had asked me to think again; but in my case thinking again did not lead to a change of mind; and I devoted most of the long, forty-page introduction to the second edition (drastically abbreviated in the chapter I wrote for Tom's collection)[96] to defending positions I had adopted long before, especially on the questions of the composition of the Gospel (which I was still convinced had taken several years to complete), and the breakaway of the Jesus-group from the traditionalists in the synagogue (where I still followed Martyn).

Besides the new introduction I inserted three additional excursuses, two of them very short. The first three chapters of the first edition, on the history of research, were dropped, and I made a few, mostly very minor, revisions. (The most important of these was due to my change of mind about the significance of the Gospel's dualism.) Having come to realize, however, that both the historical section of *Understanding the Fourth Gospel* ("Genesis") and the exegetical section ("Revelation") were deficient in important respects, I added two new chapters to correct these deficiencies: chapter 6, "The Messenger of God," and chapter 9, "The Story of Wisdom."[97]

I have already summarized the article on which chapter 6 of the new edition was based. Written in America immediately after the publication of the first edition in 1991, it first appeared in my collection *Studying John* as "Bridging Ambiguities" (where the word *bridging* is itself ambiguous).

96. Ashton, "Second Thoughts on the Fourth Gospel," 1–18.
97. Ashton, *Understanding the Fourth Gospel,* 2nd edition, 281–98, 366–86.

In the concluding paragraph (also the last paragraph of the historical part of the book) I remarked, as I noted earlier, that because John's Gospel represents one form of Christianity's emergence from Judaism, "there must have been a bridge [between the two] (particularly important but having left few obvious traces) probably connected with the more prominent bridge that leads back to the Danielic Son of Man."[98] In 2011, twenty years after I had first become convinced of the relevance to the Gospel of the Jewish angel-messenger, I was able to confirm this supposition in a new study of the title *Son of Man*.[99]

I have three comments to make on chapter 9, "The Story of Wisdom."[100] In the first place, the title indicates a concession on my part to the literary critics, expressing as it does an acknowledgement that the Gospel has a *plot*. If the Jesus of the Fourth Gospel is the embodiment of divine wisdom, then his story is the earthly story of that wisdom, that is to say the story of revelation. This means that revelation, besides providing the Gospel's dominant *theme*, as Bultmann saw long ago, also furnishes it with its *plot*. Like certain other concepts around which plays or fictions have been constructed (e.g., jealousy, ambition, revenge), revelation comes already fitted with a pattern or structure (the movement from concealment to disclosure) and already projecting, implicitly at least, a story. The happy coincidence of theme and plot goes a long way towards explaining the excellence of the Fourth Gospel as a work of literature. Like Othello, in whose speeches we detect the corrosive effects of jealousy, Macbeth, who can neither disguise nor resist the tugs of ambition, and Hamlet, who broods so often on his desire for revenge, the hero of the Gospel discourses on revelation even as he lives out its story.

Secondly (something not made clear at this point in the book), I hold that the evangelist built his Gospel upon a missionary document of uncertain length generally known as the Signs Source, plus, I believe, an appeal to the Samaritans that underlies the story of the woman at the well in chapter 4. Whether or not this hypothesis is correct it does not pose too much of a problem, because if these sources already existed as continuous compositions, the evangelist undoubtedly integrated them, as well as an early version of the passion narrative, into his own work. The real problem arises from a second hypothesis—to which I also

98. Ashton, *Understanding the Fourth Gospel,* 2nd edition, 298.

99. Ashton, "Johannine Son of Man," 508–29.

100. Ashton, "Johannine Son of Man," 366–86.

subscribe—that some major sections did not belong to the Gospel as it was originally composed, but were added later: chapter 6, part of chapter 10, most of chapter 11 (the raising of Lazarus, displacing the temple episode), chapters 15–17, and, most significantly, the prologue. Nevertheless, conceived as it was from the outset as a continuous narrative, the Gospel must have had a plot already traceable in its first version without the need to include anything added later, especially the prologue. And in fact the narrative can easily be read as the story of Jesus's unremitting efforts to get his message across. (At some point he announces that he is truth in person.) Like Hamlet, whose plans for revenge are realized only in the very last scene, Jesus's words meet with incomprehension by the Jews, and are not fully understood even by his disciples until the very end of the story. When, just before his death, they tell him, "Now you are speaking plainly" (16:29), the reader knows how limited their understanding still is.

The story of revelation (or, better, revealed wisdom), besides being observable in the body of the Gospel, also occurs in a compressed form in the prologue, which was added after one version of the Gospel, usually referred to as the first edition, had already been written. Probably the work of someone belonging to the same community as the evangelist, it has a rather different take on the wisdom tradition. The term *dwell* or *tabernacle* in 1:14, widely assumed to allude to an injunction Ben Sira addressed to the law, "Make your dwelling in Jacob" (Sir. 24:8), represents a bold transformation of the extraordinary idea that wisdom came to dwell on earth in the form of the law: it was not the Torah, but the *Logos* (a masculine surrogate of wisdom), so it is asserted, that came "and dwelt amongst us." I suspect, however, that in also affirming that "his own people did not receive him" (1:11), the writer of the prologue was summing up what he had read in the body of the Gospel (which also no doubt reflected his own experience) concerning the hostility of the Jews who refused to accept the message of Jesus.

One of the very few clear allusions to the wisdom tradition in the body of the Gospel, where incarnation is not even hinted at, comes in Jesus's response to the temple proctors (ὑπηρέται) sent to arrest him: "I shall be with you a little longer, and then I go to him who sent me; you will seek me and you will not find me; where I am you cannot come" (7:35–36). Besides reminding us of Proverbs 1:28, "they will seek me diligently but will not find me," this takes up an alternative version of the tradition according to which wisdom tried and failed to find somewhere to dwell on earth; so she "returned to her place, and sat down in the midst of the angels" (1 En. 42:2). The response is even closer to a line in an apocalyptic writing composed roughly at the same time as the Gospel: "then wisdom shall hide herself, and understanding withdraw into her treasury, and shall be sought by many but not be found" (4 Ezra 5:9–10). So the Gospel reflects a strong tradition of a hidden wisdom which defeats all attempts to find her, of which the best-known and most powerful statement comes in Job 28 (quoted *in extenso* in this chapter of my book).[101]

Besides the story of the limited success met with by revelation, there is a subplot, more easily observable, which is that of the *search*. This really begins with the reaction to the healing of the cripple: "This was why the Jews began to hunt Jesus down, because he did this on the Sabbath" (5:16), and continues with references to Jesus's attempts to avoid the Jews (7:1) or to hide from them (8:59). At one point we are told "he slipped from their grasp" (10:39). After the raising of Lazarus Jesus moved to Ephraim, but still the hunt went on (11:56). The narrative section of the first part of the Gospel concludes with the statement "he went and hid from them" (12:36). Yet the warning Jesus had just given to his disciples not to allow the darkness to catch up with them (12:35) was made in the knowledge that in one sense it was about to catch up with *him*, which it did shortly afterwards in the garden across the Kidron valley. "Whom do you seek?" he demanded of the huge force sent to arrest him—which included the ὑπηρέται (temple proctors) who had challenged him much earlier at the Feast of Tabernacles—before going on to reinforce the irony of his question by answering their query about his identity with the admission, "I am [he]," a reply emphasized by the narrator, who repeats it twice (18:5, 6, 8). On the story level, representing the forces of darkness, they had at last caught up with him, but on the higher level of understanding he had escaped them yet again.

The second edition of *Understanding the Fourth Gospel* occupied much of my time in 2007, a very busy year, but on my return from San Diego I put it aside, and for the two and a half years left to me in Paris started upon a new project, a novel commentary of Matthew that has no place in this essay. Yet the prospect of further work on John was still in my mind, because on one of my return visits to Oxford I had been surprised (and of course deeply gratified) by a suggestion of a colloquium based on my own work to be held in the University of Bangor. The suggestion came

---

101. *Understanding the Fourth Gospel*, 2nd edition, 380.

from Catrin Williams, who happened to be in Oxford on one occasion when I had dropped in to see Chris Rowland at The Queen's College. The two of them had agreed, subject to my approval, to organize a followup on a chapter of *Understanding the Fourth Gospel* called "Intimations of Apocalyptic" which I have already discussed at some length.

When I first moved to Paris there were a number of people I knew from the United Kingdom already living there. But these, one by one, began to leave, and having no firm Parisian friends, I became increasingly aware of my isolation. By the middle of 2009, I admitted to myself that I was lonely and unhappy. In early January 2010 I put my flat up for sale. Not surprisingly there was a great deal of interest. A sale was concluded within a few weeks and I immediately began to ask for bids from removal firms both in England and in France. The two burly men who turned up on the morning of the 11th of June were somewhat dismayed to find no lift: the firm's representative who had inspected the flat a few weeks earlier had misinformed them. But they showed surprising equanimity, and of course it is much easier to carry heavy loads down five flights of stairs than to carry them up.

XI: Back in Oxford (2010–14)

By the middle of June 2010 I was back in Oxford, in a flat rented from an old friend and fellow Wolfsonian. In the laborious task of shifting furniture, and unpacking and shelving thousands of books and records, I was lucky to have the generous assistance of Roger Riddell, an old friend (and another ex-Jesuit) with whom I had renewed contact in Paris. This done, I immediately set to work on preparing my talk for the colloquium at Bangor, due to be held the following month. For me the colloquium was an enriching experience, especially because it gave me the chance not only of renewing my acquaintance with old friends and colleagues— Chris and Catrin, of course; Judith Lieu, now professor at Cambridge; Ian Boxall, whom I had taught as an undergraduate years before; and Robin Griffith-Jones—but also of meeting for the first-time famous scholars whom I knew only from their books—Jörg Frey, Loren Stuckenbruck, and April DeConick—and, to name but one other, the much younger scholar, Benjamin Reynolds, the only speaker to engage directly with my own work. For various reasons the resulting volume, carefully edited by

Catrin and Chris, did not appear until 2013;[102] but whilst working on my own paper I was able to write a spinoff article on the Son of Man which was immediately accepted by John Barclay for *New Testament Studies.*[103]

By the beginning of 2011, six months after my return to Oxford, I had enough new material to form the basis of a number of lectures that could then be worked up into a book. Accordingly I approached the Oxford Faculty of Theology (of which I had ceased to be a member five years earlier) with an offer to give half-a-dozen lectures, without remuneration, at a time and place of their choosing. I thought that this offer might be accepted under the rubric of "Further Lectures offered to the Board," but this did not work out. But I gave the lectures at Strawberry Hill the following year, 2012, between March and April. As soon as they were finished I set to work expanding them into a book, and by February 2013 the text was sufficiently advanced for it to be submitted in a proposal to Fortress Press in America. Within an hour or so of receiving this proposal the editor, Neil Elliott, gave it a positive response. I completed the book soon afterwards, and it was published in March 2014.[104]

I held a lunch party at Wolfson to celebrate my eightieth birthday in June 2011. A few of those I invited were unable to attend, but among the seventy or so who could were many academic friends, along with their spouses or partners—notably Chris Rowland and Bob Morgan from Oxford, Douglas Templeton and Graeme Auld from Edinburgh, and Peter Coxon from St Andrews. Martin Sharpe (son of Rosemary, who had befriended me in Fareham years before) played his saxophone to welcome people in. My brother Michael was able to come, and also his daughter Jane and her husband Sandy. David Ebbett, Judy's husband, Tom Whyte, my partner in the Paradise project, and Cordelia Hebblethwaite, Peter's daughter, whom I had got to know well in Paris, were there. Many Wolfsonians, too many to name, came along, and I was especially pleased to greet my good friend Jim Bradley, who came all the way from Newfoundland simply for the party, and slept that night in my spare bedroom. Little did I suspect that within a year he would be dead of lung cancer.

Later in the same month I made a start on another project that I had had in mind for some time, a collection of essays in honor of Christopher Rowland, who was to retire three years later, in 2014. Although I knew

102. Williams and Rowland (eds.), *John's Gospel and Intimations of Apocalyptic.*

103. See note 99.

104. Ashton, *Gospel of John and Christian Origins.*

that another collection was already underway, celebrating his Christian radicalism and his interest in reception history,[105] I believed that his main contribution to biblical studies deserved to be commemorated in another book. He had become renowned for his work on apocalyptic, especially his pioneering study *The Open Heaven* and no fewer than three commentaries (all very different) on the book of Revelation. And of course I relished the opportunity of thanking him in an appropriate way for the Festschrift that he had presented to me years earlier. Before long no fewer than twenty-five people had agreed to contribute to the book, and although for various reasons four of these dropped out I was delighted to be able to present the book to him at a surprise party at Wolfson in June 2014,[106] eighteen years almost to the day after his gift to me on my own retirement.

In the summer of 2013 I heard from Catrin Williams that Jan van der Watt, professor of New Testament at the University of Nijmegen, was among the organizers of a conference on the prologue of John to be held that September on the island of Patmos, at which she and a number of other Johannine scholars were to present papers. At my request she put me in touch with Jan, who soon afterwards sent me an invitation to attend the conference. When the time came, after spending a night in Cos, one of the few Greek islands with an airport, I took a ferry the next morning, along with Catrin, to Patmos, where for the first time in my life I experienced the lavish luxury of a five-star hotel. For me, apart from the actual papers, the high points of the conference were first the visit to the cave where John is supposed to have written the book of Revelation, and secondly the opportunity to make the acquaintance of a German scholar whose ongoing commentary on John is, in my view, one of the best ever, and certainly the best so far in the twenty-first century.[107] Michael Theobald, who had arrived a day late, had to take a ferry to Samos before the final session, and since, as it happened, I was taking the same boat on my way to Istanbul to stay for a few days with a Turkish friend, we talked together during the crossing (he speaking German, I English) and had the pleasure of recognizing not just a shared interest but a shared

105. Bennett and Gowler, *Radical Christian Voices and Practice.*

106. Ashton, *Revealed Wisdom.*

107. Theobald, *Das Evangelium nach Johannes.*

approach to the mysteries of the Gospel. In a very short time we had become friends.[108]

Although I had not read a paper in Patmos, Jan van der Watt asked me to contribute an article on the prologue to add to the papers that were delivered there, and, if I could, another paper for a South African journal, to pay my way for a conference to be held in Ephesus the following year. Both of these are now written and have been accepted for publication, but are not yet published and so have no place in the present essay.

Soon after the pleasures of Patmos came yet another conference, in Baltimore, Maryland. Two years before, in 2011, Catrin Williams and Tom Thatcher had conceived the idea of celebrating the sixtieth anniversary of C. H. Dodd's second great book on the Gospel by inviting contributions to a new collection. Most of the contributors, along with several others, took part in a short conference held in November 2013 at St Mary's Seminary, Baltimore (where Raymond Brown had taught for many years), and the book was published soon afterwards.[109] At first I had refused to contribute to this volume, feeling that this was a subject on which I had little to say, but then, under some pressure, agreed to write a piece on Dodd's suggestion of a hidden parable in John 5:19–20. I entitled this piece "Reflections on a Footnote."[110]

Immediately after the conference on John at the seminary came the annual SBL meeting, held as usual in large hotels in the city center. For me this meeting had three highlights. The first was a chance encounter with Peder Borgen (older than I but looking much younger), whom I had got to know when he was a visiting scholar at Wolfson in the 1980s. The second was a session organized at short notice to honor the memory of the recently deceased Sean Freyne, an Irish scholar whom I greatly liked and admired, a session in which a moving tribute from Sean's fellow Irishman John Collins was followed by brief reminiscences from some of those present (myself among them). The third highlight was an evening spent in the company of my old friend and ex-student Ian Boxall, who had just started on a new job at the Catholic University of America, Washington, DC.

108. He read *The Gospel of John and Christian Origins* before publication, and his appraisal on the back is eloquent testimony both to our shared approach and to our friendship: "A marvelous book that will bring richness to the study of John."

109. Thatcher and Williams, *Engaging with C. H. Dodd.*

110. Thatcher and Williams, *Engaging with C. H. Dodd,* 203–15.

XII: Conclusion (September 2014)

All autobiographical essays are to some extent apologias, even if Newman's famous book is the only one to include the word in its title. In rounding off this essay I will start by offering a defense of each of the two editions of *Understanding the Fourth Gospel* (the basis of all my other work on John) against somewhat critical reviews, and then conclude with a summary of the findings of my recently published book, *The Gospel of John and Christian Origins*.

(a) Understanding the Fourth Gospel, 1st edition, 1991

Most of the reviews of the first edition were favorable. One reviewer, however, for whom the book proved "a bit of a nightmare," described it as "a throwback to the 1970s." He saw in it "an objectivist approach to meaning as coming either from the author or the world of the text; a further conception of meaning as univocal and retrievable, through the use of proper methodology; an evaluation of all preceding scholarship as either correct or incorrect, depending on approximation to the author's own interpretation of the Gospel."

Far from regarding its meaning as univocal, I believe that the Gospel narrative is conducted throughout on two levels of understanding. Far from demanding that other scholars conform to my own view, I think that all interpretation should be based upon argument and evidence. To take just one example, my long-held conviction that the Gospel was composed over a long period of time was first formed after reading Wellhausen, Schwartz, and Bultmann, and confirmed later by the works of Brown, Lindars, and Martyn—not because they agreed with me but because I was persuaded by them. Admittedly the evidence, more often than not, is too slight to warrant certainty on particular issues, so although some interpretations are clearly wrong, most others are no more than possible (insofar as they cannot be *shown* to be wrong), and none (including my own) is definitive.

One reviewer observed that my book "lacks proper critical acumen: not only does it fail to address critically the theoretical foundations of its own method, especially in this day and age, but it also tends to stereotype and dismiss far too lightly the contributions of the more recent critical methods, from narratology to reader response to deconstruction."

On the whole, this is an accurate observation. It is true that I made no attempt to justify the method known as historical criticism (which in any case is not so much a method as a principled approach). I thought at the time, and I still think, that it requires little or no justification: it seems to me obvious that no work of literature composed at a different time and in a different language from one's own can be properly understood without some knowledge of the language it was written in and its historical background. But this was the heyday of postmodernism. Historical criticism had already come under fire in several quarters; and just how confident its detractors had become by the end of the twentieth century is clear from the first page of M. W. G. Stibbe's introduction to a collection of essays entitled, significantly, *The Gospel of John as Literature: An Anthology of Twentieth-Century Perspectives*, which he introduces by saying of current literary critics of John: "First of all, and most obviously, they have rejected historical criticism. Nearly all the books which study the final form of John's Gospel begin with at least some brief and iconoclastic rejection of former, more historical methods."[111]

Accordingly, in the title essay of my book *Studying John*, where I quoted Stibbe on the last page, I put up a defense both of my use of historical criticism and of my deliberate eschewal of the other methods recommended by the reviewer.[112] The first of these, narratology, should rather be called narrative criticism, for narratology is properly speaking not a method but a theory. In *Studying John* I devoted a whole chapter to this topic, a chapter based on the assumption (shared by most narrative critics themselves) that the method *as such* excludes any inquiry into the history of the work in question and demands a smooth (synchronic), as opposed to a rough (diachronic) approach to the text.[113] This assumption, however, is mistaken, as I should have seen.[114] However long the Gospel took to compose, it is unquestionably a narrative, so there must be some way of treating it as such: I conceded this in my exposition of chapter 9

111. Stibbe, "Introduction," 1.

112. Ashton, *Studying John*, 184–208.

113. Ashton, *Studying John*, 141–65.

114. Gérard Genette, who devotes the greater part of his book *Figures III* (a part he entitles *Discours du récit*) to a narrative-critical study of Proust's *A la recherche du temps perdu*, starts by admitting the necessity of having recourse from time to time to earlier versions of it (Genette, *Figures III*, 67). Later proponents of narrative criticism proved more receptive to the possibility of combining it with other, non-literary methods, or at least of using it alongside them, e.g., Petri Merenlahti, who proposes "a shift from literary studies into something new" (*Poetics for the Gospels?*, 136).

of the second edition of *Understanding the Fourth Gospel,* "The Story of Wisdom."[115]

Reader response, the second of the two self-styled critical methods mentioned in the review, has made no contribution whatsoever to the understanding of the Gospel (or indeed of any other work of literature.) It hardly deserves to be called a critical method at all, since almost by definition it requires no expertise from its participants, nor even any background knowledge of the complex works of literature on which they are expected to comment. Some readers, despite their ignorance, may now and again make a perceptive remark; but that still leaves anyone seeking a proper understanding with all the work to do.

The third method, deconstruction, is the brainchild of the philosopher Jacques Derrida. He and his followers, dancing gleefully around the text, may throw some incidental light on the works they are discussing, but since the whole *raison d'être* of deconstruction is to subvert the text as it stands and defeat all efforts to find any stable meaning, such light as it sheds will never be anything other than fitful and oblique.[116]

There remain, however, three further paths to the Gospel that merit some attention (although I myself have always stepped past them with averted gaze). The first of these, ignored in the past by most of the major commentators, but adopted quite recently by a number of respected scholars, is the use of the Gospel as a source of information about the real Jesus, the Jesus of history. Although in principle there is nothing wrong with this approach—one is quite entitled to look to Shakespeare for information about the kings of England—I confess that for me it holds no attraction, and in any case it makes no contribution to the understanding of the Gospel itself.

In the second place there is the now well-established approach of reception history, an exciting new venture for those eager to observe the impact that the books of the Bible have made upon successive generations. Had I had the time to acquire the necessary background knowledge I might well have done work of this kind myself, applying, of course, in doing so the well-tried tools of historical criticism, but . . . no one has unlimited amounts of time.

---

115. See Ashton, *Understanding the Fourth Gospel,* 2nd edition, 366–83.

116. See *Studying John,* 202–203, where I offer a critique of a very entertaining essay by Stephen Moore on the story of the woman at the well, "Are there Impurities in the Living Water that the Johannine Jesus Dispenses?," 207–27.

The third approach to be considered is the application of the *social sciences* to the study of the Gospel, an approach adopted by a number of scholars, especially Jerome Neyrey and, more recently, Philip Esler. I prefaced my essay on narrative criticism in *Studying John* by remarking that "the historical critical method itself, its muscles now hardened by occasional injections of sociological theory, is still alive and running strongly,"[117] my point being that far from setting itself up as a better alternative, the social-scientific approach is simply a new and distinctive type of historical criticism. Its emphasis on the need to take into account the differences between the social circumstances of the biblical writers, on the one hand, and of present-day society, on the other, will be applauded by any historical critic worthy of the name. Such reservations as I have, relate to what I have called the problem of *weighting*—just how much importance should be attached to any particular feature of the work one is studying. I think that those who adopt the social-scientific approach run the risk of exaggerating certain aspects of the text and neglecting, or altogether ignoring, other equally relevant features.[118]

(b) Understanding the Fourth Gospel, 2nd edition, 2007

I turn next to a review by Craig Koester (the only one I have seen) of the second edition of *Understanding the Fourth Gospel*,[119] an unenthusiastic review but a fair one. Koester quite reasonably takes exception to my rash assertion that, in the previous two decades, "there has been no major advance in Johannine studies."[120] I have never thought it necessary to discuss or mention explicitly everything published on the subject, not even good books by scholars I respect, unless I have learned something from them that I could use and therefore should acknowledge, or unless, conversely, it seemed to me that the argument could be advanced by reasoned disagreement. But I do not really believe that mine are the only legitimate questions that can be addressed to the Gospel, and it was foolish of me to convey that impression. Koester was right to remark that

117. Ashton, *Studying John*, 141.

118. My suspicions were confirmed by a rapid perusal of one such study, a *Social-Science Commentary on the Gospel of John* by Malina and Rohrbraugh. Despite its many valuable insights, the commentary as a whole is decidedly thin.

119. Koester, Review of *Understanding the Fourth Gospel*.

120. Ashton, *Understanding the Fourth Gospel*, 2nd edition, 1.

"the discussion has not moved steadily forward along the lines set several generations ago but has branched off in multiple directions." He might have instanced his own fine study of the symbolism of the Gospel,[121] so much richer and more readable than the narrowly focused articles or monographs that are the staple fare of academic theological publishing.

On one issue, however, I wish to respond to his review. I had said of the passion narrative that "in the case of the Fourth Gospel 'passion' is a misnomer; Jesus controls and orchestrates the whole performance"[122] and that the reader is invited "to *see past* the physical reality of Jesus' death to its true significance: the reascent of the Son of Man to his true home in heaven."[123] Koester was left wondering how I might revise my position "in light of the numerous treatments of the Johannine passion account that have appeared in recent decades" (including no doubt his own, in chapter 6 of *Symbolism*). To which I can only say that I still think that my interpretation does much more justice to the Gospel account than those that stress the painful and sacrificial aspects of Jesus's passion. This is a good example of what I have called the problem of weighting. I place the weight upon *glory*: the evangelist, seeing Jesus's death primarily as a glorification (12:28; 13:31–2; 16:14; 17:5), does his best to eliminate the shameful aspects of Jesus's suffering, omitting, for instance, the stripping and the spitting highlighted by Mark, and selecting a term meaning to lift up or elevate to signify by what death Jesus would die (12:33). In this Gospel, moreover, Jesus deliberately refrains from begging his Father to "save him from this hour" (12:27) and ends his life with a cry of triumph.[124] Koester, by contrast, lays greater stress on the most brutal aspects of the punishments of scourging and crucifixion, and in doing so highlights precisely the aspects of Jesus's passing that, as I see it, the evangelist deliberately tones down.

---

121. Koester, *Symbolism in the Fourth Gospel*.

122. Ashton, *Understanding the Fourth Gospel*, 2nd edition, 464.

123. Ashton, *Understanding the Fourth Gospel*, 2nd edition, 471.

124. To get an idea of the remarkable variety of responses this question still elicits, one has only to turn to a collected volume published in the same year as the second edition of my own book: Van Belle, *Death of Jesus in the Fourth Gospel*, over a thousand pages, with fourteen main papers and thirty-eight shorter contributions.

(c) *The Gospel of John and Christian Origins*
(Minneapolis: Fortress Press, 2014)

Having in some respects moved beyond my earlier work, I will conclude this essay by summarizing the conclusions of my most recent book.

I have never changed my view that, on the fundamental issue of the basic theme of the Gospel, Bultmann was right to conclude that its key concept is revelation. But it is equally the case that for this author the revelation of Jesus, the truth, has replaced an earlier revelation, the law, and that Jesus has ousted Moses from his position as *the* intermediary above all others between God and his people. This extraordinary shift from one religion to another is easier to comprehend in the light of Jewish apocalyptic. The covenanters at Qumran, whilst accepting, like most of their Jewish contemporaries, the authority of the Mosaic law, also acknowledged, unlike them, that there were other seers, especially Daniel and Enoch, whose visions were an additional source of revealed mysteries. They were even invited to contemplate "the mystery of what is coming to pass," the *raz nihyeh*, which, insofar as it could be thought of as God's plan for the world, has—as I have already suggested—an evident parallel in the Johannine Logos, also an object of contemplation. Apocalyptic texts that would have been lost altogether had they not been preserved in Christian sources, are proof of the readiness, in some Jewish circles, to accept further divine revelations, and thus make Christianity itself easier to comprehend.

Over one important issue I disagree with the majority of commentators on the Gospel, namely the question of how the evangelist set about his writing. He is typically thought of as a theologian, or as a biblical scholar eagerly scouring the Old Testament (and sometimes parts of the New) in the hope of finding evidence to support his own ideas, or even, by some, as carefully clipping out phrases from the Synoptic Gospels (which he had on his desk in front of him as he wrote) and inserting them into his own composition in an order and context of his own choosing. But the fact that he was influenced by and alludes to earlier traditions is no reason to believe that he deliberately sought them out. They were part of him, in his mind and in his memory. And from the fact that synoptic-type sayings abound in his Gospel it does not follow that he had the Synoptic Gospels available to him as a written source. Dodd was right about this,[125] but any careful reader of his book can see that his own approach to

---

125. Dodd, *Historical Tradition in the Fourth Gospel.* See too Theobald, *Herrenworte*

the puzzles he deals with on almost every page is entirely literary. He does not consider the possibility that one or more of Jesus's disciples, carrying lodged in their memory a store of sayings on which they could continue to draw, became the nucleus of the Johannine community (as modern scholars were to call it) that had at some point separated from other early Christians and (probably for years) remained part of a Jewish synagogue in the diaspora.

If we accept that the evangelist could draw upon oral tradition whilst composing his Gospel, a further question arises. Where did he get the other ideas that dominate his work? In the last three chapters of my book I discuss what I believe to be the key concepts concerning Jesus that mark out the Fourth Gospel from the other three—prophet, wisdom, Son of Man—arguing that they did not all reach him in the same way.[126]

The first key concept is that of the prophet. One central element in Jesus's own prophetic message (for he knew himself to be a prophet from the outset of his career) was the fatherhood of God. This must have had something to do with the title of Son of God that was soon bestowed on him, though of course the belief that he was the Messiah (called Son of God in the Bible) was also part of the mix. Prophet, Messiah, and Son of God, titles bestowed on Jesus by his very earliest followers, reflect ideas that soon became embedded in the tradition. In Johannine circles, however, as is clear from the testimony of the Baptist recorded early in the Gospel that Jesus had come to be thought of not just as *a* prophet but as *the* prophet, the successor to Moses foretold in Deuteronomy. Much later—it is impossible to say when—he came to be regarded by the traditionalists in the synagogue as a threat, about to oust Moses from his position as the leading intermediary between God and his people. Nevertheless, Jesus's insistence throughout the Gospel that he does nothing of his own accord, that he does not speak on his own authority or seek his own will, shows that even the claim to be the prophet *par excellence* is far from being a claim to be equal with God.

The second key concept is wisdom. In the Old Testament wisdom books, including Job, there are two kinds of wisdom: human and divine. Divine wisdom is often thought of as completely hidden from mankind. Occasionally, however, when she does make herself available, she is sometimes well-received, sometimes badly. The single clear reference in

---

im Johannesevangelium.

126. Ashton, *Gospel of John and Christian Origins*, 133–44, 157–80, 181–99.

the body of the Gospel to the tradition of hidden wisdom ("you will seek me and will not find me; where I am you cannot come": John 7:34; see Prov 1:28) establishes the theme of the unsuccessful hunt for wisdom on the part of Jesus's enemies; but elsewhere in the Gospel, Jesus's success in making himself known draws on the theme of revealed wisdom. So too, though not as a story, does the statement of the incarnation of the Word in the prologue, where most agree that the term *dwell* or *tabernacle* alludes to the tabernacling of the law in Sirach 24:8. Logos is the masculine surrogate of the feminine wisdom.

The third concept is the Danielic Son of Man. Unlike his predecessors, John confers angelic status on Jesus by identifying him as Son of Man *whilst still on earth* (9:35–37; see 5:27). Yet although Jesus never proclaims himself as Son of Man either to his friends or to his enemies (an omission that reinforces our sense of his habitual reticence) he was nevertheless *accused* of claiming equality with God; and it is obvious both from the prologue and from the confession of Thomas in the last chapter that he was believed to be divine by the Johannine community. Moreover although he says repeatedly throughout the Gospel that he neither speaks nor acts on his own authority, he is so closely associated with God that he can say, "I and the Father are one." The message of the prologue is that God's plan for mankind was embodied in the person of Jesus Christ, and we have seen that at one point in the Gospel he identifies himself with the angelic figure of the Son of Man. Yet when all this has been taken into account we are still left with the biggest mystery of all: the extraordinary portrait of Jesus himself.

It commonly happens that somebody else's observation, however important, makes no impact on you—you do not even hear it—until you are ready to receive it. We all suffer from (and sometimes benefit from) a protective deafness. I first read B. H. Streeter's *The Four Gospels* a long time ago. When I reread it some months ago a sentence I had previously passed over unnoticed leapt out from the page: "The starting-point of any profitable study of the Fourth Gospel is the recognition of the author as a mystic—perhaps the greatest of all mystics."[127] Ignored by all other commentators, and dismissed out of hand by Bultmann, the suggestion that the evangelist was a mystic is, I am now convinced, by far the best overall explanation of his extraordinary picture of Jesus, of his deliberate suppression, as far as is possible, of the negative elements in the passion,

127. Streeter, *Four Gospels*, 365.

and of his vision of the crucifixion itself as an elevation. Almost from the start of the Gospel, the wedding feast of Cana, the figure of Christ is bathed in glory (2:11), and his glory never left him, even though it was to be manifested more particularly in his death (13:31–32). The Johannine community realized that the truth they prized as the source of their new life was to be identified not with the Jesus of history, but with a risen Christ free from all human weakness and resplendent in glory.

There is nothing quite like the Fourth Gospel anywhere else in Christian literature, above all in its portrait, quite without parallel, of the figure of Christ. Even when compared with the strange and enigmatic Jesus of the other Gospels, this picture of a man with an absolute assurance of his origin and his destiny, with no doubts, no hesitations, and no fears, is unique. Set in the context of Second Temple Judaism, along with the charge that this was a man who claimed equality with God, it becomes even harder to explain. In relation to other Christian writings, the Gospel of John appeared to Harnack and, later, to Bultmann, the greatest puzzle of all. But the puzzle looms even larger when we see it, as they did not, in the light of the great all-embracing question of how Christianity emerged from Judaism. This was the puzzle at the back of my mind when writing *The Gospel of John and Christian Origins*.

One Final Thought

"It would be a valuable practice for the historian," writes J. L. Martyn, "to rise each morning saying to himself three times slowly and with emphasis, 'I do not know' . . . The number of points in the history of the Johannine community about which we may be virtually certain," he continues, "is relatively small, and we need to be clear about this."[128] But historians, like politicians, are also rhetoricians, out to persuade. They may sometimes be prepared to say, "I do not know"; but for the most part they will find it hard to temper their assertions at every point with *perhaps* and *probably*, which, in strict accuracy, they should include. On the other hand, their readers, recognizing the genre of historical argument for what it is, ought to be critical enough to introduce their own modifications. *Caveat lector.*

---

128. Martyn, *Gospel of John in Christian History*, 92.

2

Really a Prologue?

THE MOST FUNDAMENTAL QUESTION concerning the first eighteen verses of the Gospel of John is whether the traditional title, prologue, can be exegetically justified. On the very first page of his splendid commentary, after the long introduction, Michael Theobald writes of *der sogenannte Prolog*.[1] True, his hesitation proceeds solely from his conviction that the real opening of the Gospel is the whole of the first chapter, which he refers to as a *großraümiges Diptychon*—an exceedingly spacious diptych; and a couple of pages further on he allows that that there are good grounds for the name *Pro-logos*. Nevertheless it still may be asked whether verses originally composed as a hymn to the Logos are a proper introduction to a narrative in which the Logos is never mentioned, and where there is not even a hint of the idea that forms the climax of the hymn, the startlingly novel concept of incarnation. In no respect, moreover, does the prologue perform the usual function of a preface or introduction, which is to summarize the content of what follows.

In this opening paragraph I have already declared my allegiance to what I will call the H camp—scholars who, following Adolf Harnack,[2] believe that the prologue was built around a previously existing composition generally known as the Logos hymn, and that at some point the evangelist substituted this for an earlier introduction to his Gospel. The

---

1. Theobald, *Das Evangelium nach Johannes*, 108. In this respect he agrees with C. H. Dodd, who refers to the whole of chapter 1 as "The Proem: Prologue and Testimony" (Dodd, *Interpretation of the Fourth Gospel*, 292).

2. Harnack, "Über das Verhältniß des Prologs," 189–231.

other camp (I will call it the B camp—B for Barrett) consists of those who maintain that the evangelist himself wrote the entire prologue for the express purpose of furnishing a proper introduction to all that follows. Between these two is a smaller group of scholars who, whilst admitting the basic truth of the Harnack hypothesis, think that the prologue is the first and only introduction to the Gospel, and that the evangelist wrote it round the Logos hymn because he saw this to be the key to his own work.

There are two points of agreement between the three groups. First there is their recognition that verses 6–8 and 15, commonly called the "Baptist" verses (although John is never called the Baptist in this Gospel) purposely anticipate what follows. (This, however, is no answer to the difficulties outlined in my first paragraph, because the link established by these verses goes no further than chapter 1.) Secondly there is a shared conviction that the central concept of the prologue, the Logos, is directly reflected in the remainder of the Gospel. If not, why is it there at all? For the most part this conviction amounts to no more than an intuition, a gut feeling neither articulated nor argued, but simply taken for granted.[3] It is a conviction, however, that I share, and the main purpose of this paper is to give it exegetical justification. I will devote the first section of my paper to exposing the flaws in what seem to me to be some inadequate defenses of this fundamental intuition: but before doing so I want to refer briefly to the work of two of the most admired twentieth-century writers on the Gospel, Rudolf Bultmann and C. H. Dodd, both of whom share the basic conviction that the key to the Gospel is to be found in what the latter calls "the Logos-doctrine."

According to Dodd, "the Logos-doctrine is placed first, because, addressing a public nurtured in the higher religion of Hellenism, the writer wishes to offer the Logos-idea as the appropriate approach, for them, to

3. E.g., Beasley-Murray, *John*, 5: "a directive to the reader how the entire Gospel should be understood"; Schnelle, *Das Evangelium nach Johannes*, 10, remarks: "Der Prolog . . . dient als Lektüreanweisung für die Leser, indem er das vom Evangelisten beabsichtigte Verstehen des Folgenden vorbereitet und prägt"; Witherington, *John's Wisdom*, 47, notes: "a key for the hearer or reader to understand what follows"; Ridderbos, *Gospel of John*, 17, sees it as "a splendidly constructed a priori introduction to the story"; Hooker, *Beginnings*, 65: "if you are so foolish as to begin reading the story at 1:19 you will have thrown away the key to what follows"; Culpepper, *Gospel and Letters of John*, 109, also regards it as "the key to understanding all that will follow"; Lincoln, *Gospel According to Saint John*, 108–9, remarks: "readers are being equipped from the start to be able to share the narrator's guiding perspective"; Thyen, *Das Johannesevangelium*, 64, also opines that the prologue "eines literarischen Werkes die Lektüre der gesamten ihm folgenden evangelischen Erzählung . . . bestimmen soll."

the central purpose of the Gospel, through which he may lead them to the historical actuality of its story."[4] Bultmann, unlike most others, recognizes that "the Prologue is no introduction or foreword in the ordinary sense of the words," for "there is no indication in it of the content or structure of what follows."[5] Yet even so he has no hesitation in declaring that "the theme of the Gospel is stated in the ὁ λόγος σὰρξ ἐγένετο,"[6] a declaration that is demonstrably false, since there is no trace in the body of the Gospel (or indeed anywhere else in the Bible apart from 1 and 2 John) of the strange idea of incarnate wisdom, the λόγος ἔνσαρκος or the λόγος σεσαρκωμένος.[7]

I. Some False Routes

A small number of scholars do attempt to defend the view that the prologue prepares readers for what follows, and is intended to do so. A close examination of their arguments will give us a better idea of the nature of the problem.

First let us look at Charles Kingsley Barrett's defense of the thesis in his Ethel M. Wood lecture, "The Prologue of St John's Gospel," delivered in February 1970. One reason why Barrett's work is particularly interesting is that the narrative critics (who now dominate what I have called the B group) joined in the game too late for him to have come across them when he delivered this lecture. He begins by expounding a number of earlier theories—those of Bultmann and Käsemann in some detail, and then another half-dozen attempts to reconstruct the original hymn, summed up in Raymond Brown's recently published commentary. Barrett rejects them all.

At the time he gave his lecture most Johannine scholars agreed with Harnack and, somewhat later, Rendel Harris,[8] in holding that some

---

4. *Interpretation of the Fourth Gospel*, 296.

5. *The Gospel of John*, 13.

6. *The Gospel of John*, 64. He returns to this theme at several points in his commentary: pp. 151, 468, 631, 632, 634, 659.

7. Scholars are surely right to find in the second phrase of 1:14, καὶ ἐσκήνωσεν ἐν ἡμῖν, an intentional allusion to Sir. 24:8, where Wisdom, soon to be identified with the Law (24:23), says, "The one who created me (ὁ κτίσας με) assigned a place for my tent (σκηνή) [also *tabernacle*]. And he said, 'Make your dwelling (κατασκήνωσον) [*Tabernacle*] in Jacob.'" But there is no question of the law taking flesh.

8. "The Origin of the Prologue to John's Gospel," 147–70, 314–20, 388–400,

kind of wisdom hymn had been adapted as the basis of the prologue we now have. In setting out to disprove this theory, Barrett starts by showing that there was no agreement concerning the verses in the prologue that should be assigned to the hymn. Nor was there any agreement about the language of the hymn: some thought it was Aramaic, others Greek. Virtually the only point of unanimity was that verses 6–8 and 15, which deal with the witness of the Baptist, were prose insertions in a poetical prologue.

This is where Barrett begins his own argument: "Let us see how we fare if, instead of treating them as later supplements, looked at last (if looked at at all), we begin with them."[9] He concludes that what the prologue says about John in verses 6–8 is a summary of the extended treatment in chapters 1, 3, and 4, and that "in 1:15 later material is quoted in an awkward manner which evidently presupposes that the reader of the Prologue must be familiar with the narrative that follows: This is he of whom I said, He who comes after me has come to be before me, for he was before me."[10] He concludes that this is how the author succeeds in placing the subsequent narrative in an intelligible setting. "This means that the 'Baptist' verses were not an afterthought, but part of a serious, connected, thought-out, theological purpose." Then, a little later, comes the decisive move in the argument:

> If this is the origin and meaning of the "Baptist" verses in the Prologue it is reasonable to suppose that this will also be the origin and meaning of the rest; that is, that, as these verses were designed to bring out the theological significance of the story of the Baptist, so the Prologue as a whole was designed to bring out the theological significance of the history of Jesus . . . The evangelist knows that however indispensable the figure of the Baptist may be . . . he is not the *beginning* of the Gospel.[11]

I have three comments to make on this argument.

1. Earlier in his lecture, Barrett had observed: "We may ask whether there are breaks in sense, which would lead us to suspect the activity of a more or less intelligent editor; but this is a matter of exegesis."[12] By

---

415–26.

   9. Barrett, *Prologue of St. John's Gospel*, 18.

  10. Barrett, *Prologue of St. John's Gospel*, 22–23.

  11. Barrett, *Prologue of St. John's Gospel*, 23, 24.

  12. Barrett, *Prologue of St. John's Gospel*, 17.

deliberately commencing his own discussion not at verse 1 but at verse 6, which is precisely where other scholars had in fact noticed a break in sense, he is ducking the obligation to answer his own question.

2. Much of what he says about the "Baptist" verses is true, but none of it counters or disproves the widespread theory that verses 6–8 were inserted into an already-existing hymn, and that 1:15 was roughly copied from 1:30.

3. In moving from what he had shown was probably the purpose of the "Baptist" verses to the assertion "that this will also be the origin and meaning of the rest," Barrett is assuming what he was setting out to prove. He offers no convincing explanation of the quite exceptional nature of all that is said here concerning the Logos. This, unlike what he calls the "Baptist" verses, has no direct parallel elsewhere in the Gospel. The Logos itself, the undisputed subject of the prologue, vanishes from sight when it is over, and never reappears.

In the second edition of his commentary, published seven years after this lecture, Barrett goes even further: "If the Prologue was intended to express in eighteen verses the theological content of twenty chapters a good deal of condensation was necessary; and much of John's Christology is condensed in the word λόγος."[13] This *if*-clause, it must be said, is nothing but an unargued assumption. I have already pointed out that the word λόγος occurs nowhere else in the Gospel in the sense it has in the prologue. How is it possible to move from the use of this single word to the complex Christology of the body of the Gospel, where there is not so much as a hint of incarnation, and Jesus's entry into the world is always referred to either as a descent (as Son of Man) or a mission?

A very different defense of the theory that the prologue was composed to introduce the Gospel is to be found in James Dunn's article, "Let John be John," first published in 1983.[14] Dunn proceeds on what I believe to be the correct assumption that "*the task of setting John in its historical context must be given a place of priority* in any inquiry into the gospel and

13. Barrett, *Gospel According to St. John*, 151. In his article, "The Pivot of John's Prologue," 2n5, R. A. Culpepper gives a list of other scholars who affirm the unity of the prologue: Eltester, Lamarche, Irgoin, Ridderbos, Borgen, Hooker, Fenton, F. W. Schlatter, and Van den Bussche, to which one might add the names of Culpepper himself, Léon-Dufour, Berger, Ruckstuhl, and (as we shall see) J. Neyrey and J. Zumstein.

14. Dunn, "Let John be John," 293–322.

the fourth Gospel."[15] And he is also right to observe that in pursuing this task "it is *the context of late first-century Judaism* which must have first claim on our attention."[16] But is he right to say that the prologue gives us the clue to the evangelist's distinctive Christology? I think not.

Dunn finds it "impossible to regard the prologue . . . as redactional (i.e., added after the Fourth Evangelist put the Gospel into its present form); the themes of the prologue are too closely integrated into the Gospel as a whole and are so clearly intended to introduce these themes that such a conclusion is rendered implausible."[17]

Read uncritically, his arguments may look quite cogent. He is certainly right to note the close resemblance of John's Logos to the figure of Wisdom in the Old Testament, "distinct from all other potential intermediaries[. . .]by virtue of *its precosmic existence with God . . .* , and precisely by virtue of *its close identity with God*."[18] But he is surely wrong to find echoes of this tradition in "the idea of being sent or descending from heaven." The ideas of mission and descent (two ideas, not one) are indeed found in the Gospel, the first associated with the Son, the second with the Son of Man. But neither of them occurs in the prologue or, for that matter, in the Jewish wisdom tradition. Moreover, the "I am" statements, to which Dunn also appeals, though they can be matched by instances of self-declaration in the wisdom literature, have no obvious connection with these.

So when Dunn concludes that it is precisely because "the Son is the incarnate Logos, God in his 'knowability' and 'visibility', that the Son can say, 'He that has seen me has seen the Father' (12:45; 14:9),"[19] he is assuming, like Barrett before him, what he needs to prove. He is confident that the key to John's distinctive Christology is to see the titles, Messiah, Son of God, and Son of Man, "primarily as *an elaboration of the initial explicit identification of Jesus as the incarnate Wisdom/Logos.*" But this is another *petitio principii*. All these titles are drawn from Jewish traditions that

15. Dunn, "Let John be John," 295 (emphasis in the original).

16. Dunn, "Let John be John," 303 (emphasis in the original).

17. Dunn, "Let John be John," 313n78. There is some confusion here, because the Gospel in its present form *includes* the prologue. And there is no reason why an introduction added after the rest of the work has been completed should not echo and reflect most of its main themes. Many operatic overtures do just that, and many literary prefaces too.

18. Dunn, "Let John be John," 313 (emphasis in the original).

19. Dunn, "Let John be John," 314.

have nothing to do with wisdom. As Jean Zumstein concludes, at the end of his own discussion of the prologue, any hope of finding a summary of the Gospel's theology in the Logos hymn is illusory.[20]

Jerome Neyrey, in his 2007 commentary, shows no interest in the long-standing and widely held belief that the prologue is built around a wisdom hymn. He refers to this theory in the past tense: "*When* scholars argued that the prologue was a wisdom hymn . . ."[21] Since that time, he implies, things have changed: "*Now* scholars stress the extensive relationship between prologue and Gospel, such that one might say that the prologue is . . . an overture, a summary of what is subsequently developed."[22] To demonstrate this, Neyrey promises to "unpack every verse of the prologue, identifying its major thematic elements and indicate some places in the Gospel where these themes reappear."[23]

This he does in nineteen paragraphs. To show the nature and the quality of his demonstration it will be sufficient (but also, I fear, necessary) to quote a substantial portion of the first three.

> 1. *Word of God and Words of God.* In the beginning was the unique Word (1:1), who alone makes God known (1:18; 6:46). Moreover, the Word of God "comes from heaven . . . and testifies to what he has seen and heard . . . He whom God has sent speaks the words of God" (3:31–34). In his final prayer, Jesus tells God how faithful he has been in revealing God's word: "I have made your name known to those whom you gave me from the world" (17:6, 26) . . .

> 2. *The Word Was "God."* In several places, Jesus is accused of being "equal to God" (5:17–18; 10:33). The name "God" will be shown to refer to God's creative power, which Jesus, who is Logos and "God," exercises in 1:1–3. The deity's other name, "Lord," is associated with the second power (i.e. eschatological power).

---

20. "Le prologue, seuil du quatrième évangile," 259. For a German version of this article, see J. Zumstein's *Kreative Erinnerung,* 105–26.

21. Neyrey, *Gospel of John,* 41.

22. Neyrey, *Gospel of John,* 41–42 (emphasis added); "a wisdom hymn," Neyrey adds, adverting to the very first version of the theory, advanced by Adolf Harnack as long ago as 1892, "stitched by the author to the front of the Gospel to make it more acceptable to Hellenistic readers." Harnack of course did not write in those terms and most of the subsequent supporters of the basic theory have not subscribed to his view of its purpose.

23. Neyrey, *Gospel of John,* 42.

Hence, at the Gospel's ending, when Jesus has demonstrated power over death, he is acclaimed "My Lord and My God."

3. *In Him Was Life.* Jesus tells us that God gave him "to have life in himself (5:26), meaning that Jesus is imperishable or immortal, just as God is. Jesus also tells us that God gave him power to lay down his life and power to take it up (10:17–18). Both of these remarks, we suggest, indicate what the author means when he says "in him was life."[24]

The arguments are feeble, the exegesis null. I will comment briefly, in turn, on just these three paragraphs.

1. It is misleading, indeed confusing, to place the preexistent Logos right at the outset alongside "the words of God," as if these were conceptually related, and as if the words recorded in the Gospel were uttered not by Jesus but by God himself. Crucially too, as I have already noted, neither in the body of the Gospel nor anywhere else in the Bible apart from the prologue and 1 and 2 John is there any trace of the startlingly novel idea of *incarnate wisdom*.

2. The accusation of *claiming* to be (not of *being*) equal to God is one that Jesus *defends himself against* in chapter 5, protesting that he can do nothing of his own accord (ἀπ᾽ ἐμαυτοῦ, v. 30). True, he does say elsewhere, "I and the Father are one" (10:30) and "he who has seen me has seen the Father" (14:9), but these apparent contradictions require careful elucidation. Moreover God's other name in this Gospel is not *Lord* but *Father*. The term *Lord* (Κύριος) is how Jesus's disciples address him, as he observes in 13:14. It is never used to refer to God in the Gospel except in biblical quotations (1:23; 12:13, 38).

3. God's bestowal of life upon Jesus *does not* include the gift of immortality, for he dies later on the cross. And when the Shepherd lays down his life for his sheep this is not ζωή, but ψυχή, which corresponds in Hebrew to נפש, not to חיים, in Latin to *anima*, natural human life, not to *vita*.

In 2008, thirty years after the publication of Barrett's commentary, Martin Hengel also declared himself in favor of the view that the prologue is related to the Gospel and "can come [*mag kommen?*] from the Evangelist himself." Unlike Barrett, however, he recognizes that what Barrett

24. Neyrey, *Gospel of John*, 42

calls the "Baptist" verses, "written in the same style as the hymn (!), have been inserted to clamp it to the Gospel." He contemptuously dismisses the many attempts to reconstruct the original shorter form of the hymn. Referring to Michael Theobald's painstaking *Habilitationsschrift*,[25] which reports some forty of these—"Naïveté or hybris on the part of exegetes," he asks, "or both?" But why should all or any of these scholarly undertakings be ascribed to naivity or hubris? In what follows, Hengel proceeds on the basis of his own conviction that this "hymn or psalm to the Logos" is the work of the evangelist himself, "who describes in stages the saving revelation of God through his Word."[26]

II. The Logos Hymn

It is of course true that of forty mutually incompatible reconstructions only one can be correct. But Hengel's response is like that of a man chafing impatiently before a locked door who, when handed forty different keys, each supposed to fit the lock, throws them all away and stalks off in a dudgeon. Inquiry into the hymn that underlies the prologue is by no means wasted effort, even if, as Michael Theobald admits, "der Streit um dessen genaue Gestalt vielleicht nie zur Ruhe kommen wird."[27] The crucial difficulty lies in distinguishing the original hymn from subsequent comments on it. If this could be done tolerably well we would have some indication of the evangelist's own understanding of the hymn and his reasons for using it as a preface to his Gospel. Although we have to admit that absolute certainty is unachievable, the possibilities are limited; and by moving within the limits we may dispel some of the fog.

Let me outline the two main problems:

1. Was the prologue composed before or after the body of the Gospel? The majority of commentators think (and most simply assume) that it was composed first, as a deliberate introduction. My own view is that this is unlikely, for two reasons—first the awkwardness of the insertions concerning John the Baptist, especially the second, and secondly the absence of any reference to the words and deeds of Jesus that make up the substance of the Gospel, or to his passion and death. If the author of the

---

25. Theobald, *Die Fleischwerdung des Logos.*

26. Hengel, "Prologue of the Gospel of John," 266.

27. Schnelle, *Das Evangelium nach Johannes*, 105.

prologue had been concerned to prepare for what follows by rehearsing its main motifs, then he would have included at the very least some reference to these—the stuff of the Gospel that follows. Yet they are not even alluded to in the prologue that we have. Accordingly, I am persuaded that the prologue was not attached to the Gospel until a recognizable version of this had already been composed (the first edition)—signs, discourses, controversies, passion, and resurrection—and that it was added for some other reason than to provide readers with a guide enabling them to understand all this material.

2. Which of the eighteen verses, and which parts of them, belong to the original hymn, and which were added later as interjections or comments? Barrett, collating earlier estimates in the course of preparing his 1970 lecture, found that altogether "a maximum of thirteen verses are ascribed to the poetic source (1–5, 9–12, 14, 16–18); the minimum figure . . . is five (1, 3, 4, 10, 11)."[28] If we accept the broad consensus that at least 6–8 and 15 were later additions, and that Ernst Käsemann was wrong to exclude 14 and 16, we would still be left with disputes over six of the eighteen verses. Yet although any attempt at greater precision is always going to be open to doubt, no one looking for evidence of the evangelist's intentions can rest content with so much uncertainty. As Michael Theobald says of those who refuse the challenge: "sie berauben sich damit wichtiger Einsichten."[29] So here I want to take one further step. One fact about the Greek text, not recognized by all commentators but highlighted by Theobald,[30] should be taken into account. In the conclusion of 1:10 ("the world did not know him"), the word translated *him* is masculine (αὐτόν). This means that it cannot originally have taken up the *light* of 1:9, which is neuter (φῶς). And 1:9, after the interruption of 1:6–8, follows on from 1:5, which, picking up the conclusion of 1:4, is also about the light. So it looks as if the reflections about the light in 1:5 and 9 are comments added by the evangelist. (Also, the rather puzzling use of the present tense φαίνει in 1:5 ceases to be problematic provided it is understood as a remark of the evangelist writing in his own present.) If, then, bracketing 1:5–9, we think of the "him" of 1:10 as taking up the "him" of 1:4 (also a masculine, referring to the Logos)], then there is no problem with the grammar: "what came to pass in him was life, and the

28. Barrett, *Prologue of St. John's Gospel*, 14.

29. Schnelle, *Das Evangelium nach Johannes*, 105.

30. Schnelle, *Das Evangelium nach Johannes*, 105–6; Theobald, *Die Fleischwerdung des Logos*, 467–69.

life was the light of men: he was in the world, and the world did not know him. He came to his own home and his own people did not receive him [another masculine]."

We may accept this grammatical argument and bracket out 1:5 and 9, or we may reject it and retain 5 and at least part of 9. In either case, provided we acknowledge that Logos (masculine) can stand as a surrogate for Wisdom (feminine in Hebrew as well as Greek) we have the beginning of what looks like a hymn in praise of wisdom. The next two verses, 12 and 13, are disputed. Following Theobald once more, I think that not only 13 but also the conclusion of 12, τοῖς πιστεύουσιν εἰς τὸ ὄνομα αὐτοῦ, is an explanatory comment added by the evangelist to emphasize, right at the beginning of his work, the overriding importance of faith. Without at least the first clause of 12, however, there is no continuation, because without an explicit acknowledgement that at least *some* people did actually welcome the coming of the Word, then there would have been no course open to him, after a fruitless visit to earth, but to follow the example of Enoch's Wisdom and return to heaven (1 En. 42:1–2). But then comes the crucial verse 14, and then, without a break, verse 16. This would give us, as a minimum, the following conclusion: "But to all who received him he gave power to become children of God . . . And the Word became flesh and dwelt among us, full of grace and truth; we have gazed upon his glory . . . And from his fullness we have all received."

This leaves us with an original hymn comprising verses 1–4, 10–11, the beginning of 12, most of 14,[31] and 16. At 17, however, with respect, I take issue with Theobald, who assigns it to the hymn. Bultmann holds that it is an exegetical gloss on 1:16, "which mentions the name Ἰησοῦς Χριστός, suppressed until now, abruptly, and without any introduction."[32] I think it is much more than a gloss on the preceding verse, but defer any comment until later.

First I want to return to the thesis that the evangelist composed his prologue from the outset as a preface to his Gospel. At the start of my essay I stressed the lamentable weakness of the arguments of three different champions of this thesis. But of course one cannot conclude that their

---

31. As Theobald, *Das Evangelium nach Johannes*, 106, points out, the phrase "glory as of the only Son from the Father" introduces an idea not to be found in the original hymn: it must have been added by the evangelist.

32. Bultmann, *Gospel of John*, 17.

thesis is wrong simply because of the weakness of the arguments they use to defend it.

Jean Zumstein, in a very interesting and original essay,[33] offers a different defense. Without naming Barrett or Dunn, he highlights very clearly the flaws in their main arguments, and lends some plausibility to his own thesis simply by skirting circumspectly around the pitfalls into which they had stumbled.

In stressing the links (*liens*, *Verbindungen*) between the prologue and the Gospel, he makes four points. I have no problem with the first three of these. (The second, based on the "Baptist" verses, is undisputed.) The fourth, however, listing what he calls "toute une série de catégories théologiques fondamentales," is less convincing, because although Zumstein provisionally accepts the thesis of an underlying Logos hymn ("à supposer que cette thèse soit fondée"), he makes no attempt to distinguish between the terms in the prologue that are shared by the Gospel and the Logos hymn and those that are not.[34] This is important, because if—the very point at issue—the bulk of the Gospel was composed before the prologue was added, then it is obviously a mistake to suppose that concepts (and words) found *both* in the original hymn *and* in the Gospel were introduced into the prologue with the express purpose of fashioning links. They were there already. Moreover the terms involved here are among the most significant of all: life, light, knowledge, truth, glory, and possibly the light/darkness antithesis too.[35] As Zumstein says himself, it is from what the evangelist has added to the hymn ("les ajouts rédactionnels") that we can learn how he reread it.

On the question of whether the prologue was composed before or after the narrative that follows, Zumstein sidesteps all earlier discussion. Ignoring the earlier arguments of Brown, Lindars, and Becker that we have to reckon with a number of different stages in the composition of the Gospel, he focuses exclusively on the extended reflection in Michael

---

33. Zumstein, "Le prologue."

34. Yet Zumstein is clearly aware of the distinction, and lists the probable additions: vv. 6–8 and 15, 12c–13, and 17–18 (Zumstein, "Le prologue," 225). Later it becomes clear that he fully accepts the old thesis: "pour commencer son oeuvre, l'évangéliste a recouru à un hymne traditionnel en usage dans les communautés johanniques" (Zumstein, "Le prologue," 228).

35. Depending upon whether one sees verse 5 and (part of) verse 9 as belonging to the original hymn or as having been added by the evangelist.

Theobald's *Fleischwerdung*.[36] Yet he gives surprisingly short shrift even to this. After briefly outlining the summary Theobald offers (on little more than a page) of his own position, he swerves aside. "L'histoire de la composition du quatrième évangile," he declares, "reste un énigme," and in response to the question whether one has to have recourse to a diachronic model to explain all the continuities and discontinuities that characterize the relationship between the prologue and the body of the Gospel, he replies, simply, "Nous le pensons pas,"[37] evidently reluctant to deal with the many reasons that multiple-stage theorists had advanced in defense of this theory.

Both Theobald and Zumstein are interested in what the former, following H. Lausberg, calls the *Metareflexivität* of the prologue. "Contre Theobald," says Zumstein, "on fera valoir que le caractère métatexte du prologue n'implique en aucune façon son caractère secondaire."[38] But Theobald would probably agree: still following Lausberg[39] he had said this: "Über die Feststellung der rein formalen 'Metareflexivität' des Prologs hinaus müssen noch andere Argumente mit ins Spiel kommen, will man für Verfasser-Verschiedenheit plädieren."[40] One of these additional arguments is the fact that apart from a few redactional passages "gibt es keinen Text im Ev, der unbedingt zu seinem Verständnis den Prolog voraussetzt." This is surely right. But when Theobald adds that it is rather the case that "der Prolog auf den narrativen Vorgaben des Corpus Evangelii aufruht und aus ihrer Terminologie gebildet ist,"[41] I have to disagree, if only because so many of the key words occur in the Logos hymn, and

36. Though drawing attention in a note to Theobald's whole argument (Theobald, *Das Evangelium nach Johannes*, 296–399, 438–93), he focuses on the two-page summary (Theobald, *Das Evangelium nach Johannes*, 371–73).

37. Zumstein, "Le prologue," 225.

38. Zumstein, "Le prologue," 225n25. What does he mean by *caractère secondaire*? If he is saying that it does not follow from the reflective character of the prologue that it was written *after* the text it introduces, then of course he is right. (Though I strongly suspect that the vast majority of prologues and prefaces, overtures and introductions, were composed after, mostly very soon after, the work that they precede.) The important question is not *when* the prologue was written, before or after the body of the Gospel, but the nature and substance of the reflections that can be discerned in it and how far they bear upon the Gospel itself.

39. Lausberg, *Der Johannes-Prolog*.

40. Theobald, *Die Fleischwerdung des Logos*, 298.

41. Theobald, *Die Fleischwerdung des Logos*, 373.

the origins of this hymn are certainly not to be sought in the body of the Gospel.

These are difficult issues. The most effective way of throwing light on them, I suggest, is to start with the time-honored theory that the evangelist made use of the Logos hymn when composing the prologue, and then to weigh up the plausibility of suggestions based upon this supposition. This is what I propose to do in the concluding part of this essay. But first . . .

III. An Historical Parenthesis

Someone once commented upon the remarkable number of skeletons that litter the graveyard of research into the Fourth Gospel. Quite a few of these turn out on inspection to be theses concerning its composition. The partitionist theories of Weisse, Schweizer, and Wendt (names that most Johannine scholars nowadays would not even recognize)[42] have been lying there, long forgotten, for the best part of two centuries. The displacement theories that succeeded them (Kümmel dates the first of these to 1871)[43] later received strong endorsement from no less a scholar than Rudolf Bultmann, and lingered on in one form or another for over a century, only receiving their final *coup de grâce* (a merciful release, as it appeared to many) with Ernst Haenchen's unfinished commentary of 1980,[44] when they were laid to rest alongside other recently deceased oddities like Gillis Wetter's "divine man" theory and Bultmann's much vaunted Mandaean source.

Meanwhile, however, a rather different explanation had been suggested of what, following the exhaustive studies of Eduard Schwartz early in the twentieth century, had come to be called the Gospel's aporias. What is sometimes known as the multiple-stage theory is built upon the hypothesis that the Gospel as we know it was not originally planned as a unified composition; the awkward bumps in the present text result from the failure of one or more editors or redactors to ensure a smooth transition at points where new material has been added. Wilhelm Wilkens, the

42. I discuss these briefly in my *Understanding the Fourth Gospel*, 1st edition, 28–29.

43. Kümmel, *Introduction to the New Testament*, 198.

44. In a section of his introduction headed "Disorder and Rearrangement," Haenchen concludes, "The time of theories of displacement is gone" (Haenchen, *John 1*, 51).

first scholar, as far as I know, to come up with a coherent version of this theory, thought of the evangelist as an eyewitness who twice revised his original work.[45] The most recent of numerous different proposals built upon the same basic premise employ the term *relecture* to indicate that in some cases the additional material is to be seen as a revision of an earlier text in the light of new situations which, according to this new modification of the theory, have arisen in the life of the community.[46]

In certain quarters the multiple-stage theory won wide acceptance, but eventually it came up abruptly against the formidable obstacle of narrative criticism. Like C. H. Dodd, who may be seen as a precursor of this new method of gospel study,[47] the narrative critics simply ignore the problems wrestled with by their predecessors. They see no point in offering new solutions to these, because once it is admitted that the exegete's real responsibility is to deal with the text as has been transmitted, then even the most intractable of the aporias are of no consequence. Narrative critics need not bother to choose from among the wide variety of multiple-stage theories that have been put forward, because the delicate task of discerning between different levels of redaction has no relevance to their own work. Clearly what holds for the body of the Gospel holds for the prologue too. Narrative critics have no need of or use for the kind of defense of its integrity we have seen offered by Bultmann and Dunn.

It is worth observing, in concluding this parenthesis, that the multiple-stage theory, unlike the earlier partitionist and displacement theories, has never been disproved. As Michael Theobald notes (opening his brief discussion of the issue under the heading, *Die sekundäre Redaktion des Buches*), the supposition that the Gospel results from a single casting (*aus einem Guß*), and that chapters 1–21 are the work of a single author, was enjoying a certain popularity at the time he was writing his own book (i.e., the years preceding its publication in 2009). But this supposition,

---

45. Wilkins, *Die Entstehungsgeschichte des vierten Evangeliums*.

46. Jean Zumstein himself is the leading proponent of *relecture*, and his *Kreative Erinnerung* (see n20) is full of fruitful suggestions arising from the insight that many passages in the Gospel, especially chapters 15–17, were composed later than others. So I find it puzzling and paradoxical that *at the same time* (for his essay on the prologue is included in *Kreative Erinnerung*) he completely rejects (p. 113) what he calls *ein diachrones Modell*. (Other scholars who have worked along the same lines include Zumstein's assistant, A. Dettwiler, and C. Hoegen-Rohls.)

47. See Culpepper, "C. H. Dodd as a Precursor," 31–65.

as he points out, mildly, overlooks the literary facts (*geht an den literarischen Befunden vorbei*).[48]

Having myself argued previously, following Raymond Brown, Barnabas Lindars, and, to a lesser extent, J. Louis Martyn, that there were at least two distinct stages (generally called *editions*) in the composition of the Gospel,[49] I was gratified to discover that Theobald, whose commentary, I am embarrassed to confess, I only discovered some years after it had been published, is in basic agreement with this thesis. Indeed, he amplifies and refines it in impressive detail.[50] I now think that the prologue was added to the Gospel just before (or at the same time as) the new material of the second edition, notably chapters 6 and 17.[51]

IV. A Real Prologue

1. The Logos Hymn

If we accept the traditional view that the evangelist has taken a Logos hymn, probably written by one of his own community, and adapted it to make a new beginning for his Gospel, then we may wonder why. What was his motive for doing so? And what is the significance of the reflections he appends at the end?[52]

Almost without exception commentators refer to this as a creation hymn. But this is wrong—most obviously wrong, perhaps, in the Latin translation of 1:3, *Omnia per ipsum facta sunt*, echoed later in the key verse, *Et verbum caro factum est*. The Latin translator, blinded by the

48. Schnelle, *Das Evangelium nach Johannes*, 70.

49. Ashton, *Understanding the Fourth Gospel*, 1st edition, 76–90, 160–66.

50. Schnelle, *Das Evangelium nach Johannes*, 70–74. Only on two points (important ones) do I find myself in disagreement. Theobald insists that the Gospel is a *Gemeindebuch*; but I see no reason to suppose, except in the case of chapter 21, that anyone other than the evangelist himself had a hand in the major secondary redactions. (1 John is a different matter.) And I have argued, following Lindars, that the whole of chapter 6 (not just verses 51c–58 and 64–65) belonged to the second edition.

51. It is in these two chapters that we find the most direct references to the prologue. 6:46 ("Not that anyone has seen the Father *except him who is from God*") reflects and corrects 1:18 ("No one has ever seen God"); 17:5 ("the glory I had with thee before the existence of the world") and 17:24 ("in your love for me before the foundation of the world") echo the key motif of preexistence.

52. I first advanced the argument summarized here nearly thirty years ago, and have recently repeated it, slightly modified, in a recently published book: Ashton, *Gospel of John and Christian Origins*, 145–55.

allusion to Genesis in the very first verse, has mistranslated the Greek verb γίνεσθαι, which does not mean *to be made*, but *to come to pass*. Compare this with the Syriac, where the translator, more alert and not misled by the initial allusion to Genesis, translates literally: "Everything came to pass in him, and apart from him not even one thing came to pass."[53] Latin, moreover, having no definite article, cannot discriminate between two very different Greek terms: τὰ πάντα, the regular term for the whole universe,[54] and πάντα, which means *everything*, but much more vaguely. One Greek writer, the gnostic Ptolemy, keenly aware of the difference, and anxious nevertheless to find support for his own conviction that this prestigious and authoritative author was as concerned as he was himself with the genesis of the universe (τῶν ὁλῶν), writes this: "he (the apostle John) λέγει εἶναι τά τε πάντα δι᾽ αὐτοῦ γεγογέναι καὶ χωρὶς αὐτοῦ γεγογέναι οὐδέν" (cited by Epiphanius, *Panarion* 33.3.6). Ptolemy recognized that the article was required before πάντα in John 1:3 to give him the sense he required, and evidently had no compunction in adding it, realizing that otherwise the prologue would provide no backing for his views.

One important early Jewish writer found support in the opening of Genesis for the belief that, as Carol Newsom puts it, "what endows the world with meaning is . . . that set of structured relationships called מחשבת כבודו, *His [i.e. God's] glorious plan*."[55] For, as she explains, where Genesis 1 is concerned with creation, in 1QS 3–4 the author of the Community Rule "is concerned with the מחשבת [i.e. the plan, literally *thought*, of God] that grounds creation."[56] "From the God of Knowledge comes all that is and shall be, כול הווה ונהייה" (1QS 3:15), a text in which the Hebrew nipʿal of היה corresponds exactly to the Syriac pʿal of *hwh* as this occurs in the Curetonian version of John 1:3 and 14, translating, in both instances, the Greek ἐγένετο. *This is precisely the concern of the author of the Logos hymn—not creation, but the plan of God.* What caught the attention of the

53. Burkitt, *Evangelion da-Mepharreshe*, 1:423. An exact parallel is to be found in 4 Ezra 6:6: "then I planned these things and they came into being through me and not another," for where the Syriac (in Michael Stone's translation) has "came into being," the Latin, just as in John 1:3, has *facta sunt*.

54. For examples of this usage in the Old Testament, see Gen 1:11; 9:3; Job 8:3; 11:10; Wis. 1:7, 14. For the New Testament, see Rom 11:36; 1 Cor 8:6; Col 1:16–17; Heb 2:10.

55. Newsom, *Self as Symbolic Space*, 84.

56. Newsom, *Self as Symbolic Space*, 86.

evangelist in this hymn and seized his imagination had little to do with creation. Rather it was the coincidence of the meaning of the word Logos (the divine plan) with the story he had just told; for he could now see that God's plan for humankind was nothing more and nothing less than the life, death, and resurrection of Jesus, and all his words and deeds, as he had recounted them in his Gospel.[57]

But what of the actual author of the hymn itself? If we have to confess ignorance of his (or her) identity, the same is true of the evangelist—who was surely no less dazzled than his own readers have been by the brief flash of religious and poetic genius, no more than a few lines, that he was to absorb and assimilate into his Gospel. The amazing conviction that God's wisdom had taken flesh was first of all not his own insight but another's. It was not he but another who declared, "We have seen his glory." The theme of glory permeates the Gospel: seen by his disciples as early as the marriage feast of Cana, Jesus's glory never left him. The constant awareness of Jesus's glory, evident throughout the Gospel, cannot be explained simply as a literary expansion of a motif taken over from the hymn. Here, surely, was an experience that the two writers shared, and that brought them together. But they experienced it differently. What astounded the author of the hymn was his vision of wisdom in the flesh, whereas what preoccupied the evangelist was such an overwhelming sense of the divine glory of the man whose story he was telling that it led him to play down the purely human traits found in abundance in the other three gospels.

2. Moses and the Law

Let us leave aside both the light/darkness antithesis in verse 5 (which may have been added by the evangelist precisely in order to prepare his readers for the dramatic opposition that colors the whole of the first half of his book);[58] and also the gloss in verse 12 on "those who received him, to whom he gave power to become children of God," by "who believed in his name." Both of these deserve fuller comment, but the two concluding verses of the prologue are more important still, for it is here that the

57. See n52 above. The passage to which that note refers is an excursus entitled "The Prologue: God's Plan for Humankind."

58. Bultmann thinks that verse 5 summarizes the first part of the Gospel, chapters 3–12, and that the other side of the theme, summarized in verses 12–13, is presented and developed in chapters 13–17 (Bultmann, *Gospel of John*, 48).

evangelist gives the strongest indication to his readers of the significance they should attach to the hymn he has taken over.

Verse 17 reads, ὅτι ὁ νόμος διὰ Μωυσέως ἐδόθη, ἡ χάρις καὶ ἡ ἀλήθεια διὰ Ἰησοῦ Χριστοῦ ἐγένετο. Two of the key words here, χάρις καὶ ἀλήθεια, are taken from the hymn, in which ἀλήθεια occurs once, in verse 14, and χάρις three times, once in verse 14 and twice (χάριν ἀντὶ χάριτος) in verse 16. The use the evangelist makes of these two motifs, however, could scarcely be more different. He seizes upon the first, χάρις, "grace," because it enables him to make the strongest possible contrast with the Mosaic law. Michael Theobald, agreeing here with Raymond Brown,[59] thinks that there is no antithesis intended in this verse, noting the absence of a *but* between the two clauses,[60] and arguing from the use of the verb διδόναι that the law is seen as a gift.[61] I disagree. By the time the prologue was written the Johannine community had severed relations with the Jewish synagogue where they used to worship alongside their fellow Jews, though understandably they attached all the blame for this breach to their antagonists (9:22). And they had evidently accepted the designation *disciples of Jesus* as opposed to *disciples of Moses* (9:28). The only value ascribed to the law in this Gospel is as a testimony to Jesus (5:39). It may well be, as Barnabas Lindars argues,[62] that in joining the terms χάρις and ἀλήθεια the evangelist was consciously alluding to the traditional Jewish view of the law as a gift and a grace; but if so it was to assert that, contrary to this tradition, the *only* grace, the *only* truth has come through Christ. Not only is the law being completely rejected in this verse, but Moses, according to Jewish tradition the prime intermediary between God and his people, has been ousted by Jesus Christ.

Truth, however, like glory, is a favorite idea of the evangelist himself. And the use he makes of it, in different contexts and different forms, is so individual, so imaginative, so extensive, that it is hard to believe that he borrowed it from someone else.[63] If he did, he certainly made it his own.

59. Brown, *Gospel According to John*, 16.

60. The steward at the wedding at Cana, noticing how differently the bridegroom is acting from everybody else when it comes to serving the good wine, remarks on it without a *but* (2:10).

61. Schnelle, *Das Evangelium nach Johannes*, 134.

62. Lindars observes that according to rabbinic exegesis the grace and the truth of God are revealed in the Law and refers to a midrash on Psalm 25:10 that includes the phrase חסד ואמת (ḥesed weemeth) (Lindars, *Gospel of John*, 97).

63. According to Brown (*Gospel According to John*, 1.19), what ἀλήθεια means in

It may well be that in this instance the author of the hymn, whom we must think of, after all, as a member of the same community, had himself taken it over from the evangelist. No doubt these two were good friends. Perhaps they had reflected over the truth that was Jesus whilst praying together, or over a glass of wine. Who knows?

3. Revelation

In 1:18 we read, Θεὸν οὐδεὶς ἑώρακεν πώποτε μονογενὴς θεὸς ὁ ὢν εἰς τὸν κόλπον τοῦ πατρὸς ἐκεῖνος ἐξηγήσατο. This verse performs many functions.

First, within the prologue itself, we are told that the Logos, now identified with Jesus, after sojourning for an unspecified period among those who welcomed him, is now resting with God. (The Greek phrase εἰς τὸν κόλπον has a surprising physicality, weakly rendered by the English "in the bosom of the Father," a rendering that does nothing to convey the image demanded by the Greek of a father hugging a greatly loved son close to his chest.)

Second, the assertion that no one has seen God is effectively directed against Jewish claims on behalf of Moses.

Third, the readers of the prologue and of the Gospel that follows are told how they are to understand the claim in the hymn, now endorsed by the evangelist on behalf of his own community, that he and they have gazed on the incarnate Logos. This did not involve a direct vision of God—nobody has ever had that—but that is of no consequence, for God can be and has been fully revealed in the person of Jesus. This message will be most perfectly expressed in the words, "Whoever has seen me has seen the Father," and "I am in the Father and the Father in me" (14:8, 10). The standard English translation of the very last word of the prologue, ἐξηγήσατο, "he has made him known," obscures its real meaning; for in the Gospel that follows Jesus conspicuously refrains from saying anything at all about God except in references to the relationship between them: sender/sent, Father/Son. Properly understood, however, this final word is an admirable summary of the message of the whole Gospel: the Jesus of the story that follows—all that he says and does, his life, death and resurrection—is God made manifest, God fully revealed.

---

the prologue is not truth but "endurance, fidelity."

3

John and the Johannine Literature

The Woman at the Well

Introduction

OF ALL THE WRITINGS of the Bible none is more obviously an integrated whole than the Gospel of John. The first-time reader lionized by reader-response critics is sure to find it, as David Friedrich Strauss famously did, a "seamless garment." Its themes (judgment, mission, revelation, truth) and symbols (light, water, bread, healing, life) are skillfully interwoven into the familiar gospel story of Jesus's brief career as a teacher and won-der-worker, with its dramatic ending of death and resurrection. In this, the fourth version of the story, the parts are more than usually represen-tative of the whole. Besides the sustained self-allusiveness consequential upon the evangelist's interpenetrative technique, the reason for this is that once under way the story is dominated throughout by the powerful pres-ence of Jesus, who keeps introducing fresh variations on the single theme of life-giving revelation. This is what justifies the synecdochic approach of the present essay. In John 4 the Samaritan woman, passing from incre-dulity to belief, invites a similar response from the readers of the Gospel. Those acquainted with the whole Gospel know that the same invitation is issued on almost every page: any episode of comparable length could be used, as this one is here, to illustrate models of interpretation.[1]

---

1. The same cannot be said, unfortunately, of the Johannine Epistles, whose precise relationship with the Gospel is still disputed by scholars. Judith Lieu discusses this

All the writers whose work is assessed here are responding to the same text. Almost all have decided upon its meaning after reading it carefully over and over again. Most have made careful appraisals of their predecessors' opinions. Many have pondered the same evidence and the same arguments. Yet each has his or her own point of view: a point of view implies an angle; an angle implies a slant. In one or two cases, not more, the slant might reasonably be ascribed to blinkered vision; but if this is true of only a few, how are we to account for the remarkable divergences of the rest?

Part of the reason is the sheer complexity of the text itself, the rich ambiguities that make the very idea of a definitive exegesis palpably absurd. But if we are to get beyond a helpless shrug of the shoulders we must begin by outlining a number of interpretative options that no student of the Gospel can entirely evade. Some of these permeate the whole of biblical criticism; others are especially relevant to John. Even the most particular elements (a tiny example is the meaning of the verb συγχράομαι in verse 9)[2] indicate the *kind* of choice that faces us wherever we look.

Rough Versus Smooth

The most significant of all the issues on which Johannine scholarship continues to be split involves what has come to be known, after the great linguistician Ferdinand de Saussure, as the distinction between synchronic and diachronic approaches to the Gospel. Those who adopt a synchronic or "smooth" approach insist upon reading the text as it has been transmitted, without delving into its prehistory. A diachronic or "rough" approach, on the other hand, demands both a recognition of the presence of successive layers in the text (usually attributed to source, author, and redactor) and some attempt to prise these apart. These two approaches are rarely combined, though why this should be so is something of a mystery, since the possibilities of dialectic enrichment are, one would have thought, fairly obvious. Commentators occasionally make some grudging acknowledgement of the justification of source and redaction

---

question with fairness and lucidity in *The Theology of the Johannine Epistles*.

2. David Daube has suggested an alternative meaning to the usual "have dealings with," that is, "use the same utensils as" ("Jesus and the Samaritan Woman," 137–47). In my view this would not significantly affect the interpretation of the episode as a whole.

theories, but the vast majority, when they get down to business, prefer the smooth approach. As for articles and monographs, I know of only two "rough" studies of John 4:1–42, the first by Luise Schottroff,[3] a pupil of Bultmann, the second, much more recent, a doctoral thesis by Andrea Link.[4] A first-time reader of the other books, articles, and extracts discussed below would certainly conclude that there is nothing at all to be said for a diachronic analysis of the text.

History Versus Exegesis

Are we to approach this passage as exegetes, simply asking what it means, or as historians, more interested in what it can tell us about the origins and growth of the community for which it was composed? Here too, although in theory the alternatives are not mutually exclusive, they are rarely combined in practice. Yet we should at least remain alert to the possibility that a purely historical insight might open a window on to a fresh interpretation.

Background

Introducing his commentary on John (subtitled "how he speaks, thinks, and believes") Adolf Schlatter observes that he has been variously regarded: "as a Greek, a Paulinist, a philosopher of religion, a poet, a mystic, and a gnostic."[5] His own work is suffused with his perception of John as a Palestinian. An abyss yawns between him and Rudolf Bultmann,[6] for whom the evangelist is a converted gnostic with a redeeming message for all mankind; and an even deeper chasm separates him from C. H. Dodd,[7] convinced that John is a Greek whose work was intended in the first place for the perusal of well-educated Hellenistic pagans. Our views on this matter cannot but affect our own understanding of the Gospel text. These days, thanks largely to the pioneering efforts of Raymond Brown[8] (for Schlatter's work had little impact), the Jewish provenance of

---

3. Schottroff, "Johannes 4,5–15," 199–214.
4. Link, *Was redest du mit ihr?*
5. Schlatter, *Der Evangelist Johannes*, vii.
6. Bultmann, *Gospel of John*.
7. Dodd, *Interpretation of the Fourth Gospel*.
8. Brown, *Gospel According to John*.

John is mostly taken for granted; but we should not forget that this too is an interpretative choice.

Readership

John's intended readership may have changed more than once during the composition of the Gospel, and in any case its nature is hard to determine with any precision. This is nevertheless the kind of problem that historical critics take in their stride: it causes them no discomfort. On the other hand, they are likely to bristle at the sound of the term "ideal reader" as this comes ringing down from the citadel of narrative criticism. Whatever our point of view, whether it be old-fashioned and traditional, modern or postmodern, we are living at a time when the notion of the reader has become no less problematic than that of the author. In the present context the question is further complicated by the fact that individual interpreters may themselves have different readerships in mind—expert or lay, critical or uncritical, committed or uncommitted. All of which prompts a warning: *caveat lector.*

Genre

One of the drawbacks of selective exegesis, the isolation of a single passage for close scrutiny, is that it may cause the reader to forget the relevance for interpretation of the genre of the whole work. John's Gospel is a proclamation of faith in narrative form, paradoxically recounting Jesus's earthly career in order to persuade its readers to accept him as their Risen Lord. This means that it has to be read on two levels, first the story level and secondly the level of spiritual understanding.[9] The riddles of the Gospel, its symbols, and its ironies are all aimed at reinforcing this purposeful ambivalence. That is why the most helpful studies are generally those that highlight one or more of these features, those for instance of G. R. O'Day,[10] emphasizing the irony of the gospel, or D. A. Lee,[11] focusing on its symbolism.

9. For a full defense of this view of the Gospel, see chapter 11 ("The Gospel Genre") of Ashton, *Understanding the Fourth Gospel,* 1st edition, 407–42.

10. O'Day, *Revelation in the Fourth Gospel,* 49–92.

11. Lee, *Symbolic Narratives of the Fourth Gospel,* 64–97.

Context

A second possible disadvantage of selective exegesis in the sense in which I am using this term is the risk of neglecting the many links, both structural and thematic, that tie the various episodes of the Gospel together. A small example is Jesus's assertion, in John 4:34, that his "food" is "to accomplish the work" of the one who sent him. The singular "work" is also used in this strong sense in 17:4, where Jesus speaks of "having accomplished" the work that he had been given to do (see too 6:29). A very teasing question of a different kind is posed by the statement, in John 4:22, that "salvation comes from the Jews." How could the Fourth Evangelist, elsewhere so hostile to those he portrays as Jesus's adversaries, have written that? It is all too easy to miss internal allusions and contextual difficulties if you are preoccupied with the interpretation of a single chapter.

Of more immediate significance (and indeed noticed by many interpreters) are all the binary oppositions that set this passage off against the Nicodemus episode in chapter 3—Pharisee/Samaritan, named/unnamed, man/woman, night/day, secret/open, indoors/outdoors; but the resemblances are important too, especially John's use in both chapters of his favorite device of the riddle. In each case the riddle is contained in a single expression, ἄνωθεν in chapter 3, ὕδωρ ζῶν in chapter 4. English has no word that does justice to the double meaning of ἄνωθεν (from above/a second time), so the ambiguity is always in evidence. Yet when it comes to chapter 4 all translations without exception render ὕδωρ ζῶν, even where it first occurs, as "living water," thus missing the deliberate ambiguity of the Greek (where the first meaning of the term is simply fresh or running water) and making it impossible for the Greekless reader to sympathize with the woman's initial confusion.

Weighting

We now come to yet another choice that confronts anyone seriously attempting to understand a text from which he or she is separated by a temporal or cultural gap (which is what makes interpretation necessary in the first place). This is what may be called the problem of weighting, felt here most acutely in the problem of how to deal with Jacob's well. That the location of the encounter between Jesus and the woman has some bearing on the meaning cannot be doubted. But when we ask *how* it should be brought into the interpretation opinions differ widely; and there is no way of arbitrating between them that would satisfy all the contestants. Yet we must suppose that the allusion would have been picked up quickly, almost instinctively, by John's first readers. Nineteen centuries later it is impossible, surely, to state with any confidence just what significance they may have attached to it.

This kind of apparently trivial problem crops up everywhere. It is as if, planning a journey to a distant country, we were to depend on a compass reading that we could only glimpse with blurred vision from a long way off. The slightest mistake will lead us far astray; and the same is true for any other traveler. Tiny differences in perception may have great consequences.

Literal Versus Symbolic

Here is another sort of problem on which it is impossible to reach any agreement. "You have had five husbands," Jesus tells the woman (verse 18), and there is nothing else in the Gospel to advise us whether we should take this information literally or symbolically. All are agreed that the preceding dialogue concerning living water must be interpreted symbolically. What then are we to make of the five husbands? Some favor an allegorical reading: the five gods of the Samaritans, the five books of the Pentateuch, even the five senses—though in that case, as A. Loisy dryly enquires, how are we to identify the woman's present partner (a sixth sense, perhaps?).[12] Feeling that none of these suggestions fits in very easily with the preceding dialogue, we may opt instead for a literal reading. But in that case how do we explain the abrupt shift from the symbolic to the literal mode? We shall see that there are various ways of tackling this problem.

Many other questions may come into our minds as we dig deeper into the story, but these are the ones best capable, in my judgment, of dividing "soul from spirit, joints from marrow."

Method

There are probably as many methods of biblical criticism as there are kinds of music, and as many new methods as there are kinds of pop music. The champions of the new methods are likely to dismiss the censures

12. Loisy, *Le quatrième évangile*, 354n1.

of old-fashioned historical critics just as abruptly as admirers of, say, heavy metal are likely to brush aside the remonstrances of those who prefer the classical tradition. The result is a *dialogue de sourds*, with each side convinced of the deafness of the other. How in such circumstances can an unreconstructed and (so far) undeconstructed historical critic hope to give a reasonably impartial account of modern approaches?

Analysis

The interpreter's task is threefold: analysis, application, and explanation. Though distinguishable, the three tasks are not always distinct. Usually, though not always, analysis is absorbed into explanation, and very often application is too. Even where a writer is chiefly interested in analysis on the one hand or application on the other, some explanation is always felt to be indispensable.

To analyze a text is to spell out one's understanding of its structure and meaning. Analysis used to be carried out without tools: all one needed was a good eye and a sensitive nose. The modern form of analysis, text-linguistics, is a much more complex affair, but its aims are the same. Here too analysis does its utmost to rely exclusively upon information provided by the text itself. Hendrikus Boers states quite frankly: "If the analysis were to suggest something which cannot be recognized by a sensitive reader *without* the analysis . . . I would consider the analysis to have introduced alien material into the text."[13] After this candid admission he justifies and explains the elaborate procedures of the first part of his book (backed up by nearly eighty diagrams, some of a truly daunting complexity) by comparing them to the laborious business of reading a foreign language with the aid of a grammar. First he offers a quite simple preliminary analysis. Thereafter, appealing to the semiotics of A. J. Greimas and J. Courtés, he discusses what he calls the textual syntax of the episode, clarifying it on the three levels of its surface narrative, syntactic deep structure, and discursive syntax. A comprehensive analysis of the deep structure leads him to the conclusion that "contrary to an analysis of only the surface by traditional means, John 4 is a syntactically tightly cohesive text."[14] He then tackles the semantic component of the chapter, starting with "the concrete figures" and moving on to "the more abstract level

13. Boers, *Neither on This Mountain*, 148.
14. Boers, *Neither on This Mountain*, 77.

of the values expressed by these figures,"[15] the values of sustenance, life, obedience, human solidarity, and salvation. He explains in great detail how these are interrelated within the story. The second part of the book attempts to flesh out the preceding analyses in a full interpretation,[16] and the concluding pages summarize the meaning of the passage as "the process of revelation of Jesus as the savior of the world."

Employing rather different procedures, but equally dependent upon a synchronic reading and equally committed to the use of text-oriented techniques, Birger Olsson[17] and J. Eugene Botha[18] have arrived at rather different results. Although each of the three is offering an "objective" analysis of the same text, they all find it impossible in the long run to detach analysis cleanly from explanation.

Application

All texts carry meaning; many, including the Bible, also carry a meaning for their readers. "Meaning for"—significance in the strong sense—is traditionally covered by the Latin term *applicatio*. In pre-critical days the application was generally caught up in the interpretation. Historical critics are for the most part anxious to exclude it. Raymond Brown, for instance, prefaces his remarkable two-volume commentary by confessing a "stubborn refusal to make a biblical text say more than its author meant to say." He can do this because of his sense of "the clear difference between the thoughts of the various biblical authors (which are the concern of the biblical scholar) and the subsequent use and development of those thoughts in divergent theologies (which are the concern of the theologian)."[19] Since then, however, the legitimacy of separating explanation and application has increasingly come under question.[20] Whoever is right on this contentious issue, all agree on what application means in a hermeneutical context: it is the appropriation of a biblical text in

---

15. Boers, *Neither on This Mountain*, 79.

16. Boers, *Neither on This Mountain*, 144–200.

17. Olsson, *Structure and Meaning in the Fourth Gospel*.

18. Botha, *Jesus and the Samaritan Woman*.

19. Brown, *Gospel According to John*, vi.

20. Notably by Christopher Rowland in his inaugural lecture as Dean Ireland Professor of the Exegesis of Holy Scripture, University of Oxford: "Open thy Mouth for the Dumb," 228–45.

such a way that it speaks to its readers directly in their own situation and demands from them an active response. We may distinguish two main kinds of application in the interpretation of John 4:1–42: the psychologizing and the feminist.

Psychology

The first of the psychologizing explanations, that of François Roustang,[21] now nearly half a century old, draws its inspiration more from Hegel than from Freud or Jung. It uses the "woman at the well" episode as a model of the transition from indifference to faith, and its tone is in some respects less psychological than philosophical or theological. Yet Roustang's brilliant analysis of the woman's progress from appearance to reality and from falsehood to truth depends, like many of Hegel's ostensibly "logical" moves, upon enduringly valid psychological insights into the difficulties human beings encounter when trying to confront and acknowledge the truth. This is a bold study, elaborating upon John's text much as a skilful composer develops the potential of a single melodic line; and it may well, as Roustang fears, offend the purists: "professional exegetes are unlikely to follow us here."[22] Yet it does less violence to the text than many other interpretations, and merits respect for its religious sensitivity.

Unlike Roustang, who directs a polite nod towards those he calls "les exegetes de métier" before boarding his own train, Eugen Drewermann has no time for traditional biblical scholarship. Towards the beginning of his huge two-volume work, *Tiefenpsychologie und Exegese*, he launches a fierce attack on the historical-critical method as generally practised. Viewed hermeneutically, he says, it is extremely limited; viewed theologically it is downright wrong (*geradezu falsch*). He goes on to accuse professional exegetes of hiding behind the so-called objectivity of their theoretical reconstructions.[23]

In Roustang's interpretation the conclusion of the story (verses 35–38) provides an effective counterpart to the preceding section by outlining the conditions of the possibility of an act of faith. Drewermann breaks off before this conclusion, but like Roustang he follows what he calls a *Zerdehnungsregel*: this allows him to stretch out and slow down the

21. Roustang, "Les moments de l'acte de foi," 344–78.
22. Roustang, "Les moments de l'acte de foi," 344.
23. Drewermann, *Tiefenpsychologie und Exegese*, 1:23–25.

very rapid movement of the text itself and to read from it the story of a gradual coming-to-faith in the Messiah that he sees as equivalent to the step-by-step process of Jungian individuation (which is what, for him, genuine religion is all about). The term "spirit" in the phrase "spirit and truth" (verse 23) he takes to mean personal conviction (as opposed to tradition) and "truth" to mean personal integrity. Jesus acts as a kind of Jungian analyst, enabling the woman to find her true self.[24] Drewermann ends by asserting that theological exegesis cannot get by ("nicht auskommen kann") without the help of depth psychology.

Where Roustang turns for help to Hegel (though without naming him) and Drewermann to Jung, Stephen Moore[25] appeals to Lacan and Derrida. In his Lacanian reading of the episode he goes beyond all other interpreters by placing the emphasis not on the woman's thirst but on that of Jesus himself. The interchange between the two is driven, Moore insists, by *Jesus's* longing to instil in the woman a desire for the living water he has come to bring: "Only thus can his own deeper thirst be assuaged, his own lack be filled."[26] With Lacan's assistance Moore is able to plunge much deeper into the well, theologically speaking, than the rest of us, still clinging to the ropes of traditional exegetical methods, can possibly manage. He then calls upon Derrida's deconstructions to help him highlight the change of register in the crucifixion scene. Two levels of meaning of the water symbol (physical and spiritual) that had been quite properly held apart in the dialogue suddenly collapse into one.[27] The newly discovered meaning, however, cannot hold, and the result is the deconstruction of the text and the disorientation of the reader.

Feminism

Certain readers (who may, as we have seen, be psychologists but are more often theologians) approach the Bible brandishing an axe. When applied to the passage which concerns us here this is generally a feminist axe, and it is wielded in three ways. First, by a proceeding analogous to what is generously called positive discrimination, it is possible to hew a meaning out of the text in the service of a higher cause. A second tactic is to point

---

24. Drewermann, *Tiefenpsychologie und Exegese*, 2:686–97.

25. Moore, "Are There Impurities in the Living Water?," 207–27.

26. Moore, "Are There Impurities in the Living Water?," 208.

27. Moore, "Are There Impurities in the Living Water?," 222.

out the underlying androcentrism of the biblical authors themselves, a characteristic that men, in the nature of the case, are less likely to notice than women. Sometimes the claim is made that the reading now being proposed is the right one and that only the prejudices of earlier scholars blinded by phallocentrism or misogyny have prevented them from seeing it.

The little interchange between Jesus and the woman beginning "Go and call your husband" (verse 16) is an excellent example. Some scholars attach a symbolic significance to the five husbands; even so it is arguable that the text itself exhibits a misogynistic bias. Others, mostly male, opt for a literal reading: the woman's marital life is in total disarray. This exposes them to the charge that their unconscious bias has led them to shift the interpretation from the symbolic to the literal without first trying to give a coherent reading of the whole episode by remaining on the symbolic level appropriate, as all agree, to the dialogue concerning living water. Stephen Moore, feminist as well as deconstructionist, has some fun citing a series of commentators thundering moral disapproval of the woman's behavior ("profligacy and unbridled passions," "a tramp," "an illicit affair," "bawdy past," "immoral life," etc.).[28] He then points out that the commentators in question, only too ready to underline the woman's failure to grasp the symbolic import of "living water," "effectively trade places with her by opting to take Jesus' statement in 4:18 at face-value."[29]

Sandra Schneiders, equally dismissive of literal readings of the five husbands, writes of the episode as "a textbook case of the trivialization, marginalization, and even sexual demonization of biblical women."[30] But whereas Moore signally fails to follow up his own criticisms of literal readings with a symbolic interpretation of his own, Schneiders is braver. "The entire dialogue between Jesus and the woman," she urges, "is the 'wooing' of Samaria to full covenant fidelity in the New Israel by Jesus, the New Bridegroom."[31] Like many other interpreters she stresses the symbolic significance of the meeting by the well (we shall return to this theme), but goes further than some by asserting that "Jesus has already been identified at Cana as the true Bridegroom who supplied the good wine for the wedding feast (John 2:9–11) and by John the Baptist

28. Raymond Brown is less censorious, finding the woman "mincing and coy, with a certain light grace" (*Gospel According to John*, 175).

29. Moore, "Are There Impurities," 212.

30. Schneiders, "Case Study," 188.

31. Schneiders, "Case Study," 191.

as the true Bridegroom to whom God has given the New Israel as Bride (John 3:27–30)."[32] (A much cruder reading, drawing on some of the same evidence, is Lyle Eslinger's suggestion that the woman was employing a series of *double entendres* whilst making "sexual advances" to the attractive stranger in an attempt to seduce him.)[33]

In her seminal work *In Memory of Her* Elisabeth Schüssler Fiorenza makes a brief but important contribution to the debate. "The dramatic dialogue," she observes, "is probably based on a missionary tradition that ascribed a primary role to a woman in the conversion of the Samaritans"[34]—an exceptionally interesting comment because the Samaritan woman now takes on historical significance as the leader of an early Christian mission to the Samaritans (who took their name from the capital city of ancient Israel). The evangelist, reluctant to leave her in the center of the stage for too long, is quick to add that true faith consists in listening to Jesus himself (verse 42); but in underlining the plain statement that many of her fellow-citizens "believed on the strength of her word" (verse 39), Schüssler Fiorenza performs the service of reminding us that the Gospel is available to the historian as well as to the exegete.

Explanation

The business of exegetes is to use all the information at their disposal to explain the text in question. To illustrate the explanation of the "woman at the well" episode I have chosen three works published within the last decade: a doctoral thesis by a Nigerian sister, an extract from a grandly conceived "reading" of the whole Gospel by the veteran French scholar, Xavier Léon-Dufour, and a thesis from within the German tradition by Andrea Link.

Teresa Okure, alone among present-day exegetes, regards the evangelist as an eyewitness of the events he records.[35] Having selected an episode in Jesus's own life that corresponds to the situation of the audience he is addressing, he goes on to portray him in the exercise of the mission given him by God.[36] The readers John has in mind may be insiders, but

32. Schneiders, "Case Study," 187.
33. Eslinger, "Wooing of the Woman at the Well," 167–83.
34. Schüssler Fiorenza, *In Memory of Her*, 327.
35. Okure, *Johannine Approach to Mission*, 272–73.
36. Okure, *Johannine Approach to Mission*, 292.

they too, Okure insists, fall within the sphere of the evangelist's own missionary endeavor, standing as they do "in special need of being reminded
of Jesus' uniqueness as God's eschatological agent of salvation . . . and
of the resulting need for their total dependence on him."[37] As her title
suggests, she concentrates entirely on the theme of mission. By the end
of her book this theme, which started as a leitmotif of the gospel,[38] has
become *the* leitmotif.[39]

Léon-Dufour, a past master in the French art of *haute vulgarisation,*
offers a discursive (and synchronic) reading of the Gospel that manages
to integrate a wide range of reference, especially to the Old Testament,
into a searching exegesis.[40] He explains this episode, which he sees as "a
symbolic narrative," with the aid of his own theory of two levels of understanding, of Jesus and of the church. On the first level the living water
symbolizes the revelation that Jesus has come to bring, on the second
level, the spirit, that has to wait upon his going. He refuses to choose between a literal and a symbolic reading of the five husbands: certainly the
woman is the symbolic representative of her people as they move from
idolatry to the service of the true God; but at the same time she has her
own importance as an individual standing in urgent need of the life and
salvation brought by Jesus. Major biblical references are inserted into the
discussion rather than being crammed into footnotes: here is unobtrusive scholarship directed to an uncomplicated reading of the text.

Andrea Link is the only commentator in recent times to take a
diachronic approach. In the first half of her book, she summarizes and
criticizes earlier views. Then, after a long verse-by-verse study of the
redactional history of the episode,[41] she devotes a shorter, concluding
section to what she calls *Theologiegeschichte.*[42] This focuses on the theological differences between the three levels of redaction: first the source or
Grundschrift, and then the work, successively, of evangelist and redactor.
The source is a missionary document in which "the woman from Sychar"
figures as a dialogue partner of Jesus, a disciple of Moses and an active

37. Okure, *Johannine Approach to Mission,* 287.

38. Okure, *Johannine Approach to Mission,* 2.

39. Okure, *Johannine Approach to Mission,* 291.

40. Léon-Dufour, *Lecture de l'Évangile selon Jean,* 339–95. For other examples
of "discursive readings," see O'Day, *Revelation in the Fourth Gospel;* Lee, *Symbolic
Narratives.*

41. Link, *Was redest du mit ihr?,* 178–324.

42. Link, *Was redest du mit ihr?,* 325–71.

missionary eager to promote faith in Jesus.[43] It also portrays Jesus as a prophet closely resembling Elijah (verse 19) and as Messiah (verse 25). The evangelist goes beyond the source in seeing Jesus as revealer (verses 10–15) and savior of the world (verse 42). Although Link's redactor has some affinities with Bultmann's ecclesiastical redactor (he is interested in sacramentalism [verse 2] and futuristic eschatology [verse 14]), his most important obsession, anti-docetism, was first ascribed to him by Georg Richter.[44] Link also detects his interfering hand in the transformation of the woman into a Samaritan (verses 7, 9) and above all in the assertion that "salvation is from the Jews" (verse 22). Ultimately, however, she agrees with Okure about the missionary thrust of the story, as it insists that the goal of all missionary endeavor is "to lead humans to the direct experience of God in Jesus Christ."[45]

Conclusion

Of all the methodological options that dominate present-day exegesis of the gospels, the most deplorable, it seems to me, is the almost unanimous rejection by English-speaking scholars of a diachronic approach to the text. Leaving aside all the other "aporias" that keep rearing up from beneath John's deceptively smooth surface text, the startlingly abrupt transition in 4:16 should be enough to arouse the suspicions of any alert reader that some cutting and pasting has been going on. "Go and fetch your husband" is a decidedly odd response to a request for water. Many commentators ignore the difficulty. Some have idiosyncratic explanations of their own. C. M. Carmichael,[46] for instance, judges that "the switch in conversation would be inexplicable if it were not for the underlying marital theme," a suggestion that fits in with an unusually lavish treatment of that particular motif. Dorothy Lee, after acknowledging the apparent abruptness, takes the opposite view that "the image of the second scene is dependent on the primary image of water/the well in the first scene."[47] M.-J. Lagrange[48] engagingly proposes that the woman's incredulity must

43. Link, *Was redest du mit ihr?*, 352.

44. Richter, *Studien zum Johannesevangelium.*

45. Link, *Was redest du mit ihr?*, 365.

46. Carmichael, "Marriage and the Samaritan Woman," 332–46.

47. Lee, *Symbolic Narratives*, 74–75.

48. Lagrange, *Évangile selon saint Jean*, 109.

have shown in her face and prompted Jesus to change tack ("prendre un autre ton"). J. E. Botha[49] credits Jesus with a particularly subtle strategy: having failed thus far to coax the woman on to his own wavelength, he determines to flout three key maxims generally observed in two-way conversations, those of relevancy, manner, and sequencing: "this 'break' created by the flouting of maxims indicates to the other character that the current line of discussion should be terminated, and it gives Jesus the opportunity of continuing the conversation and introducing a new program or topic."[50] Thus Botha cleverly justifies the apparent dislocation in terms of his speech-act theory, paradoxically underlining the extent of the difficulty as he does so. Boers disagrees: only a naive reader would be bothered by the apparent inconsequence: "at the deeper level Jesus' command prepares for the revelation of his miraculous ability which the woman mockingly denied him by challenging him with Jacob's miracle."[51] This may indeed be the right solution *on the level of the final redaction*, but not, I think, otherwise. Jürgen Becker[52] proposes that in the source what is now verse 16 followed verse 9; so too Link. This suggestion has much to be said for it, as long as we see that in the text as we have it the dialogue on living water (verses 10–15) helps to account for the woman's amazed admiration: "I perceive that you are a prophet" (verse 19).

To adopt this solution is also to dodge Stephen Moore's strictures on those who, on reaching the five husbands, slide unreflectingly from the symbolic to the literal mode. Yet none of the suggested symbolisms is very impressive. By far the most popular of them, the false gods of the Samaritans, is open to the objection that according to 2 Kings 17 the Samaritans had seven false gods, not five, and not all male. Where arguments are inconclusive exegetes will continue to wrangle. I myself am inclined to accept Andrea Link's suggestion that the number five (which she speaks of as "ein Annäherungswort"—an approximation) simply serves to reinforce the reader's sense of the urgency of the woman's need for the salvation proffered by Jesus.[53] This conversion story provided John with a framework for his own symbolic dialogue concerning living water.

49. Botha, "John 4:16a," 183–92.

50. Botha, "John 4:16a," 188–89.

51. Boers, *Neither on This Mountain*, 170.

52. Becker, *Das Evangelium des Johannes*, 165.

53. Link, *Was redest du mit ihr?*, 269.

The weakness of Link's work lies not in her approach or her method but in her failure to invest her redactor with the slightest verisimilitude: how could any wholehearted anti-docetist have made such a botched job of the Gospel as a whole? The conclusion of verse 9 ("Jews have no truck with Samaritans") may, it is true, be the work of a glossator, but the remainder of the narrative is much better explained as the combination by the evangelist of two stories, one his own, one taken from a source. The best account of the problem posed by verse 22, I persist in thinking, is that of Klaus Haacker (known seemingly to only a few later commentators).[54] Haacker argues that it reflects the kind of controversy between Jews and Samaritans that is seen in Ecclesiasticus 50:25–26 and *Testament of Levi 7*. But this need not have prevented it from figuring in a document used by missionaries who were carrying the gospel from Judaea, already recognized as Jesus's native-land, into Samaria.

What then of Jacob's well? The most informative discussion of this topic, with abundant references to Jewish sources, is Jerome Neyrey's "Jacob Traditions."[55] Neyrey is one of the first among an increasing number of modern scholars[56] to take the view that the story in John is a variant of the classical Jewish betrothal scene, as found in Genesis and Exodus. But although this suggestion cannot be ruled out, a simpler explanation is ready to hand. Jacob is mentioned because he is the father of both Judah, from whom the Jews took their name, and Joseph (cf. v. 5), the greatly revered ancestor (through Ephraim and Manasseh) of the Samaritans. Jacob's dying blessing embraced both Judah and Joseph, describing the latter as "a fruitful bough by a spring" (Gen 49:9–10, 22; cf. Deut 33:13–17). No doubt this view reduces the significance of the well by making it serve simply as a natural backdrop for a dialogue about water; but, as Haacker saw, it also furnishes a plausible setting for the opposition between the two sacred mountains, Gerizim and Zion.

54. Haacker, "Gottesdienst ohne Gotteserkenntnis," 110–26. For a full discussion of the significance of the phrase in the context of the whole gospel, see Ashton, *Studying John*, 44–49.

55. Neyrey, "Jacob Traditions and the Interpretation of John 4:10–26," 419–37. The fullest information on the various ideas associated with water is to be found in Odeberg, *Fourth Gospel*, 149–70.

56. Bligh, "Jesus in Samaria"; Carmichael, "Marriage and the Samaritan Woman"; Eslinger, "Wooing of the Woman"; Schneiders, "Case Study."

A Note on Commentaries

Boers artlessly informs his readers that from the vast array of commentaries at his disposal he limited himself to "35 of the most promising." Time, he adds resignedly, "can be better spent."[57] Truly much perusal of commentaries is a weariness of the flesh.

Publishers approve of commentaries, especially those that belong to a series. It is easy to see why. They sell well, especially to libraries. Occupying as they do so much space on the shelves, no interpreter of interpretations can afford to neglect them entirely.

Writing nearly a century ago, in 1904, the great Hermann Gunkel[58] made some trenchant remarks about biblical commentaries of his own day. He was struck by the vast array of information that they provide, in an almost limitless profusion ("eine fast unübersehbare Fülle") that can only bewilder beginners and is hardly likely to satisfy more experienced readers. He gloomily concluded that despite the extraordinary variety of the fare on offer one thing is in danger of being left behind, and that is the text!

Gunkel was writing primarily of the exegesis of the Old Testament, but said himself that most of his comments apply equally well to the New. In the case of John's Gospel there is only one commentary that escapes the pitfalls he so ruthlessly reveals, and that is Rudolf Bultmann's magisterial *Das Evangelium des Johannes*,[59] which did not appear in English until three decades after its publication in Germany during the war (1941). Despite the many criticisms that can be made of this work, Bultmann penetrates to the heart of John's message with extraordinary insight, focusing unerringly on the evangelist's special interest in revelation, not least in the passage under discussion. Convinced as he is of the abiding relevance of Jesus's life-giving message, he conveys it to his own readers, if they allow themselves to be led by him, with great urgency and power. This is probably the greatest commentary on any New Testament writing in the second millennium, and leaves one wondering what may be expected from the third.

---

57. Boers, *Neither on This Mountain*, 144n1.

58. Gunkel, "Ziele und Methoden," 11–29.

59. Bultmann, *Gospel of John*. For a critical appreciation of Bultmann's work on John, see chapter 2 of Ashton, *Understanding the Fourth Gospel*, 1st edition, 44–66.

4

Riddles and Mysteries

The Way, the Truth, and the Life

IT HAS LONG BEEN recognized that the riddles in the Fourth Gospel constitute the main element of what Herbert Leroy has called the Johannine Community's *Sondersprache*,[1] the special or private language it employed to reinforce its sense of identity and the conviction of its superiority to the outside world. James Kelso notes that "'riddle' is a comprehensive term for a puzzling question or an ambiguous proposition which is intended to be solved by conjecture."[2] The Fourth Evangelist's riddles make use of ordinary everyday words to convey a meaning that the outsider can only guess at. It is worth stressing from the outset that the riddle, by its very nature, is a confrontational form, opposing the riddler to the (would-be) solver, although the nature of the confrontation will differ from one case to another.

Most of the FG's riddles, like the symbols with which they frequently overlap, cluster around the central motifs of "revelation" ("the truth") and the "life" that acceptance of this revelation ensures. Two of the most important, the "living [or fresh] water" in John 4 and "the bread of life" in chapter 6, make this association explicit. But one could say the same of other key riddles, such as *anōthen* ("again/from above"), the term that so confuses Nicodemus (3:3), and the more frequent *hypagō* ("depart"),

1. Leroy, *Rätsel und Missverständnis*.
2. Kelso, "Riddle," 765.

as the answers to these riddles involve the entry of the revealing word of God into the world and his eventual withdrawal from it. In spite of the fact that Pilate's question to Jesus, "What is truth?" (18:38), is the only example in the FG of the interrogative form generally associated with Western riddles, *alētheia* ("truth") also belongs to the private language of the FE's community. When the Jews show themselves perplexed by Jesus's declaration that "the truth will set you free" (8:32), their failure to understand concerns the nature of the truth just as much as that of the promised freedom. "Life" carries the same ambiguity in the FG. Clearly, the FE prefers the term "eternal life," in which ambiguity is replaced by oxymoron: "eternal life," like "centralized democracy," "realized eschatology," and—as Chistopher Ricks once wryly observed to me—"literary theory," is a term in which the adjective appears to conflict with, even to negate, the noun it qualifies. But the word *zōē* ("life") appears often enough on its own in the FG, and when it does the reader is well aware that it carries the same kind of special meaning as, say, *anōthen* or *hypagō*.

The overlap between symbol and riddle in the FG is not incidental. Life, the gift of inestimable worth promised to those who accept Jesus's message, is the Johannine equivalent of the synoptic kingdom of God. And just as the picture language of the synoptic parables (images especially of growth, light, abundance, and value) describes the kingdom of God without ever saying what it actually is, so the everyday symbols of the FG, water and bread, even when they figure as riddles, are immediately associated with the staples of human life and thus subtly conjoin the natural and the supernatural. This kind of association between the natural and supernatural is fairly typical of the myths, metaphors, and riddles of many religious groups. The language of the riddles of the *Rig Veda*, for instance, is drawn from the everyday experience of an Indian dairy farmer, his tools (the plough, the wheel, the cart), the animals associated with them (horses and oxen), plus other familiar living things (birds, animals, trees), and climatic phenomena (clouds and rain). The effect of these riddles is to establish indissoluble links binding the mysterious happenings of the natural universe to the daily life of the farmer, as has been demonstrated in a wide-ranging article by Walter Porzig in which he also shows how the Brahmins used these riddles for the instruction of the young with a view to ensuring the survival of the priestly sect and of its privileged status.[3] The druids too are said to have included in

3. Porzig, "Das Rätsel im Rigveda," 646–60.

the final trial to which they subjected their neophytes the task of "answering complicated riddles before a committee."[4]

It would not be difficult to provide formal solutions to the riddles of the FG. But a list of such answers would hardly grant us access to the thinking of the Johannine Community. What the FG demands of its readers is what Jesus also demands of his hearers, and that is not knowledge, but *faith*. Faith is a response not to instruction but to revelation, and revelation is concerned with mysteries rather than riddles. Yet the riddles are closely connected with revelation, and so we must investigate the nature of the link between them. This means proceeding beyond the form-critical investigation of the original compositional setting of the FG's riddles into a deeper analysis of the mystery in which they are enclosed.

In order to keep this ambitious program within the compass of a single essay, I will restrict my remarks to the crucially important theme of Jesus's return to the Father, which is signified in the FG by the word *hypagō* ("go away/depart").[5] For practical purposes, I will focus on two passages in which this theme occurs: John 8:21–24 and 13:31–14:6.

John 8:21-24—Life and Death

> Again he said to them, "I am going away, and you will search for me, but you will die in your sin. Where I am going, you cannot come." Then the Jews said, "Is he going to kill himself? Is that what he means by saying, 'Where I am going, you cannot come'?" He said to them, "You are from below, I am from above; you are of this world, I am not of this world. I told you that you would die in your sins, for you will die in your sins unless you believe that I am he [*hoti egō eimi*]." (John 8:21–24)

As the opening of verse 21 indicates ("Again he said"), this is not the first mention of Jesus's impending departure in the FG. An earlier statement (John 7:33–36) had provoked a similar (though not identical) misunderstanding on the part of the Jews. Both passages take up the

---

4. Ashe, *King Arthur's Avalon*, 30.

5. See Ashton, *Understanding the Fourth Gospel*, 1st edition, 191–92, 448–52, 492–93.

important motif of the quest for Jesus, begun in 5:18, that is one facet of the larger Johannine theme of revelation.[6]

The form of the ensuing dialogue between Jesus and the Jews, the judicial trial, is closely related to the riddle. In the chapter on riddles in his classic study *Einfache Formen*, Andre Jolles compares the judicial trial with another form closely resembling the riddle, the scholastic examination.[7] In the latter case, there is someone "in the know" whose job it is to put questions to the examinee in an attempt to elicit the right answers. In the case of the judicial trial (Jolles is thinking of the system employed in continental Europe wherein the accused is examined by a magistrate), it is the judge or magistrate who needs to know and the accused who has the knowledge (of his guilt or innocence) and poses the riddle. Should the judge fail to solve it, he ceases for all practical purposes to be the judge. In the FG, this judicial dialectic is most evident in the trial before Pilate, but it is important to recognize that John 8 is also much more than just a "controversy dialogue," the term Leroy uses to describe even the exceptionally bitter exchange that concludes the chapter.[8] While this may be an adequate categorization of the arguments in the Synoptic Gospels, which typically conclude with a clever rejoinder from Jesus that leaves the Pharisees red-faced and discomfited, the angry confrontations between Jesus and the Jews in the FG portray the latter no longer as mere interlocutors, but rather as hostile interrogators anxious to secure an admission that will justify a death sentence On the other hand, Jesus himself, who in the FG always initiates the dialogue, also has no qualms about prophesying the death of his adversaries.

The confrontation in John 8 begins abruptly: "I am going away, and you will search for me, but you will die in your sin. Where I am going, you cannot come.' Then the Jews said, 'Is he going to kill himself?'" (8:21). Both parties speak of death: first, Jesus: "you will die in your sin"—a direct consequence of the Jews' unsuccessful search; then the Jews: "Is he going to kill himself?"—a crass misunderstanding of Jesus's announcement, which, by an extra irony lost on the Jews, does indeed refer in one sense to his approaching death.

The threat of death in this context is counterbalanced by a promise of life: "Whoever keeps my word will never see death" (John 8:51). An

6. Ashton, *Studying John*, 168–82.

7. Jolles, *Einfache Formen*, 131–32.

8. Leroy, *Rätsel und Missverständnis*, 87.

identical promise appears at the beginning of the Gospel of Thomas (1; cf. 18, 19), although there it is made, significantly, not to those who "keep" the words of Jesus but to those who "find the interpretation [*hermeneia*]" of them, that is, who find solutions for his many riddles. Throughout the wisdom literature, "life" is the ultimate prize: "For he who finds me [Wisdom] finds life and obtains favor from the Lord; but he who misses me injures himself; all who hate me love death" (Prov 8:35–36). In the opening of Proverbs 8:36, the LXX substitutes *hoi de eis eme hamarta-nontes* ("those who sin against me") for the Hebrew "he who misses me," thus bringing the saying closer to Jesus's threat in John 8:21.

John 8:21 is, in fact, an example of what the Germans evocatively call a *Halsrätsel* or *Halslöserätsel* ("neck riddle"), a riddle so dangerous and threatening that one literally risks one's neck by undertaking to solve it. The best-known example of this is the Greek legend of the Sphinx, but almost equally familiar nowadays is the story of the opera *Turandot*, adapted for the stage by Schiller and Brecht and set to music by Puccini and Busoni. The FE's irony is many-layered, for both the threat and the promise (8:51) are cloaked as riddles: neither the death the Jews are risking nor the life that is tantalizingly offered to those among them who keep Jesus's word is quite what they think it is.

Crucial for the understanding of this passage is the recognition that, in this instance, the solution to Jesus's riddle is itself the successful outcome of the quest. To grasp the full significance of the term *hypagō* ("go away"), which covers what later came to be called the "Paschal mystery," is *ipso facto* to have penetrated the heart of the mystery. For to know where Jesus is going is to have found him.

Like the answer to all riddles, the real significance of Jesus's departure is available only to the initiated, that is, to Johannine Christians. But the life-threatening aspect of this particular riddle entitles us to compare it with the central myths of other societies, those that Joseph Goetz calls "the really great myths, the ones that catch man at the depth of his being." Goetz notes that such myths are generally concealed from outsiders, for history proves that divulging them to the uninitiated either leads to their death or perhaps assumes that they are dead already. The modern interpreter often prefers to say nothing, since it is impossible to explain these myths except to people who have lived them from within. In approaching the myths that are central to a community, "we are right at the heart of the problem of religious communication."[9] Surely the FE would say the same.

John 13:31–14:6—The Way of Wisdom

When we turn to the departure riddle at John 13:31—14:6, which refers back directly to the one we have just been considering (8:21), the situation could hardly be more different. Now Jesus is surrounded not by his enemies but by his most intimate disciples.

> "Little children, I am with you only a little longer. You will look for me; and as I said to the Jews so now I say to you, 'Where I am going, you cannot come . . . '" Simon Peter said to him, "Lord, where are you going?" Jesus answered, "Where I am going, you cannot follow me now; but you will follow afterward. . . . And you know the way to the place where I am going." Thomas said to him, "Lord, we do not know where you are going. How can we know the way?" Jesus said to him, "I am the way, and the truth, and the life. No one comes to the Father except through me." (John 13:33, 36; 14:4–6)

We have already noted that "truth" and "life" belong to the special vocabulary of the Johannine Community. Jesus's hearers fail to penetrate his true meaning either because they are culpably blind to it (the Jews) or because they have not yet been initiated into the inner circle (Nicodemus and the Samaritan woman). At the end of the Book of Signs, after going into hiding for the last time (John 12:36), Jesus commences a new kind of dialogue in the Upper Room. The first-time reader of the FG is likely to be surprised by the realization that the disciples, who should be able to grasp Jesus's message without difficulty, exhibit a considerable degree of misunderstanding. This is because a new distinction has now been introduced: the temporal distinction between those who, listening to Jesus during his lifetime, cannot yet bear the full burden of what he is saying (16:12), and those others, paradoxically privileged, who are to be led into the wonderful realm of "the truth" under the guidance of the Paraclete after Jesus is gone (16:13).

In the Book of Signs (John 2–12), Jesus had spoken both of "truth" and "life" but never of "the way." The implication of the statement we are now considering (14:6) would seem, at first glance, to be open and

9. Goetz, "Mythe," cols. 1985–86.

direct. Jesus is the truth and Jesus is the life, both statements that can be readily comprehended by those who know the FG. But "I am the way" is a new assertion, and not an easy one, following as it does the initial pronouncement that "you know the way where I am going." At 14:4–5, "the way" refers to the goal of Christian experience. But now in 14:6 "the way" seems to be the journey or experience itself; notably, Jesus drops "where I am going" from Thomas's question and replaces it with "no one comes to the Father, but by me."

In the remainder of this essay, I will argue that the Johannine motif of "the way" originates in the Jewish wisdom tradition and that this understanding enables us to assess its significance for the Fourth Gospel as a whole. The combination of the motifs of "wisdom" and "revelation" that characterizes the wisdom literature was taken over and absorbed by a quite different genre, Jewish apocalyptic. It is to this genre that we now turn for clues to the answers of the FG's riddles.

Apocalyptic Wisdom

Michael Stone has called attention to the "Lists of Revealed Things" in a number of ancient apocalyptic writings. In these passages, "the subjects of the lists are far from self-evidently unknowable. Indeed, they are revealed or catalogued or shouted out in praise."[10] Second Enoch, for instance, claims to have "measured all the earth, and its mountains and hills and fields and woods and stones and rivers, and everything that exists" (40:12). "What song the sirens sang," Sir Thomas Browne famously remarked, "or what name Achilles assumed when he hid himself among women, though puzzling questions, are not beyond all conjecture." But the same cannot be said, surely, of Enoch's measurement of everything that exists. Although many, perhaps most, of the items on the apocalyptic lists would fit comfortably in an encyclopedia of scientific lore, this is not true of all of them, for some involve information that is inherently supernatural in nature and origin.

For example, Uriel—the tough-minded angelic guide in 4 Ezra—has evidently perused a list of "revealed things" and can therefore declare that "those who dwell upon earth can understand what is on earth, and he who is above the heavens can understand what is above the height of heaven" (4:20; cf. John 3:12). Uriel is astute enough to pull this list

10. Stone, "Lists of Revealed Things," 83.

apart, distinguishing those items that might in principle be possible and legitimate objects of human inquiry from those that cannot be understood short of a revelation from heaven or an ascent to heaven. From the former group he selects three items and transforms them into riddles (Latin *similitudines*; Syriac *matlîn*, reflecting the Greek *parabolai*; and Hebrew *mesalîm*, unsatisfactorily rendered by the NRSV and Stone as "problems.") He then challenges Ezra to answer any one of them: "Go, weigh for me the weight of fire, or measure for me a measure of wind, or call back for me the day that is past" (4:5). Ezra, not surprisingly, is aghast, and protests that no mere mortal could be expected to answer any of these riddles. But Uriel retorts that the fire, the wind, and the day (unlike the sea, the deep, the exits of hell, or the entrance of paradise) are "things through which you have passed" and therefore should be well within the seer's competence to discover.

Although the items on the apocalyptic lists are not "riddles" in the Johannine sense (because they are not couched in the equivocal language employed by the FE), they function in much the same way by setting the privileged guild of seers over against the rest of humankind, clearly distinguishing the "knows" from the "know-nots." There is something decidedly odd, however, about the knowledge involved in apocalyptic wisdom, as evidenced by the previous examples. How, before the invention of anemometers, does one set about measuring the wind? And would you get the same result every time you did? With what instrument does one "weigh fire"? Notably, when Uriel proudly proclaims his knowledge, he does not say specifically what he knows. Instead, he gives a list of questions to which he claims to know the answers without saying what those answers are. So by a rather circuitous route we have found our way back to the kind of dilemma that confronts us in the FG. In both the FG and the apocalypses, the answers to the riddles we are concerned with seem much too shallow to justify the revelatory claims implicit in each.

Stone further points out that "many of the elements mentioned in the lists in 4 Ezra and in 2 Baruch are drawn from the important chapters 28 and 38 of the Book of Job."[11] But those chapters of Job make it clear that true wisdom is not to be found in the parts of the universe Enoch claims to have successfully researched—not in the deep, not in the sea—for "the place of understanding . . . is hidden from the eyes of all [the] living" (Job 28:20–21). And by asking Job who determined the measurements of the

---

11. Stone, "Lists of Revealed Things," 421.

earth (38:5), God is implying that this information is unavailable, even by way of revelation, to scientists or seers. So it is Uriel, posing unanswerable riddles to Ezra, who is the true heir to the Job tradition. Stone is right to argue that Uriel's list of questions "amounts to a denial, daring, perhaps even polemical, of the availability of certain types of special knowledge, a denial therefore of a specific part of the apocalyptic tradition."[12] But this denial is at the same time a reaffirmation of the message of Job, in which God alone understands (LXX, "understood") the way to wisdom (*autēs tēn hodon*) and knows its place (*ton topon autēs*) (Job 28:23). In 4 Ezra, as in Job, the way of God is the heart of the mystery, different in kind as well as in degree from the natural phenomena that surround it. Uriel, fully aware that Ezra will be baffled and frustrated by the riddles he is setting him, knows perfectly well that unlike these natural things the way of God, his plan for the world, is *inaccessible even in principle* to mere mortals. Like Job, he places God's way at the center of his list of things that the seer cannot be expected to comprehend: "for the way of the Most High is created immeasurable" (4:11, Syriac text). This picks up on Ezra's complaint, toward the end of the previous chapter, that God has not shown anyone how "his way" might be understood (3:31).

We return now to the FG. To introduce the theme of "the way" in John 13, the FE seizes on the same wisdom tradition and boldly reverses it. The prologue ended by picturing the Logos, who had tabernacled on earth like "the book of the covenant of the Most High God" (Sir. 24:23), nestling in the lap of the Father (John 1:18). Now Jesus reveals himself as "the way" to God. I have argued elsewhere that the real theme of the Johannine prologue is not creation but revelation, and that "Logos" refers to God's providential plan for the world, a meaning regularly carried in the Hebrew Bible by the terms for wisdom (*hochma* or *sophia*) and, occasionally, for "word " or "thoughts" (*mahsebôth*).[13] "The way," as both Job and 4 Ezra show, is an alternative formulation of the same principle.

Toward the beginning of her discourse in Proverbs 8, personified Wisdom, standing "on the heights beside the way" and "beside the gates in front of the town" (vv. 2–3), proclaims that her mouth will utter truth (v. 7), while toward the end of the chapter she announces that whoever finds her finds life (v. 33). Hence, the way to wisdom is concealed from all except God (Job 28:12–23), but the way to God is wisdom. In asserting

12. Stone, "Lists of Revealed Things," 420.
13. Ashton, *Studying John*, 17–31.

that he in his own person is the way, the truth, and the life, the Johannine Jesus is giving a marvelously inclusive summary of the benefits and
graces that wisdom has to offer.

The FG and the Wisdom of Solomon

By choosing to enter the domain of the FG through a door the FE would
have wished to reserve for initiates—its riddling language—we have been
able to see how he managed to appropriate for his own purposes the
central motifs of the Jewish wisdom tradition and then reapply them,
with astonishing boldness, to the person of Jesus. In doing so, he was at
the same time laying claim to territory staked out over a century earlier
by the author of the Wisdom of Solomon. Whether the FE was actually acquainted with this apocryphal work (written, like his own, in the
Greek language) cannot now be determined. But the two writings exhibit
a number of striking similarities that deserve to be emphasized, for a
comparison will shed light on the central purposes of each.

In the first place, both the FE and the author of Wisdom of Solomon
can be seen to be reflecting directly on the genre exemplified by their
respective works.[14] But whereas the FE is working with the quite recent
(and quite limited) gospel tradition, the author of Wisdom of Solomon
is able to draw on the literary corpus of the entire Hebrew Bible. He is
not the first Jewish writer to have acted in this way: the narrative section
of Deuteronomy is largely a midrash of Exodus and Numbers; Deutero-
Isaiah, working with the preexilic prophetic tradition, was able at the
same time to reflect on the essential characteristics of prophecy itself.
Our author, whom we might call Deutero-Solomon, standing outside the
Hebrew canon but clearly harking back to it, is bolder still, incorporating
in his work elements from all the major biblical genres. His last chapter
even includes apocalyptic, and an earlier passage is highly reminiscent of
Stone's "lists of revealed things" (Wis 7:17–20).

In the second place, both Deutero-Solomon and the FE use a private language to bolster the pride and confidence of what was no doubt
a tightly knit group of fellow believers surrounded by a hostile majority. In the case of Greek Solomon, we may suppose that if his Egyptian
hosts had even guessed at the nature and extent of the vilification he was
heaping on them they would have reacted with anger and hostility. And

14. Ashton, *Understanding the Fourth Gospel*, 1st edition, 434–37.

whereas the Jewish readers for whom he wrote would have greeted the recasting of the biblical legends in the second half of the book, along with their attribution to a series of unnamed men and women, with delighted recognition, their pagan fellow citizens must have responded with blank incomprehension. They are even less likely to have identified the man who pleased God and was "perfected in a short time" (Wis 4:13) as the 365-year-old Enoch, or to have seen in the claim for immortality made on behalf of the righteous man at the beginning of the book (who boasted that God was his father; 2:16, cf. 18:13) an acknowledgment of God's determination to rescue his chosen people from all adversity. Yet the key to all these riddles lies in the Hebrew Scriptures.

Third, in both books a reflective section is followed by an extended narrative section, with the figure of Wisdom playing a major role in each. In the first (meditative) half of Wisdom of Solomon, an exhortation to seek Wisdom (6:1–21) is followed by a long disquisition on Solomon's quest for wisdom that culminates in a midrashic version of his great prayer (9:1–18; cf. 1 Kings 8). This intricately patterned passage is punctuated by numerous reminders of hymn-like praises of Wisdom from the earlier tradition: Proverbs 8:22–31, Sirach 24:1–21; and 2 Baruch 3:9–4:4. The second half of the book begins with a narrative (summarized in 9:18) listing the achievements of personified Wisdom. In the FG, the meditative section is restricted to the prologue, often seen as a hymn to the Logos, Wisdom's masculine surrogate, while the hero of the long narrative that follows (who now has the human name "Jesus") is to be seen among other things as a figure of Wisdom.

Finally, we should remember the place each of these authors gives to the theme of "life," found everywhere in the Hebrew Bible from its first appearance as the tree of life in the garden of Eden, but especially common in the wisdom literature. I suspect that "life" almost always carries some of the extra resonance already discernible in the symbol of the tree of life. This, of course, holds out for human beings the enticing prospect of immortality, an idea taken up directly by Greek Solomon when he promises *athanasia* to everyone who heeds the laws of wisdom (Wis 6:15; cf. 1:12, 15; 4:1; 5:15; 6:18; 8:13, 17). The Odes of Solomon, claiming the authority of the same name, add a slightly different nuance by speaking of the "deathless life" that "rose up in the land of the Lord, and . . . became known to his faithful ones, and was given unsparingly to those who trust in him" (15:10; cf. 28:31; 38:3; 40:6). The promises of the Odes are more than matched by the FE; there is no need to list the numerous passages in the FG that guarantee eternal life to those who believe in Jesus. But John goes further. When Jesus says of his adversaries, the Jews, that they "search for life in the scriptures," he could well be speaking to the readers of Wisdom of Solomon, insofar as this book, as we have seen, sets out to encapsulate the whole biblical tradition. But, declares Jesus uncompromisingly, "*I* am the one to whom they [the Scriptures] bear witness" (John 5:40; my italics). The Scriptures are the hermeneutical key to Jesus, and Jesus is the hermeneutical key to the Scriptures. There could be no more direct expression of the challenge Christianity poses to Judaism.

5

"Mystery" in the Dead Sea Scrolls and the Fourth Gospel

TWENTY YEARS AGO I argued that although the actual words *mystery* and *revelation* are not found there, the Gospel of John is nonetheless related and indeed heavily indebted to Jewish apocalyptic, where the concept of a revealed mystery is all-important. In this essay I wish to return to this subject by emphasizing that certain ideas found in the Dead Sea Scrolls, especially in one key document that had not been published when I was engaged in the composition of *Understanding the Fourth Gospel*, are also important to John.[1]

In the first part of this essay, I want to focus on the phrase רז נהיה, asking (1) what, in this particular context, it *denotes* or refers to, and (2) what it *means*, and how it should be translated. The all-too-frequent confusion of these two questions is a major source of difficulty. The examination of this phrase will lead into a study of its association with the concept of *wisdom* and an inquiry concerning what this can add to our understanding of the Johannine notion of the Logos. The second part of the essay will address two related issues: (1) what is the relationship between Qumran's רז נהיה and Israel's revealed Law?, and (2) what is the understanding at Qumran and among the Johannine community of the new heavenly revelation ("truth") and of the special life that it confers?

---

1. Ashton, *Understanding the Fourth Gospel*, 1st edition, chapter 10.

113

Mystery

I begin with an overview and analysis of various contexts in which the term רז נהיה appears in the Qumran documents. The first appearance is in 1QMysteries:

> They know not *the mystery to come* (רז נהיה) nor do they understand the things of the past. They know not that which shall befall them, nor do they save their soul from *the mystery to come*.[2]

Ever since 1955, when Milik and Barthélemy published 1QMysteries in the first volume of *Discoveries in the Judaean Desert*, the term רז נהיה has been the occasion of some puzzlement. Milik's rendering, *le mystère future*,[3] is accepted by most translators and interpreters of this document (including, initially at any rate, García Martínez: "the future mystery").[4] One major problem with this passage is that elsewhere the term רז נהיה always has a positive connotation. Whether we render it as "the mystery to come" or "the future mystery" it remains decidedly opaque. If we accept Milik's transcription, then in this instance it must represent some dreadful fate or punishment awaiting the wicked, whereas the good, presumably, will be saved.[5] Yet such a negative denotation is not found anywhere else in the scrolls.

If we leave 1QMysteries on one side, there are two other important texts that must be taken into account if we want to get a clearer understanding of this expression: the Community Rule and 4QInstruction. Vermes translates the relevant verse from the Rule as follows: "For my light has sprung from the source of His knowledge; my eyes have beheld His marvellous deeds, and the light of my heart, *the mystery to come*" (1QS 11:3).[6] For García Martínez the term has a future meaning in this context also (as well as in 1QMysteries): "the mystery of the future."[7] But it is hard to make any sense of this: neither the denotation nor the meaning

2. Translation Vermes, *Complete Dead Sea Scrolls*, 389.

3. Milik and Barthélemy, *Discoveries in the Judaean Desert*, 103.

4. García Martínez, *Dead Sea Scrolls Translated*, 399. Yet on the very next page, the same phrase in another copy of the same document is translated as "the mystery of existence"!

5. Unless, like John Collins and Torleif Elgvin, we adopt the bold expedient of translating the Hebrew מן as "by": "they will not save themselves *by* the רז נהיה" (Collins, "Mysteries of God," 289; Elgvin, "Wisdom at Qumran," 2:162).

6. Vermes, *Complete Dead Sea Scrolls*, 115.

7. García Martínez, *Dead Sea Scrolls Translated*, 17.

is at all clear. In any case some commentators disagree about the meaning of the key term here. Alexander Rofé, for instance, understands it to refer to "the secrets of what has happened, i.e. the innermost significance of events" and notes (there being no past participle in Hebrew) that he "would construe *nihyeh* as a perfect, rather than as a participle."[8] He does not, however, attempt to explain the syntax required by this translation. Eduard Lohse, in his selection of Qumran texts, points נהיה with a *qamets* instead of a *tsere* and translates the whole phrase as "das Geheimnis des Gewordenen."[9] James Charlesworth, in the first volume of a major project involving a commentary and translation of all the scrolls, retains the future meaning but modifies it slightly: "the light of my heart beheld the mystery of what shall occur and is occurring forever."[10] In an even later publication, García Martínez translates it as "the mystery of existence."[11] Here, I suspect, he is transferring to the Community Rule a rendering that he uses for another, very different, document, 4QInstruction.

The year 1999 saw the appearance of one of the last volumes in the splendid series *Discoveries in the Judaean Desert*, published by the Clarendon Press. Volume 34, edited by John Strugnell, Daniel Harrington, and Torleif Elgvin, contains a number of fragments (1Q26, 4Q415–418, 4Q423) of a document known originally as "Sapiential Text A" and subsequently as "4QInstruction." This document had been available to scholars since its preliminary publication by Ben-Zion Wacholder and Martin Abegg in 1991, and it forms the centerpiece of Harrington's study "Wisdom Texts from Qumran." The "understanding child" is enjoined to gaze and meditate day and night upon the רז נהיה.

> 6 By day and by night meditate upon the mystery that is to be/
> come and study it always. And then you will know truth and
> iniquity . . . 7 . . . Then you will discern between good and evil
> according to their works. For the God of knowledge is the foun-
> dation of truth, and by the mystery to be/come 9 He has laid out
> its foundation, and its deeds he has prepared with [. . .] wisdom,
> and with all cunning He has fashioned it. . . . 18 . . . And you,
> O understanding child, gaze on the mystery that is to be/come.
> And know 19 the paths of everything that lives and the manner

8. Rofé, "Revealed Wisdom: From the Bible to Qumran," 2 n.3.

9. Lohse, *Die Texte aus Qumran*, 41.

10. Charlesworth, *The Dead Sea Scrolls*, 47.

11. García Martínez and Tigchelaar, *The Dead Sea Scrolls Study Edition*, 1.97.

of his walking that is appointed over his deeds. (4Q417 frag. 2 6–19).[12]

Harrington comments that the רז נהיה

> seems to be a body of teaching that concerns behavior and es-chatology. It is probably an extrabiblical compendium, not the Torah. It may have been something like the "instruction on the Two Spirits" in 1QS iii 13–iv 26. Or it may have been the "Book of Meditation" (see 1QSa i 6–8) by which a prospective member of the movement was instructed (at home?) between the ages of ten and twenty. Or it may have been the "Book of Mysteries" (1Q27, 4Q299–301), which uses the term frequently in a cosmic context.[13]

But against this it should be said that the use of רז נהיה "in a cosmic context"—a use also evidenced in the line from the Community Rule cited above—makes it unlikely that the term refers to a written document, however prestigious and however prized. This is just possible if it was accorded the same authority as the Torah itself, identified with Wisdom in a famous passage in Sirach (24:23–24); but even this possibility vanishes if 1Q27 is taken into account. 4QInstruction (4Q416 frag. 2 3.18; 4Q418 frags. 10 a-b 1, frag. 123 2.4, frag. 184 2, frag. 190 2; 4Q423 frag. 5 2) speaks of "opening the ears (of the student or disciple) רז נהיה." Harrington translates this in its first occurrence, "they [i.e., the student's parents] uncovered your ear *to* the mystery that is to be/come."[14] But "to" seems an improbable rendering of the preposition ב. (The difference in meaning between ב and ל is well illustrated in Job 36, where in verse 10, "he opens their ear *to* instruction," the preposition is ל; whereas a little further on, in verse 15, "he opens their ear *by* adversity," the preposition is ב.) Elsewhere, it is true, in one of the songs of praise (1QH 9.23), we read, "Thou has opened my ears *to* marvelous mysteries." But the Hebrew here, לרזי פלא, is unambiguous; whereas in yet another passage, where ב is used, Vermes (1997) translates, "thou has given me knowledge *through* thy marvellous mysteries" (1QH 9.23; 15.30; 19.13). In the official edition of the text, DJD 34, Harrington allows an alternative rendering: "In this phrase, the preposition ב in ברז may indicate the subject matter of the revelation (i.e. 'about the mystery'), or the hermeneutic principle used

---

12. Harrington, *Wisdom Texts from Qumran*, 52–53.

13. Harrington, *Wisdom Texts from Qumran*, 49.

14. Harrington, *Wisdom Texts from Qumran*, 44.

for interpreting a revelation."[15] As a translation of the Hebrew ב, the latter
suggestion ("by" rather than "to") seems much more likely to be right but
raises once again the problem of how to determine the denotation of the
term רז נהיה.

Fortunately, however, Harrington comes to our assistance here
with another helpful suggestion. Rejecting the translation "mystery of
existence" as "too metaphysical and static," he compares the term in its
elusive indeterminacy to the phrase "kingdom of God" in the Synoptic
Gospels.[16] (As Jesus uses this phrase, despite strenuous efforts by New
Testament scholars to restrict its reference either to the present or to the
future, both references have to be retained.[17]) Harrington's suggestion occurs at the end of a paragraph in which he still favors the likelihood that
the רז נהיה is a written document, but of course "kingdom of God" is not
a text but a *concept* (a very powerful one), and the same is true, I believe,
of the רז נהיה. This is not a new proposal. Elgvin thinks of רז נהיה as "a
comprehensive word for God's mysterious plan for creation and history,
His plan for man and for the redemption of the elect,"[18] a suggestion cited
approvingly by Menahem Kister.[19] John J. Collins is also inclined to favor
the idea that רז נהיה is "a comprehensive term for the entire divine plan,
embracing past, present and future;"[20] and elsewhere Elgvin nicely sums
up his own suggestion as "the unfolding mystery of God."[21]

If we accept provisionally that this, or something very close, is what
the term רז נהיה *denotes*, the question of what it *means*, how it should
be translated, still has to be answered. Here too there have been many
different proposals. The first word, *raz*, is in one sense unproblematic:
it means, unquestionably, "mystery." Wacholder and Abegg, in their
Preliminary Edition, rendered the Hebrew term רז נהיה by "the mystery
of existence,"[22] a rendering retained by Loren Stuckenbruck in an essay

15. See Strugnell et al., *Qumran Cave 4*, 34:537.

16. See Harrington, "Two Early Jewish Approaches to Wisdom," 272; Harrington,
Wisdom Texts, 89–90.

17. See Sanders's excellent chapter, "The Coming of the Kingdom," in *Historical
Figure of Jesus*, 169–88.

18. Elgvin, "Wisdom and Apocalypticism," 235.

19. Kister, "Wisdom Literature and Its Relation," 31.

20. Collins, "Eschatologizing of Wisdom," 55.

21. Elgvin, "Mystery to Come," 133.

22. Wacholder and Abegg, *Preliminary Edition*.

linking 4QInstruction with Enoch,[23] and by García Martínez in his translation of the whole corpus of the scrolls.[24] Along the same lines is an
earlier modification of his original suggestion—"the secret of the way
things are"—which has received the support of Philip Davies as "perhaps
the most felicitous" of all possible choices. Davies argues that the phrase
"surely connotes the ultimate but hidden clue to the riddle of existence
itself, and especially human existence."[25] But is this how the sectarians
themselves conceived it? The rendering "mystery of existence" had already been dismissed as too philosophical by Harrington and Strugnell
in their very critical review of the *Preliminary Edition*,[26] and indeed the
term has an almost Heideggerian ring. Armin Lange's alternative proposal, "das Geheimnis des Werdens,"[27] is interestingly different in its
stress on "becoming" or "arising," but it too is scarcely satisfactory as a
rendering of the Hebrew, for the word נהיה is not an abstract noun but a
participle—that is to say, a verbal adjective.

Moreover, in the context of 4QInstruction, where "the understanding child" is invited to contemplate and meditate on the mystery day and
night, it is even harder to admit a future meaning. The contemplation of a
mystery, in principle unintelligible without a special revelation, is already
paradoxical. To propel the mystery into the long grass of an indefinite
future is to carry the paradox, in my view, to the point of incomprehen-
sibility. The niph'al participle can bear a present meaning just as easily
as a future, and accordingly I prefer to translate רז נהיה as "the mystery
that is coming to pass." Following Harrington's imaginative comparison,
I believe that the term implies the same sort of inaugurated eschatology
as the gospel phrase "kingdom of God."[28]

Implicit also in the concept of the רז נהיה is an assurance of the
providence of God. The universal Jewish belief in God as Creator has

23. Stuckenbruck, "4QInstruction and the Possible Influence," 245–62.

24. García Martínez, *Dead Sea Scrolls Translated*, 383–90.

25. Davies, "Death, Resurrection, and Life after Death," 197n1.

26. Harrington and Strugnell, "Qumran Cave 4 Texts," 491–99; see also Harrington, "Two Early Jewish Approaches," 272.

27. See Lange, *Weisheit und Prädestination*.

28. Some time after reaching this conclusion I consulted the more recent edition of
4QMysteries in DJD 20, *Qumran Cave 4.XV* (1997). On the term רז נהיה the editors
remark simply: "This refers to the secret of that which is in the process of coming
into being," adding that "this usage of Nip'al is common in Qumran Hebrew" and
comparing the usage in 4QMysteries to Sir. 42:19 and 42:35," where נהיות is parallel
to נסתרות, 'secrets'" (105).

broadened into an awareness of human history as the unfolding mystery of the divine plan. By means of the רז נהיה, the God who is the foundation of truth "has laid out its foundation [i.e., creation] and its works [מעשיה, i.e., history]" (4Q417 frag. 1 1.9).

Wisdom

4QInstruction combines the kind of paranetical instruction familiar from, say, Proverbs and Sirach with longer wisdom discourses built round the phrase רז נהיה. Torleif Elgvin, who has written extensively about the document (and indeed was responsible for the edition of one of the fragments included in DJD 34), proposed that it "represents a conflation of two literary layers."[29] Other scholars have rejected this proposal, but the very fact that it could be seriously entertained indicates the unusual nature of the document as a whole. Nevertheless, in this respect it resembles the book of Proverbs, which largely consists of dozens of (frequently platitudinous) aphorisms on how life is to be lived: "A cheerful heart is good medicine; but a downcast spirit dries up the bones" (17:22). But alongside these aphorisms, which may be grouped together under the heading of *accessible* wisdom, are ranged deep reflections upon a hidden, *remote* wisdom that can be accessed, if at all, only through a special revelation originating in God. In 4QInstruction *accessible* wisdom is represented largely by observations on how to cope with poverty: "Do not satiate yourself with bread when there is no clothing. Do not drink wine while there is no food. Do not seek luxury when you lack bread" (4Q416 frag. 2 2.19–20).[30] *Remote* wisdom has its own name in this document: רז נהיה, "the mystery that is coming to pass."

Any group that attaches special importance to an extra revelation above and beyond the Law, such as the רז נהיה, is properly speaking sectarian, because it thereby diverges from those whom we may call, with some hesitation, the representatives of mainstream Judaism. These, the direct ancestors of the writers of the Mishnah, thought of revelation very differently from the sectarian Jews of the Qumran community and the authors of some of their most cherished writings, such as 1 Enoch.

What looks like a party line is already discernible in Deuteronomy:

---

29. Elgvin, "Wisdom and Apocalypticism," 226.

30. Translation from Vermes, *Complete Dead Sea Scrolls*, 406.

> For this commandment which I command you this day is not
> too hard for you (לֹא־נִפְלֵאת הִוא מִמְּךָ) neither is it far off. It is not
> in heaven, that you should say, "Who will go up for us to heaven,
> and bring it to us, that we may hear it and do it?" Neither is it
> beyond the sea, that you should say, "Who will go over the sea
> for us, and bring it to us, that we may hear it and do it?" But the
> word is very near you; it is in your mouth and in your heart, so
> that you can do it. (Deut. 30:11–14)

Indeed, Deuteronomy *identifies* wisdom and understanding with the
Law: "Keep [these statutes and ordinances] and do them; for that will
be your wisdom and understanding in the sight of the peoples" (4:6).[31]
After reciting the ten commandments that God had dictated to him, Moses concludes, significantly, "and he added no more" (5:22). In fact, any
subtraction from or addition to the Law had been denounced in advance
(4:2). What the author calls the "secret" or "hidden" things (הנסתרות,
LXX: τὰ κρυπτά) are reserved for God; "but the things that are revealed
(הנגלות, τὰ φανερά) belong to us and to our children for ever" (29:28).

The famous passage in Job 28 that speaks of a wisdom that is in principle inaccessible to mortal man, "concealed from the eyes of every living
thing and hidden [נטתרת] from the birds of the sky" (28:21), would have
met with the approval of the Deuteronomists. Not so the claim of the sage
of Qumran to "have gazed on that which is eternal [בהויא עולם] on sound
insight [תושיה] hidden [נסתרה] from men, on knowledge and wise design
[hidden] from the sons of men" (1QS 11.5–7). This claim, which surely
concerns the רז נהיה, is properly speaking apocalyptic, asserting as it does
the revelation of hidden wisdom and rejecting the tradition common to
Job and Deuteronomy of a wisdom that remains permanently out of human reach. In fact the term "apocalyptic" is most appropriately bestowed
on works that highlight revelations over and above the Law, reserved for

31. The word translated "too hard for [i.e., *beyond*] you" in the passage from Deuteronomy quoted above (30:11), the niph'al participle of פלא, reappears at Qumran
in the hymnic conclusion to the Community Rule in a passage where it is parallel
to the רז נהיה: "my eyes have beheld his *marvelous deeds* [נפלאותיו] and the light
of my heart the mystery of what is coming to pass" (1QS 11.3). But this is simply a
coincidence, for the term is a standard one, especially in the Psalms (with the solitary
exception of Psalm 131), for the marvelous works that God has done and will continue
to do on behalf of his people. The meaning "too hard for" depends upon the following מן, as in Deut 17:4; 2 Sam 13:2; Job 42:3; Ps 131:1; Prov 30:18; Jer 32:17, 27. The
reflections of Menahem Kister on this verb, which include references to the Qumran
material, are, to say the least, tendentious (Kister, "Wisdom Literature," 21–22).

the writer and his readers; and by analogy the community to which these belong may reasonably be called apocalyptic also.[32]

The Johannine Logos

Is there anything in these reflections on the concept of mystery in the scrolls that can further our understanding of the Gospel of John? Another few lines from the hymnic conclusion to the Community Rule may help us to answer this question.

> All things come to pass by his knowledge [כול ובדעת נהיה]; he establishes all things by his design [כול הווה במחשבותו יכינו]; and without him nothing is done [יעשה]. (1QS 11.11; cf. 1QH 9.9–12)[33]

The terms "come to pass" (נהיה) and "is done" (יעשה) both refer to human history and scarcely differ in meaning. They allude to divine providence, God's unremitting activity on behalf of his creation, which we have seen to be implicit in the concept of the רז נהיה. Rudolf Bultmann cites this passage without comment as a parallel to John 1:3 (πάντα δι᾽ αὐτοῦ ἐγένετο, καὶ χωρὶς αὐτοῦ ἐγένετο οὐδὲ ἓν ὃ γέγονεν), but I suspect that the parallel may be closer than he realized.[34] In the first place,

32. A classic example of apocalyptic is 1 Enoch, on which George Nickelsburg observes that "the text as a whole is presented in a self-conscious way as a document that is revealed wisdom . . . Thus, while the prophets claimed to reveal how God would work out the divine will in the world's future, the function of revelation and the forms in which it is presented in *1 Enoch* justify using the term *apocalyptic* to distinguish the text's eschatology from that of its canonical predecessors" (Nickelsburg, *1 Enoch 1*, 55). It is something of an anachronism to speak of Enoch's "canonical predecessors" in this context, and the term *apocalyptic* should not be confined to the sect's eschatology, but the distinction is still valid. On the notable differences between the apocalypticists, most but not all of whom embraced the tradition of hidden wisdom, see the seminal article of Michael Stone, "Lists of Revealed Things," 414–52. *Accessible* wisdom, obviously, and *divine* wisdom too can easily be accommodated by writers such as Baruch and Ben Sira who stands in the Deuteronomic tradition. Not so *hidden* wisdom: "hidden wisdom and unseen treasure, what advantage is there in either of them?" (Sir. 20:30). Compare Sirach 18:4–6 and 3:21–23, which refers directly to Deuteronomy: "Seek not what is too hard for you, nor investigate what is beyond your power."

33. נהיה, the niph'al form of היה, is translated here by Vermes as a present, by García Martínez as a future ("By his knowledge everything *shall* come into being"), and by Lohse as a past ("durch sein Wissen *ist* alles enstanden"). The divergent translations are perhaps some indication of the temporal inclusiveness of the activity of God.

34. Bultmann, *Gospel of John*, 37n5.

the word πάντα corresponds very precisely to the Hebrew כול. That is to say, it refers not to the created universe (always τὰ πάντα in the New Testament and usually so in the Septuagint) but to the events of human history.[35] In the second place, the verb γίνεσθαι is used regularly in the sense of "happen" or "come to pass" and corresponds well to the niph'al of היה and the pe'al of הוי. This is also how this verse from the prologue was understood by the gnostic author of the Gospel of Truth, who, commenting on the revelation of the word ("the first to come forth"), asserts that "nothing happens without him, nor does anything happen without the will of the Father" (37:9–44). More significantly still, this is also how the verb γίνεσθαι was understood by the early Syriac translators (though the Sinaitic manuscript is deficient at this point). Unlike the vast majority of modern commentators, they were not misled by the parallel between the first two words of the prologue and the opening of Genesis into thinking that in what follows the writer is referring to the created universe. Thus, Burkitt's translation of the Curetonian version of John 1:3 reads, "Everything came to pass in Him, and apart from Him not even one thing came to pass in Him."[36] This is also the sense required in 4 Ezra 6:6: "But I planned these things and they came to pass [Syriac הוי plural] through me and not through another." See too Judith 9:5: "the things thou didst intend came to pass [ἐγενήθησαν]."

Relevant here are two more texts from the scrolls. The first, from 4QInstruction, concerns the student of the רז נהיה, who "will know the hidden things of his [God's] thoughts [נסתרי מחשבת] when he walks in perfection in all his deeds. Seek them always, look at all their outcome. Then you will have knowledge of eternal glory with his marvelous mysteries and mighty deeds" (4Q417 frag. 2 1.11–13). The second is the passage already quoted above from the Community Rule (1QS 11.5–11) that refers to the thoughts of God and the wisdom concealed from men. The word מחשבות, literally "his thoughts," is often used of God's plans or designs (e.g., Jer 29:11; 51:29; Mic 4:12; Ps 33:11), above all in the famous epilogue to the prophecy of Second Isaiah, "For as the heavens are higher than the earth so are my ways higher than your ways and my

35. One of the rare instances in the LXX where πάντα refers to the created universe is Psalm 8:7. This is quoted twice in the New Testament (1 Cor 15:7 and Heb 2:8) and in both of these passages the anarthrous πάντα is *corrected* into τὰ πάντα. Further evidence may be found in a long note (n37) in my article, "Transformation of Wisdom," 161–86.

36. Burkitt, *Evangelion da-Mepharreshe*, 1.423.

thoughts than your thoughts" (Isa 55:8–9), an assertion directly followed by the affirmation of the universal fruitfulness of "every word that goes forth from my mouth" (v. 11), an affirmation that harks back to the same author's proclamation in the introduction to his work that "the word of the Lord abides for ever" (40:8). Thus the "thoughts" of God, his plan or design, are expressed in his "word." We could hardly be closer than this to the Fourth Evangelist's conception of the Logos.[37]

The Logos, moreover, like the רז נהיה for the Qumran Community, was an object of contemplation for the Johannine Christians. The verb θεᾶσθαι in John 1:14 is generally translated as "see" ("we have seen his glory"), but it really means "gaze at" and in some contexts—for example Plato, *Phaedo* 84b, where the object of the verb is "the true and the divine and what is above mere opinion—it is best translated "contemplate." "We contemplated his glory" may not be far from what is meant here. And since John 1:3, as we have seen, probably does not refer to creation, as most scholars suppose, but to everything that happens or comes to pass, then what is being asserted might be exactly what the author of the hymnic conclusion to the Community Rule proclaimed in the passage that we have just looked at: "all things come to pass by his knowledge and he establishes all things by his design." If so (and I for one find this suggestion both plausible and attractive), the glory of the Logos is nothing less than the mystery of God's plan as, no longer hidden, it has finally been incarnated and revealed.

Qumran and the Law

Given the importance attached by the Community to the רז נהיה, it remains to be asked how they could reconcile this with their abiding attachment to the Law, understood as God's revelation to Israel. Unlike those whom we might call the Enochic sectarians, who, as Nickelsburg puts it, "leapfrogged Moses and identified Enoch as the primordial recipient of

---

37. This thesis was first set out a quarter of a century ago in the article cited above (Ashton, "Transformation of Wisdom," see n35 above), in which I modified and expanded the earlier work of T. E. Pollard, I. de la Potterie and P. Lamarche. To the best of my knowledge it has never never been the object of any scholarly comment, either favorable or unfavorable. A slightly revised version of the article was printed some years later in my *Studying John*, 5–35.

all heavenly wisdom,"[38] they did not, apparently, subordinate the Law to their other source of revelation.

None of the writings composed by the Qumran sectarians themselves is strictly speaking an apocalypse, for visions and angelic interpreters are missing from them all. But the number of manuscripts of 1 Enoch and Jubilees, plus a quantity of Aramaic texts found in their library, testifies to their appreciation of the genre, and their own work is suffused with their sense that they are the privileged recipients of a special revelation unavailable to ordinary mortals. This does not mean that they reject the Torah, and the presence among the scrolls of various halakhic texts, especially 4QMMT, shows how seriously they took its interpretation. But because of the value they attach to their own revealed mysteries, the Torah may have been no more significant to them than this new truth. For Enoch, as we have just seen, the new revelation takes pride of place. In this regard both groups of writers differ widely from Ben Sira who, though respecting and indeed prizing the wisdom traditions he has inherited, subsumes them all under the Law.

> Come to me, you who desire me, and eat your fill of my produce. For the remembrance of me is sweeter than honey, and my inheritance sweeter than the honeycomb. Those who eat me will hunger for more, and those who drink me will thirst for more. Whoever obeys me will not be put to shame and those who work with my help will not sin. All this is the book of the covenant of the Most High God, the law which Moses commanded us and an inheritance of the congregations of Jacob. (Sir. 24:19–23)

There are then two distinct attitudes towards revelation at Qumran, but even where the Law continues to occupy a central position there is still a need for interpretation. In the Rule of the Community everyone entering the community has to swear to revert to the Law of Moses; but this is "in compliance with all that has been revealed concerning it [לכול הנגלה ממנה] to the sons of Zadok, the priests who keep the covenant and seek [interpret?] his [God's] will [דורשי רצונו]" (1QS 5.9) through a revealed knowledge of the true interpretation of the law that is unavailable to outsiders. The Damascus Document interprets the well in Numbers 21:18 as the Law, "and those who dug it were the converts of Israel [ישראל שבי] who went out of the Land of Israel to sojourn in the land of Damascus." The staffs or staves with which the well was dug are envisaged

38. Nickelsburg, 1 Enoch 1, 52.

as having been instructed to do so by "the staff," that is, the interpreter of the Law (המחוקק הוא דורש התורה; CD 6.2–11). The prophets too required interpretation, contrary to the opinion of Ben Sira, who says for instance of Isaiah that he revealed "hidden things before they came to pass" (Sir. 48:25). Hence the prevalence at Qumran of the so-called *pesharim*, applications of prophetic texts to the present situation of the community. Thus it is said of the Teacher of Righteousness that God made known to him "all the mysteries of the words of his servants the prophets." But when the author of (one of) the Thanksgiving Hymns praises God for having instructed him in his wonderful mysteries (ברזי פלאכה; 1QHᵃ 12.27–28) this is something new: it was not enough for him to have the Law engraved on his heart (שננתה בלבבי; 1QH 12.10). And of course the רז נהיה (which I have already discussed at some length) was something other than the Law.

Unlike Enoch and the Qumran community, the Gospel of John abandons the Law completely. The Law is not just superseded but canceled: "for the law was given through Moses; grace and truth come through Jesus Christ" (John 1:17), and it is Jesus, so he himself asserts, to whom the Scriptures bear witness (5:39). He has succeeded the Law and replaced it as the object of revelation.

Life in a Community of the Elect

Both the Qumran Yahad and the Johannine community saw themselves as the recipients of a special revelation. One word used in both their writings to underline this gratifying conviction is "truth." Before asking about their sense of the benefits this conveys, it is worth considering how they thought of the revelation itself.

The Community Rule speaks of "those in Israel who have freely pledged themselves to the House of Truth" (1QS 5.6) and goes on to speak of "the multitude of the men of the Covenant who together have freely pledged themselves to his truth" (5.10). Considering this truth to be a privileged possession bestowed on them by God (1QM 13.12), the covenanters saw it as something not lightly to be divulged to others, recommending instead "faithful concealment of the mysteries of truth" (1QS 4.6) in the well-known passage already mentioned that pits the spirit of light against the spirit of darkness and falsehood and claims for the community the title of "sons of truth in this world." The community is also often referred to in the Thanksgiving Hymns as "the sons of his/ thy truth" (1QH 14.32; 15.32–33; 17.35; 18.29; 19.14) and elsewhere as "the community of truth" (1QS 2.24). "I know that no riches equal to thy truth," sings the poet (1QH 7.35–36).

A further point is this: *the knowledge of the truth is seen to depend upon the revelation of divine mysteries.* A passage from the Habakkuk *pesher* elucidating an instruction to the prophet to transcribe one of his visions (1QpHab 2.2) speaks of the Teacher of Righteousness, to whom God made known "all the mysteries [רזים] of the words of his servants the prophets" (1QpHab 7.1–5; cf. CD 1.11–13; 1QH 9.26). And the author of the Hodayoth (possibly the very same Teacher of Righteousness) declares explicitly that he has been made "a discerning interpreter of marvelous mysteries [מליץ דעת ברזי פלא] on behalf of the elect of righteousness" (1QH 10.15). And again: "I [thank thee, O Lord] for thou has enlightened me through thy truth. In thy marvelous mysteries, and in thy loving kindness to a man [of vanity, and] in the greatness of thy mercy to a perverse heart Thou hast granted me knowledge" (1QH 15.29–30).

In another passage, having identified himself as the Instructor (משכיל) he says that he has known God through the spirit which he gave him and that through the same spirit "I have faithfully hearkened to thy marvelous counsel" (לסוד פלאכה; 1QH 20.15).

The term סוד, which also occurs in similar contexts elsewhere in the Hymns (1QH 12.28–39; 13.11; 19.7; cf. 4Q437 6.1; Job 15:8), suggests the same kind of privileged access to the most intimate secrets of God as the Jesus of the Fourth Gospel claims for himself (see John 10:15; 17:25), and in both cases it is this privileged communication that permits the two teachers to pass on what they know to others. But for the Fourth Evangelist the truth has an even greater significance than it has for the Qumran community: it belongs to the special vocabulary of the Johannine group, and its inner meaning is hidden from outsiders such as "the Jews," who fatally misunderstand the promise that "the truth will make you free" (John 8:32), and Pilate, who fails to recognize the truth when it is standing in front of him (18:38). For "the truth" in the Fourth Gospel is actually identified with the person of Jesus: "I am the way, the truth, and the life" (14:6).

In the Farewell Discourse in John 14–16, as often elsewhere in the Fourth Gospel, Jesus appears as to be a second Moses. On this occasion, about to take leave of his disciples, he surveys what for them is the equivalent of the Promised Land. This is what he calls "the truth." Just as

Moses in the book of Deuteronomy, who is to die before he can himself conduct his people into the "the whole land of Judah as far as the Western Sea, the Negeb and the Plain" (34:1–4), stands at the top of Pisgah, casts his eyes "westward and northward and southward and eastward" (3:27), and commissions his successor, Joshua, to carry out the task he is destined not to fulfill himself, so too Jesus, unable while alive to transmit his revelation to his disciples in a way that they can understand, but clearly foreseeing all that this revelation will come to mean to them, appoints the Paraclete, the spirit of truth, to guide them into the spiritual territory that he calls, simply, "all the truth" (John 16:12). As Hans Windisch observed long ago, the Paraclete is, among other things, Jesus's caliph or successor, who will teach his disciples all things and bring to their remembrance all that he had said to them (14:26).[39]

We may now turn to a consideration of the benefits brought to both communities by the gift of the truth. Put very succinctly, the most important benefit is *life*. At Qumran, moreover, this involves sharing in the life of the angels.

> From the source of his righteousness is my justification and from his marvelous mysteries is the light of my heart. My eyes have gazed on what is eternal, on wisdom concealed from men, on knowledge and wise design (hidden) from the sons of men; on a fountain of righteousness and on a storehouse of power, on a spring of glory (hidden) from the assembly of flesh. God has given them to his chosen ones as an everlasting possession, and has caused them to inherit the lot of the Holy Ones. He has joined their assembly to the Sons of Heaven to be a Council of the Community, a foundation of the Building of Holiness, and eternal Plantation throughout all ages to come." (1QS 11.5–8)[40]

The sheer familiarity of this passage can blind us to the remarkable confidence with which the writer lays out his extraordinary claims. A list of rules and regulations astonishing in its overall severity is succeeded immediately by a solemn and insistent hymn of thanksgiving and then, without a break, by confident assertions concerning a privileged relationship with God based on a very special knowledge that marks out the writer and his community from the rest of mankind and justifies the assertion that they are not merely associated with "the sons of heaven," the angels, but virtually identified with them.

39. Windisch, "Jesus und der Geist," 303–18.
40. Translation from Vermes, *Complete Dead Sea Scrolls*, 115.

The present participation in the life of the angels is affirmed through-out the scrolls as a pledge of great peace "in a long life [כאורך ימים]," "eter-nal joy in life without end [שמחת עולמים בחיי נצח]," and a "garment of majesty in unending light [באור עולמים]" (1QS 4:6–8). I used to believe that scholars such as Aune, Nickelsburg, and Collins were wrong to fol-low H. W. Kuhn in finding in the scrolls, especially in the Hodayot, a belief in present participation in angelic life, coupled with the expecta-tion of fulfillment in the future.[41] But I am now persuaded that my earlier reservations were mistaken. This view derives strong support from the sheer variety of the documents testifying to the community's sense that it was living among angels. Apart from the Hodayot (1QH 11.22–24; 14.15–17; 15.17–18; 19.14–17), the most important of these is the Songs of the Sabbath Sacrifice (4Q400–405; 11Q17), which was unavailable to Kuhn and his first supporters. But there is other evidence besides.

First, there is the promise at the end of the Community Rule (quoted above) where "the chosen ones" are assured that God has "caused them to inherit the lot of the Holy Ones" and "joined their assembly to the Sons of Heaven to be a Council of the Community." Next there are the purity rules found both in the War Scroll (1QM 7.6) and in the Rule of the Con-gregation (1QSa 2.2–10) that exclude men suffering from pollution or any kind of physical blemish from belonging to the army ("for the holy angels are together with their armies") or from taking their place among "the men of renown" of the assembly ("for the holy angels are among their congregation"). To this we may add the evidence of 4QInstruction, which promises to the neophyte a place in the heavenly court: "among all the godly ones he has cast your lot" (4Q418: frag. 81 4–5), whether the Sons of Heaven, "whose lot is eternal life" (4Q418 frag. 69 2.13), are the human righteous, as is argued by Crispin Fletcher-Louis,[42] or the angelic host. Lastly, we may point to a short document in which the final destiny of the wicked is contrasted with a promise to the good that they will be counted "as a congregation of holiness in service for eternal life and [shar-ing] the lot of his holy ones ... each man according to the lot which he has cast ... for eternal life [לחיי עולם]" (4Q181; cf. CD 3.20; 1QH 4.27; 7.29; frag. 23 2.10). Reminiscent though it may be of John's ζωὴ αἰώνιος, this promise is different from the immediate reward offered by Jesus to those who believe. There is certainly an analogy, to put it no more strongly,

41. See Aune, *Cultic Setting of Realized Eschatology*; Nickelsburg, *Resurrection, Im-mortality and Eternal Life*; Collins, "Apocalyptic Eschatology," 21–43.

42. Fletcher-Louis, *All the Glory of Adam*, 119–20.

between the assurance of the Johannine community that they enjoyed a new kind of life, which might be characterized as the life of the new age, and the Qumran community's sense of having been admitted into the society of the angels. Yet perhaps one should not press the comparison too far. There is certainly no obvious resemblance between the Qumran and the Johannine communities, and nothing could be further from the calm sublimity of the discourses of Jesus in the Fourth Gospel than the curious mixture of self-loathing and exaltation that characterizes the Hodayot.

It should not be necessary to add that for the Fourth Evangelist all the large concepts I have discussed here—mystery, wisdom, Logos, truth, life—are summed up in the person of Jesus, who encapsulates in his own person the divine plan of God set out for the contemplation of the Johannine community, much as the רז נהיה was proposed for the contemplation of the "wise child" at Qumran. The actual term "mystery" is, of course, missing from the Fourth Gospel, but the concept of mystery is unquestionably present, an apocalypse in reverse, since it is played out not in heaven but on earth.

Conclusion

This essay was prompted by an exchange between Daniel Harrington and Joseph Fitzmyer in a volume dedicated to the memory of Raymond Brown. Responding to Fitzmyer's essay, Harrington raised the question whether the background shared by the Qumran literature and the Fourth Gospel was merely, as he put it, "apocalyptic Judaism," or something more concrete. To which Fitzmyer rather testily rejoined, "I should want to know what one means by 'apocalyptic' Judaism. That the Essenes were composing apocalyptic writings is clear, but when that adjective is applied to Judaism as such I do not know what that means."[43] Nevertheless, it is a word that has been used by other scholars, too, for example John Collins: "By an apocalyptic worldview I mean the view that human life is shaped to a significant extent by supernatural (angelic or demonic) powers and subject to a final judgment, not only on nations but also on the individual dead. . . . This view stands in sharp contrast to the worldview of the Mishnah and Talmud but is shared, broadly speaking, by the sectarian scrolls and most of the New Testament writings."[44] Similarly, Frank M. Cross, in

43. Fitzmyer, "Qumran Literature and the Johannine Writings," 129.
44. Collins, "Qumran, Apocalypticism, and the New Testament," 133.

one of the earliest general commentaries on the relevance of the scrolls to the Bible, had spoken of these as the literature of an "apocalyptic community," which Collins rightly took as a reference to "the belief of the Qumran community that it had already made the transition to a new form [of] life, while still in this life, in history."[45] Following Collins, I have tried in this essay to indicate reasons for believing that Jewish sectarians at Qumran—and the Johannine community—were apocalyptic both in the sense in which earlier scholars understood that term and in the more specific sense of living lives shaped by a revealed mystery.

45. Cross, *Ancient Library of Qumran*, 56; Collins, "Apocalyptic Eschatology," 26.

6

The Johannine Son of Man

A New Proposal

CLOSING THE INTRODUCTION TO his seminal study, *The Prophet-King* (1967), Wayne Meeks argued for the validity of a new approach in the study of Johannine christology "in the face of Bultmann's elaborate theory that had seemed to account so cogently for the total christological picture in John," an approach that his own work was intended to exemplify. Instead of a comprehensive explanation of the whole, he suggested, "it is appropriate in the study of the Fourth Gospel to focus upon a single phenomenon or group of closely related phenomena."[1] Subsequently there have been many such studies which, like his own, employ a history-of-traditions approach to the material, but the source of the one motif that seemed to Meeks to furnish the strongest argument for a gnostic background to the Fourth Gospel, the descent/ascent motif associated with the title Son of Man, is still something of a mystery.[2] No satisfactory explanation has yet been offered for the striking differences between the synoptic and the Johannine Son of Man. In his famous "Man from Heaven" article,[3] Meeks himself successfully outlined the significance

1. *The Prophet King*, 16.

2. All commentators discuss the title, many in considerable detail, but only in order to explain its use and significance in the Gospel itself. This is also true of other studies, including the chapter "Son of Man" in my own book, *Understanding the Fourth Gospel*. What is probably the most thorough discussion to date (Reynolds, *The Apocalyptic Son of Man in the Gospel of John*) sets out to prove that John is everywhere indebted to Dan 7, but goes not further.

3. "The Man from Heaven in Johannine Sectarianism," 44–72.

of the motif within the Gospel, but made no attempt to account for its origin.

Towards the end of *The Prophet-King*, in fact, Meeks had felt able to say that the pattern of the descent/ascent of a heavenly messenger "has been and remains the strongest support for the hypothesis that the Johannine christology is connected with gnostic mythology."[4] In 1969, two years after the publication of Meeks's book, this support was skillfully and ruthlessly dismantled by Carsten Colpe in a long article in *TWNT*.[5] There is indeed in some gnostic texts a sort of descent/ascent myth; but this involves the descent and subsequent ascent of a being called Man, who represents the totality of mankind. Colpe argued that there is nothing to show that this being stands behind the Son of Man in John. It is not that the idea of humankind as a collective soul has been (deliberately) left out of the Gospel (*weggelassen*), but that "the Evangelist, being interested in neither cosmology, nor anthropology, nor the destiny of the soul, was simply not acquainted with it."[6] The gnostic Man is in no sense an ancestor of the Johannine Son of Man; indeed, if any relationship is involved, it must be the other way round. To account for the up-and-down conundrum of the descending and ascending Son of Man in John what we need, paradoxically, is lateral thinking.

1. The Descent and Ascent of the Son of Man

Where should we begin? No doubt with the very first occurrence of the title in the Gospel, John 1:51, which presents commentators with the knotty little puzzle of how to explain Jesus's use of the title in his allusion

4. Meeks, *Prophet-King*, 297. Meeks adds that except for an isolated statement in Philo "this pattern of descent/ascent of a heavenly messenger has no direct parallel in the Moses tradition." This conclusion has been strongly challenged by Jan-Adolf Bühner, who argues that much of the material actually quoted and commented on by Meeks, not just from Philo but also from rabbinical and Samaritan sources, proves that Moses' commission by God was thought of as the descent and subsequent ascent of a heavenly messenger: *Der Gesandte und sein Weg*, 306–13. Moreover, focusing as he does exclusively on the Moses tradition, Meeks takes no notice of the possible influence of traditions concerning other heavenly messengers. These are treated in some depth by Bühner (*Der Gesandte und sein Weg*, 322–41).

5. Colpe, "ὁ υἱὸς τοῦ ἀνθρώπου," 400–77.

6. Colpe, "ὁ υἱὸς τοῦ ἀνθρώπου," 415 (translation modified). In the printed English version *nicht weggelassen* is translated, unintelligibly and unintelligently, as "not refuted."

to Jacob's ladder.[7] He speaks of angels ascending and descending upon the
Son of Man—himself, of course; but the use of this term here, as well as in
its next occurrence, in 3:13 ("No one has ascended into heaven except the
one who descended from heaven, the Son of Man"), is obviously different
from the indirect self-reference found occasionally in the synoptic gospels, where it is at least arguable that Jesus himself employed an Aramaic
idiom that still lies under the surface of the clumsy Greek expression we
know so well. But who was the first to associate the title Son of Man with
the motif of descent and ascent? If we rule out the gnostics, what about
the evangelist himself? But then we need to ask what there was about the
title that could have induced him to make this association.

It was with some such question at the back of my mind that when
composing the chapter "Son of Man" for my book, *Understanding*, I
turned to an article by Charles H. Talbert in which he deliberately sets out
to refute the suggestion of Meeks and others that John drew upon gnostic
sources.[8] Talbert cites a huge number of texts from both pagan and Jewish writers to show just how widespread was the myth of a descending
redeemer in Mediterranean Antiquity. The most pertinent of these are
the apocalyptic and pseudepigraphical Jewish texts he discusses under
the heading "Archangels." He concludes that "in certain circles of Jewish
angelology . . . there existed a mythology with a descent-ascent pattern, in
which the redeemer figure descends, takes human form and then ascends
back to heaven after or in connection with a saving activity."[9]

After giving qualified approval to this article, I argued (following a
brilliant suggestion by Hugo Odeberg) that in the verse under discussion
(John 3:13) what the evangelist has in his sights is not the idea of a heavenly figure descending to earth but the idea of a human being—other

7. I have given a detailed comment upon this verse in *Understanding the Fourth
Gospel*, 1st edition, 342–48, and will say no more about it here.

8. "The Myth of a Descending-Ascending Redeemer in Mediterranean Antiquity,"
418–43. See *Understanding the Fourth Gospel*, 1st edition, 350–53, where this article
is summarized and assessed. Bühner (*Der Gesandte und sein Weg*, 335–41) adds some
important rabbinical material to the texts discussed by Talbert.

9. It may be worth including at this point the most striking of these: the visit of
the angel Raphael to Tobit and his son Tobias. About to take his leave, Raphael first
summarizes his healing mission, and then tells them to give thanks to God, "for I am
ascending to him who sent me" (ἀναβαίνω πρὸς τὸν ἀποστείλαντά με, Tob. 12:20).
"This text," comments Bühner, "gives the clearest indication of the possibility that Johannine christology may have taken over some elements of Jewish angelology" (*Der
Gesandte und sein Weg*, 337, translation mine).

than Jesus—ascending to heaven.[10] So for further enlightenment I turned to an article by Peder Borgen published in 1977, in which he maintained that the verse is to be explained against the background of a strong rabbinical tradition according to which Moses, after climbing Mount Sinai to receive the tablets of the law, actually went on as far as heaven itself.[11] According to Borgen, what John actually maintains in 3:13 is "that the historical Jesus represents the reverse phenomenon [to the idea of Moses' ascent into heaven] of descent from heaven and subsequent exaltation"; and he goes on to propose that the ascent of the Son of Man in 3:13 is what he calls "a pre-existent installing in office." This proposal is not borne out, however, by the passages he invokes in its support. There is no reason to think that when Jesus claims divine authority for all he says (3:34; 7:16; 8:43; 12:49; 14:24; 17:6) he is referring to a commission given to him prior to the incarnation. Jesus often declares that he was sent by God, but this need not imply an installation in office beforehand (Moses, the archetypal prophet, was sent from where he stood); and in any case the idea of a preexistent ascent is incoherent, for a preexistent being like the Logos is with God already (πρὸς τὸν θεόν, 1:1) and has neither need nor opportunity to climb any higher: Jacob's ladder reached as far as heaven but not beyond. Borgen's convoluted paraphrase of 3:13 ("only he who descended from heaven to execute his office, the divine being, the son of man, has ascended to heaven for the installing in office prior to his descent")[12] is unpersuasive.

Placing the articles of Talbert and Borgen side-by-side, I concluded that

> what we have in the Gospel is *a fusion of two mythological patterns*, one angelic, starting in heaven (stressed by Talbert), the other mystical, starting from earth (stressed by Borgen). How great a conceptual leap is involved in this fusion may be gauged from the fact that in at least one document, *The Testament of Abraham*, the two patterns lie virtually side-by-side, without the least suggestion that the archangel Michael, who illustrates the first pattern, could ever be confused with Abraham, who

10. Odeberg, *Fourth Gospel*.

11. Borgen, "Some Jewish Exegetical Traditions," 243–58.

12. Borgen, "Some Jewish Exegetical Traditions," 254. Biblical texts cited by Borgen ("Some Jewish Exegetical Traditions," 251–52) referring to the ascent of God (1 Sam 2:10; Pss 47 [46]:6; 68 [67]:19) are irrelevant in the context of a preexistent installing in office.

illustrates the second. The blinding realization that in Jesus angel and seer are one and the same marks one of the most significant advances in the whole history of Christian thought: its ramifications are endless. Although both elements are abundantly attested in the Jewish tradition, their fusion has consequences that Judaism could not contain. Taken separately neither pattern presented any threat: the blending of the two meant a new religion. The conviction that the heavenly being was human and the human being heavenly was the conceptual hub round which the huge wheel of Christian theology would revolve for centuries to come.[13]

Over twenty years on this still seems to me a clever idea (although I now see that I had misinterpreted Borgen, who thought that the starting-point was already in heaven). What is more, a wheel does not revolve *around* a hub, since the hub is at the centre of its revolution. In any case the blinding realization was mine, not the evangelist's. But although I no longer think that he arrived at his insights simply by setting two series of texts side-by-side, I am still convinced that these may help us to understand his Gospel.

John did of course believe that Jesus descended from heaven and then went back up again. That is no more than a summary of the career of the Logos, identified as Jesus Christ at the end of the prologue. (I will return to this topic later.) James Dunn objects to Talbert's use of Jewish angelology to explain the evangelist's portrayal of Jesus's life-giving mission on the grounds that the angels were all short-term visitors.[14] But from John's perspective so was the Logos. His was a theophanic appearance, displaying the glory of God.[15] Yet in the body of the Gospel when John combines the notions of descent and ascent it is in relation to the Son of Man, not the Logos.

This is what he does in 3:13, after the dialogue with Nicodemus. But, once again, why? Having extricated ourselves from the long and tortuous cul-de-sac of gnosticism, we still find ourselves in an impasse. For nowhere else apart from the Fourth Gospel is the figure of the Son of Man associated with the notions of ascent or descent, not in the synoptic

---

13. Ashton, *Understanding the Fourth Gospel*, 1st edition, 355.

14. Dunn, "Let John Be John," 309–39.

15. Admittedly Ben Sira uses the word κατασκηνοῦν (literally, "to tabernacle") of what he thought of as the enduring presence of wisdom/torah on earth. But the word is used more naturally (as in the *Prayer of Joseph*) of short stays, since the σκήνη, the Tent of Meeting, was designed (unlike the temple) for brief and occasional divine visits.

gospels, not in the Enochic corpus, and not in Daniel 7, which is where the tradition began. The reason for this is obvious. The one resembling a human being in Daniel's dream (literally, but only literally, "like a son of man") is actually a divine being, an angel (quite possibly the angel Michael, a suggestion supported by a few lines in the War Scroll, 1QM 17.7–8).[16] His home is in heaven, not on earth: he has no need to ascend into heaven and no reason to descend to earth. Unlike the angels in Zachariah, who tell the prophet's *angelus interpres*, standing among the myrtle trees, that they have been patrolling the earth (Zech 1:10–11), and the sons of God in the opening chapters of Job, who present themselves before God ready to do his bidding (Job 1:6; 2:1), the Son of Man is not sent on a mission. Although he is given "dominion and glory and kingship" (Dan 7:14) he has no need to come down to earth in order to exercise his authority any more than "the people of the holy ones of the Most High" who are given the same authority (7:27) have to go up to heaven in order to exercise theirs. In the Gospel there is no suggestion that the Son of Man was *sent*, like other angel-messengers, to carry out a particular commission.

The fact, then, that the Son of Man is so clearly located in heaven in this key text (as well as in the references to it in the synoptic gospels)[17] is a major source of difficulty for the interpretation of the Fourth Gospel, where Jesus passes down from heaven and back again. No doubt this is why so many of the early commentators were tempted to turn for an explanation to gnostic documents in which the Heavenly Man did in some fashion descend and then reascend. By the time that the Fourth Gospel was fully composed, Jesus, now known to the Gospel's readers as the Son of Man, spoke readily of his ascent and descent: "What if you were to see the Son of Man ascending where he was before?" (6:62).[18] A little earlier the Jews had enquired, "Is not this Jesus, the son of Joseph, whose father and mother we know? How does he now say, 'I have come down from heaven?'" (6:42; cf. 6:38). The combination of descent and ascent explains both why the recollection of the ascending and descending angels in

16. See Rowland, *Open Heaven*, 181–82, plus n47. Divine beings in apocalyptic visions are regularly represented as human, just as human beings are regularly represented as animals or beasts. The name Michael (who is like God?) is peculiarly appropriate to the role played by one like a man in Daniel 7.

17. And indeed in one variant of John 3:13, where some manuscripts add the words ὁ ὢν ἐν τῷ οὐρανῷ to qualify ὁ υἱὸς τοῦ ἀνθρώπου. Some commentators, including C. K. Barrett, Nils Dahl, and Jarl Fossum, hold this to be the correct reading.

18. I am here assuming that (as I argued in *Understanding the Fourth Gospel*, 2nd edition, 44–48) chapter 6 belongs to the second edition of the Gospel.

Jacob's dream prompted a reference to the Son of Man, and why when John came to use the manna tradition in his account of the feeding of the five thousand he could build upon it with the descent/ascent pattern now associated with the Son of Man (6:50–51, 62).[19] But the allusions in chapters 1 and 6 still require explanation. Why did the Fourth Evangelist think of Jesus as a *heavenly* figure?

Let us return to 3:13: "No one has ascended into heaven except the one who descended from heaven, the Son of Man." What is the context of this saying within the Gospel? Having first (v. 7) corrected Nicodemus's misunderstanding of the meaning of the word ἄνωθεν, Jesus turns in verse 11 to explain how he has the authority to speak of heavenly things: he is speaking of what he knows and of what he has seen, having ascended to heaven and then come down (to convey his knowledge to others). Armed, or rather blinkered, by our knowledge of the rest of the Gospel, we can easily miss this, the natural reading of verses 11–13. Rudolf Bultmann, who recognizes the obvious implication of these verses, nonetheless objects that verse 13

> cannot bear the meaning which is normally attributed to it, that "no one has ever ascended into heaven, in order, that is, to bring back knowledge of the ἐπουράνια, except the one who descended from heaven." For Jesus did not first ascend into heaven to bring such knowledge back to earth again. Rather he first came down from heaven with the message entrusted to him by the Father and then he ascended into heaven. The evangelist cannot have thought of his ascent as a means for him to gain knowledge of the ἐπουράνια.[20]

Like the vast majority of commentators, Bultmann uses his knowledge of the general thrust of the Gospel and of the prologue in particular as a conclusive argument for rejecting the straightforward interpretation of these three verses. (His own solution to the problem is that the evangelist found them in his revelation discourse source.)

An alternative solution, which we have just glanced at, is Peder Borgen's ingenious suggestion of a *pre-ascension* that took place before the incarnation. Yet another is Christopher Rowland's observation that 3:14 acts as a commentary on the previous, enigmatic, verse and relates it to

---

19. See Bühner, *Der Gesandte und sein Weg*, 406n1.

20. Bultmann, *Gospel of John*, 150–51.

the cross: "12:33 shows that 'ascent' means being lifted up on a cross."[21] But in 12:33, as in the other references to the crucifixion in this Gospel, the verb used is not "ascend" but "exalt." Moreover Rowland is ignoring the fact that the ascent spoken of in 3:13 has already taken place. Why would an event said to have already happened in the first half of a verse be then *predicted* to take place in the second half? The later parallels (8:28; 12:23) do indeed show that the prediction of exaltation in 3:14 refers to Jesus's being raised on the cross; so the reversal of tenses is intolerably harsh: ascension in the past, crucifixion in the future. The same objection can be made against Jörg Frey's revival of the suggestion of Loisy and Bauer that the words "no one has ascended except" are spoken from the standpoint of the Christian community.[22] The extra nuance of Frey's theory of *Horizontverschmelzung* in no way eases the problem of the temporal dislocation. There are plenty of instances elsewhere in the Gospel that display two levels of understanding, the first the story level, the second the level of the Gospel's Christian readers. But here, if Frey is to be believed, the story-level meaning is missing altogether, *which never happens elsewhere in the Gospel*. I am equally unconvinced by Benjamin Reynolds's suggestion of a gnomic perfect ("No one ascends except the Son of Man, the one who descended").[23] We must accept that John meant what Jesus said: "No one *has* ascended except" and somehow account for the anomaly.

It is hard to overemphasize the magnitude of this problem.[24] The device of two levels of understanding, whereby Jesus's hearers are able to put one interpretation on his words, and John's readers a very different one, works on the whole very well. Here it does not work at all, for the verb is in the past, and in the time-frame of the Gospel there was no opportunity in Jesus's career for a heavenly ascent prior to Nicodemus's visit. But how could poor dim Nicodemus, who has hitherto shown little aptitude for abstruse theological discussion, possibly be expected to understand

---

21. Rowland and Morray-Jones, *Mystery of God*, 128.

22. Frey, *Die johanneische Eschatologie*, 252–55. See Bultmann, *Gospel of John*, 150n2.

23. Reynolds, *Apocalyptic Son of Man*, 115. There is no other example of the gnomic perfect in the Gospel, and none of the four NT texts cited by Reynolds (cf. Blass and Debrunner, *Greek Grammar*, §344) allows a historical expectation to the gnomic generalization. See Schnackenburg, *Gospel According to St. John*, 1:393.

24. Somewhat surprisingly Meeks makes no mention of it in his "Man from Heaven" article.

the past perfect ἀνεβέβηκεν to refer to an event in the future? Yes, all John's readers know that such an ascent did indeed take place. But the suggestion of Bultmann and others that the statement in 3:13 alludes to Jesus's final ascension into heaven seems to require an impossibly violent disruption of the storyline.

What I believe to be the right answer to the problem was sketched out before I was born by Hugo Odeberg. The evangelist is taking over a tradition that Jesus had indeed ascended into heaven during his lifetime, and the affirmation concerning such an ascent was made in the teeth of rival claims of other Jewish groups on behalf of a variety of prophets and patriarchs.[25] The meaning of the saying is the one Bultmann rejected as impossible: "no one has ever ascended into heaven, in order, that is, to bring back knowledge of the ἐπουράνια, except the one who descended from heaven." Rightly, I think, Bultmann saw a sequential connection between verse 13 (ascent into heaven) and verse 12 (speaking of earthly and heavenly things).[26] But having offered this suggestion, Odeberg fails to follow it up. How could such a tradition have arisen, and how can it be placed within the development of the christology of the Fourth Gospel?

A particularly ingenious answer to this problem is to be found in the generally excellent study of Jan-Adolf Bühner, *Der Gesandte und sein Weg*, that I have already mentioned. Bühner thinks that this logion is drawn from an early layer of the Johannine tradition according to which Jesus went up to heaven as a visionary seer so as to receive secrets to bring down to earth. Whilst in heaven he was transformed into a heavenly being (the Son of Man) and then descended to earth again *as* the Son of Man.[27] So for Bühner the ascent, in this early tradition, was the ascent of the human Jesus into heaven and the descent was the descent of the now

25. Odeberg, *Fourth Gospel*, 72. Cf. Bultmann, *Gospel of John*, 150n1; and Meeks, *Prophet-King*, 301n1, who praises Odeberg's "unusual perception." In *Understanding the Fourth Gospel*, 1st edition, 350, I wrongly stated that Odeberg does not mention Moses. He does so in *Fourth Gospel*, 97, along with Enoch, Abraham, Elijah, and Isaiah. J. Louis Martyn argues that Elijah was among the evangelist's targets (Martyn, *Gospel of John in Christian History*, 20–21). Also, I think, Enoch.

26. Schnackenburg, reorganizing this chapter, effectively severs this link. But there is no good reason for any such reorganization.

27. Bühner cites numerous examples from the apocrypha and rabbinical writings, as well as the Dead Sea Scrolls, of a human seer being transformed into an angel as a crucial part of an argument concerning the fusion of the concepts of prophet and מלאך (Bühner, *Der Gesandte und sein Weg*, 341–75). He is clear about the relevance of this argument to the association of the descent/ascent motif with the Johannine Son of Man.

heavenly Jesus down to earth. He also thinks that according to the same tradition the experience of this heavenly journey was what entitled Jesus to affirm, as he does repeatedly in the course of the Gospel, that he had "seen the Father."[28]

This is a bold and attractive reading, which breaks new ground. This may be why, so far as I can ascertain, it has been completely ignored by other scholars, including myself. For it is hard to divest oneself of the notion that the ascent into heaven mentioned in this verse must, somehow or other, be a final end-of-life ascent, and equally hard to think of the descent as anything other than the coming down to earth of the Logos.

For a long time one difficulty standing in the way of Bühner's proposal seemed to me insuperable. On the face of it the passage states very clearly that it was the Son of Man who ascended into heaven, having previously descended to earth. If that were right there could be no question of Jesus's transformation into an angelic being *after* his ascension. For the Son of Man is already an angelic being in his own right. But although this seems the obvious and most straightforward reading it does not work. For having once come down to earth, the Son of Man has no need to reascend into heaven in order to obtain secret knowledge unavailable to earthbound mortals. I have somewhat reluctantly come to accept that Bühner must be right: "No one has ascended into heaven except the one who descended *as* the Son of Man." What I previously thought was a targum-like interpretation not justified by the text now seems to me the reading that presents the least difficulties.

Let us take another look at the problem. If Odeberg was right about John 3:13 then the opening words ("No one has ascended") allude not to an end-of-life ascent but to the ascent of an apocalyptic seer for the purpose of receiving special revelations. But the verse as it stands appears to imply that the seer's descent preceded his ascent, which makes no sense. Bühner has a particularly ingenious solution to this problem, one for which he draws upon his extensive knowledge of the abundant rabbinical material concerning the figure of Moses. This is how he concludes a long section headed "Der Prophet als שליח Gottes":

> The single most important result [of our enquiry] has been to establish that under the influence of [reflection upon] the שליח

---

28. Bühner, *Der Gesandte und sein Weg*, 374–99. This is how Bühner sums up his reading: "Jesus ist in einer Art Berufungsvision anabatisch in den Himmel gelangt, dort zum Menschensohn gewandelt und als solcher in seine irdische Existenz hinabgestiegen" (398).

(emissary) the prophetic element in the Moses tradition has changed into the project of a journey that starts with a commission high up on the mountain and ends with the emissary's final report to God in heaven. This results in a pattern of descent and sub-sequent ascent.[29]

Earlier Bühner had suggested that the actual order of the two verbs, "ascend" and "descend," in John 3:13 may point to an earlier form of the saying in which the ascent did indeed precede the descent: "The possibility of such a reversal from the point of view of religious history is supported by the rabbinical tradition that ties Moses' commission on Sinai together with his descent and subsequent ascent to God."[30]

In the course of his argument in support of this contention, Bühner made use of Meeks's study (in *The Prophet-King*) of how the biblical tradition of Moses' double ascent was developed. Very often it is simply taken for granted that after climbing Sinai Moses proceeded to ascend as far as heaven itself, as for instance in a midrash on Psalm 106:2 quoted by Meeks: "Not even Moses who went up to heaven to receive the Torah from God's hand into his own could fathom heaven's depth."[31] What is more, in the abundant material concerning Moses in both the Jewish and the Samaritan tradition we find that very often Moses' final ascent of Mount Nebo to receive a last revelation before his death is blended into his ascent of Sinai, where he received the tables of the Law. One example discussed by Meeks is a passage from the Midrash Tannaim that sets a verse from Exodus (34:28) referring to Sinai side-by-side with a verse from the end of Deuteronomy (34:5) referring to Nebo, in which the one and only point of resemblance is that both verses say that Moses was *there* (שם). Meeks finds this connection "very strained," and concludes that Moses' final ascension must have already been connected with his ascent of Sinai. The bringing-together of two texts on the basis of the coincidence of a single word is a fairly common rabbinical ploy; but there are other examples too of a close association between the two ascents. In a particularly striking instance from the Samaritan *Memar Marqah*, Moses, addressing the people, tells them that "Three times my Lord said to me, '*Go up to it*,' and I went up with the mind of prophethood on the first two occasions. I delivered the first and second tablets and on

29. Bühner, *Der Gesandte und sein Weg*, 271–315.

30. Bühner, *Der Gesandte und sein Weg*, 307.

31. Bühner, *Der Gesandte und sein Weg*, 205.

this (third) occasion I receive the portion that He presented me through Adam. Twice I ascended and descended as God commanded me; on this occasion I go up and will not come down."[32] There is no direct reminder here that the mountain climbed on the third ascent (when "the portion through Adam" must have been Moses' death) was different from the first two; but it was. For Philo, who has a very different approach to the biblical texts, each ascent is a visionary experience, indeed a mystical translation in which Moses, as Meeks puts it, "leaves the mortal, bodily realm to enter the 'incorporeal and intelligible.'"[33]

Bühner, who brings these three sources together, points out that from different perspectives they all link Moses' ascent of Mount Sinai to his final ascent and death.[34] Two of the three are late, and the third, Philo, is hardly likely to have influenced the Fourth Evangelist. But there is a much earlier instance of the same phenomenon in the *Exagoge* of the playwright Ezekiel, where Moses tells Reuel, his father-in-law (Ραγουηλ in the play), that he "had a vision of a great throne on the top of Mount Sinai," where upon his reception of a royal crown he beheld "the whole earth all around, and beneath and above the heavens," a vision that Reuel interprets to mean that he will see "what is now, what has been, and what shall be" (68–69) thus extending and expanding not, evidently, the revelation on Sinai but the final revelation on Mount Nebo.[35] Like the later writers Ezekiel collapses the two revelations and the two ascents together.

Of course it is impossible to be sure that the Fourth Evangelist was influenced, consciously or not, by any of these different strands of tradition. But he may well have been, and if he was then he will have been much less bothered than his later readers are likely to be by the ambiguity of "No one has ascended." He would wish to insist upon the exclusive claim of his own hero, and deny outright that any other Jewish seer, above all Moses, but also Enoch and Elijah, had either mounted up to heaven as an apocalyptic visionary or had been translated there at the end of his life. The core of the difficulty presented by John 3:13 is the essential and

32. MacDonald, *Memar Marqah*, 2:198 (quoted by Meeks, *Prophet-King*, 245).

33. *Mos.* 2.288; *Virt.* 53.76; QG 1.86. See Meeks, *Prophet-King*, 124.

34. Bühner, *Der Gesandte und sein Weg*, 311–13.

35. What is more, Reuel's interpretation is remarkably anticipatory of the warning in m. Ḥag. 2.1 against indulging in dangerous speculation on things beyond one's competence, namely "what is above, what is beneath, what was before time and what will be hereafter"—the passage that provided Christopher Rowland with the main topics of his trailblazing *Open Heaven*. Cf. Meeks, *Prophet-King*, 208.

ineradicable ambiguity of the tradition of Moses' ascent. But it may be that this ambiguity, besides giving rise to our perplexity, can also help to dispel it.

Yet there remains a serious problem in Bühner's reading. For him, as we have seen, the tradition represented by 3:13 belongs to the very earliest stage (or level, *Schicht*) of Johannine christology. But this fails to account for the challenge to the primacy of Moses implied by the saying. During its early days, indeed during its early years, the Jesus group, co-existing in the synagogue alongside more conservative members, would have had no reason to reject any Jewish traditions that had developed about Moses, certainly not in the aggressive tone that marks the blunt exclusiveness of John 3:13. Yet if the claim that Jesus and no one else (not Moses, not Elijah, nor any other Jewish seer) had ascended into heaven to receive heavenly secrets was indeed advanced by the Jesus group in the synagogue, it must have been made at a time in the history of the community when what Ernst Käsemann calls "die göttliche Herrlichkeit des über die Erde schreitenden Christus"[36] had not yet trampled over most of the remaining traces of the human Jesus of the early tradition, to leave at this particular point only the vestigial footprint we have just been contemplating. In particular it must have been made before the evangelist and his community had become convinced that Jesus's sojourn on earth followed a long period in heaven alongside God—at a time when the Jesus group in the synagogue had not yet come to think of him as divine, but saw him simply as the Messiah and a great prophet, a remarkable, but still recognizably human, human being: before, that is to say, the prologue was added to form a new introduction to the Gospel. The challenge to Moses' privileged position must have come at a time in the history of the Jesus group when it had begun to argue with the disciples of Moses in the synagogue, but before it had confronted them with an assertion of Jesus's equality with God.

In attempting to wriggle out of this tangled skein let us start by putting the prologue on one side so as to reflect on the simplest form of what Odeberg and, following him, Bühner, thought to be the tradition lying under the surface of John 3:13: that Jesus whilst on earth had had some form of apocalyptic vision, that he was, in other words, a visionary seer. As I have said, this in itself is a very bold suggestion.

---

36. Käsemann, *Jesu Letzer Wille nach Johannes 17*, 26.

But it is arguable that Bühner does not go far enough. According to his hypothesis the Johannine community had inherited a tradition that Jesus's transformation into the angelic being called the Son of Man took place during his ascent into heaven as a visionary seer; but he does not even consider the possibility that there might be an authentic memory lying behind this tradition.

One point in all three synoptic gospels seems to offer the perfect occasion for this hypothetical journey to heaven, namely the transfiguration. The Fourth Gospel as we have it has no room for a transfiguration story. Jesus had "manifested his glory" as early as the marriage-feast at Cana (2:11), and this glory did not leave him. But the united testimony of the synoptic gospels is strong evidence for an episode in Jesus's life when he might have been the recipient of heavenly secrets. Surprisingly, no one has ever made this suggestion, not even Bühner.

The transfiguration story has often been dismissed as purely legendary. The early form critics regarded it as a kind of anticipatory resurrection appearance, displaced from its original position: "that Jesus should have been seen in a vision (*das visionäre Schauen Jesu*)," says Bultmann, "whilst still corporally present, is scarcely credible (*eine kaum glaubliche Sache*)."[37] Although the three synoptic accounts speak of the transfiguration (or, more precisely, transformation, *metamorphosis*) of Jesus rather than of a heavenly ascent, it is likely that just as some Jewish writers interpreted Moses' ascent of Sinai as an ascent into heaven, the same move was made in some Christian circles of Jesus's choice of a high mountain to display his glory. The gospel story of the transfiguration was fundamentally, as Bruce Chilton has argued, "a visionary representation of the Sinai motif of Exodus 24,"[38] and so it is quite natural to suppose that the Jewish concept of the divinization of Moses was at some point transferred to Jesus. Indeed Jarl Fossum has suggested that this is how we should understand the event that underlies Mark's version of the story: "Jesus is not only transformed, but is also installed into office as God's prophet-king with the implicit charge of proclaiming God's will. The Moses pattern

---

37. Bultmann, *Die Geschichte der synoptischen Tradition*, 278n1. One of the earliest scholars to challenge this view, Morton Smith, reinforces his argument with the sour reflection that "to suggest that the blessed Evangelists, not to mention early Christians in general, wanted to tell what they believed to be the truth, is to strike at the very root of Formgeschichte": Smith, "Origin and History of the Transfiguration Story," 43.

38. Chilton, "Transfiguration," 122 (author's italics).

continues to hold good."[39] If so, then the Fourth Evangelist will have known of this tradition, and although he could not reproduce it he could at least allude to it: I think he did so here, in 3:13.[40]

Had it occurred to Bühner that there might be an authentic memory lying behind the tradition of heavenly transformation he had discerned, then no doubt he would have found additional support in Jesus's words to his disciples as they were coming down from the mountain, when "he charged them to tell no one what they had seen until the Son of Man should have risen from the dead" (Mark 9:9). If indeed Jesus did descend from the mountain aware of the transformation that had taken place, it would be necessary to revise the widespread opinion that his self-identification with the Son of Man was simply proleptic. From that moment on any of the prophecies made of the Son of Man in Mark's Gospel, not just the explicit reference to Daniel's vision in the eschatological discourse, might actually have been uttered by Jesus!

If I am right in my supposition that the evangelist adopted this ancient tradition at a relatively late stage in the history of the Jesus group within the synagogue, there is still room to ask how it was that the descent/ascent motif associated with the Son of Man became so important for him. Another place in the Gospel is relevant in this connection: the story of the healing of the man born blind in chapter 9. John had inherited from his source, whatever name we give to this, a memory of a miracle-working Jesus. In the course of time the Jesus group in the synagogue was confronted by a denial on the part of the Pharisees that Jesus had performed his healing miracles with divine authority. This was the point at issue in the controversy over the man born blind. The Pharisees insisted that a man who broke the Sabbath could not be from God. Whereupon others demanded, "How can a man who is a sinner do such things?" (9:16). The man himself, asked what he thought, replied simply, "He is a prophet" (9:17)—in other words, his authority is from God. Asked a second time, he replied angrily, "I have told you already. Why do you want to hear it again? Do you want to become his disciples?" (9:27), a reply that infuriated his questioners, who responded by emphasizing the ineradicable hostility between the two opposing camps: "You are his disciple, but

39. Fossum, "Ascensio, Metamorphosis," 76.

40. There are other passages too where the evangelist alludes to traditions that for one reason or another he does not include in his own story, e.g., Jesus's baptism in 1:32–33 and the Gethsemane episode in 12:27–30. (I owe this observation to Judith Kovacs.)

we are disciples of Moses" (9:28). They were clinging to the old assurance that God's definitive revelation had been given to Moses; but the man they were interrogating fought back immediately with the unassailable argument, "If this man were not from God, he could do nothing" (9:33), a remark that so angered his adversaries that they immediately expelled him from the synagogue. The otherwise imperceptive Nicodemus, it may be noted, had a similar insight to that of the man born blind: "no one can do these signs that you do unless God is with him" (3:2).

The debate here evidently originated in a challenge to Jesus's authority to perform acts of healing, but the lesson eventually drawn by the evangelist, very much later,[41] focused upon Jesus's self-identification, in response to a question of the man he had just healed, as the *Son of Man* (9:35); and this in turn led to the assertion: "For judgment I came into this world," a declaration reinforced by an explicit recollection of the miracle: "that those who do not see may see, and that those who see may become blind" (9:39). Here is a claim far exceeding the authority to perform healing miracles: the claim that precisely *as Son of Man* Jesus was entitled to exercise *on earth* the authority to judge that in Daniel's vision had been bestowed upon the Son of Man *in heaven*. This means that *the evangelist himself had concluded that the heavenly figure of the Son of Man had come down to earth in the person of Jesus.* The descent of a divine redeemer figure attributed by Bultmann to a gnostic myth was something John had seen for himself. And he did so in consequence of a row with those who called themselves the disciples of Moses.

After his extraordinary encounter with Jesus the man born blind did not return to his adversaries in order to confront them with his newfound faith, or at any rate the evangelist does not tell us that he did. Had he done so he would no doubt have been greeted with a fresh outburst of indignation, something like the high priest's response to Jesus's prediction in Mark's version of his trial (14:62–64) that the Son of Man would come with power on the clouds of heaven. In John's much briefer account of the trial (before Annas, not Caiaphas) there is no such prediction; and it is noticeable that in his Gospel Jesus's strongest statements linking ascent and descent with the Son of Man (1:51; 3:13) are made to friends and sympathizers. Moreover the *question*, "What if you were to see the

---

41. In *Understanding the Fourth Gospel*, 1st edition, 179–81, I argued that the central section of the chapter, 9:18–23, was added on subsequently to the original story, and suggested that the same is true of the conclusion, 9:35–41. I am now no less confident of the first suggestion and rather more confident of the second.

Son of Man ascending where he was before?" (6:62), is addressed to his disciples.[42]

The lesson concerning Jesus's authority to judge is also drawn, if anything even more clearly than in chapter 9, from the other great healing miracle, in chapter 5, where a number of strands of the tradition and a number of christological titles have been woven together. Here too the initial protest is against an infringement of the Sabbath rest; here too the initial claim involves a participation in the life-giving activity of God; here too the debate soon comes to focus on the additional claim of authority to judge; here too that claim is associated with the authority conferred upon the Son of Man in Daniel's vision; here too the debate is between the disciples of Moses (portrayed in this story as searching the Scriptures for an assurance of eternal life) and Jesus (now making the counter-claim that Moses was really writing of him). But in this scene the association with Daniel's vision is strengthened by the omission of the definite article from the title (reproducing more faithfully than elsewhere the old Greek version of Daniel 7:14), when Jesus, as in the conclusion of chapter 9, is left to summarize the significance of his act of healing: "For as the Father has life in himself so he has granted the Son also to have life in himself, *and has given him authority to execute judgment, because he is [the] Son of Man*" (5:26–27).

"Manifestly," says Bultmann, in one of his rare comments on the historical setting of the Gospel, "the two stories in chs. 5 and 9 must be understood against the same historical background. Both reflect the relation of early Christianity to the surrounding hostile (in the first place Jewish) world."[43] But the history was a long one, and the task of placing the two stories more precisely within it is not easy. Clearly, as it stands now chapter 9 points to a definitive breakup of the two parties within the synagogue; but I have argued that before that happened there was an angry dispute over Jesus's authority to perform miracles, followed by a

---

42. In his *History and Theology in the Fourth Gospel*, 130–31, J. Louis Martyn has a brilliant insight into the evangelist's use of the two-level drama of apocalyptic. Yet the preceding argument ("From the Expectation of the Prophet-Messiah like Moses . . . To the Presence of the Son of Man") overlooks the claims to equality of God that trigger off the murderous fury of "the Jews" in chs. 5, 8 and 10, and depends on two false assumptions: first that "the titles Son of Man and Son of God have become interchangeable for John" (128 n. 193); and secondly that there is in the Gospel "an emphasis on confessing Jesus as Son of Man" (129 n. 195). Not only is there no emphasis upon confessing Jesus as Son of Man; there is no confession at all.

43. *The Gospel of John*, 239.

dawning realization that his healing deed was also a judgment, showing that he had acted with the powers bestowed by God upon the Son of Man. I concluded that in all likelihood this was the first full awareness on the part of the Johannine community that Jesus was something more than an exceptional human being: that he was in fact a heavenly or angelic being who had descended to earth invested with divine authority.[44] Chapter 5 represents a further stage in the same history: the synagogue authorities ("the Jews") saw that what was being now claimed for Jesus was equality with God, and "this was why they sought all the more to kill him" (5:18).

After reminding ourselves that the *Sitz-im-Leben* of both of these key episodes is *controversy*—specifically controversy between the disciples of Moses on the one hand and either Jesus (chapter 5) or his disciples (chapter 9) on the other—we are perhaps in a better position to understand Jesus's vehement assertion that "no one has ascended into heaven except the one who descended from heaven, the Son of Man" (3:13). For although he places this assertion very early in his Gospel, the evangelist is taking for granted the conviction he shares with his readers that the angelic figure of Daniel's dream had descended to earth invested with an authority already conferred upon him in heaven.

So what I am suggesting is that the evangelist, enabled by his new understanding of Jesus as the Son of Man, now saw that for the old Jewish tradition—that Moses had gone on from Sinai as far as heaven to receive God's definitive revelation to his people, and that at the end of his life he also ascended into heaven—must be substituted an identical claim made on behalf of Jesus. That he should have made these claims of Jesus *as Son of Man* is of course paradoxical in the extreme, but there is plenty of evidence within the Gospel to prove that Jewish beliefs concerning Moses' central place in God's grand design were appropriated for their own purposes by the Jesus group within the synagogue.

At this point we must return to consider the prologue, which some readers might think of as, in current parlance, the elephant in the room. Those scholars who assume with Bultmann that because the prologue comes first the evangelist must have written it first, and consequently that

44. It should be added that the evangelist may have found an additional impetus in one or both of two types of Son of Man sayings in the other three gospels: first those in which the title Son of Man refers to Jesus's activities on earth (although these have no connection whatever with Daniel's dream); and secondly those that refer to the coming of the Son of Man in judgment, such as Mark 13:26 and 14:62 (although in these verses, like the passage in Daniel that they recall, the Son of Man is thought of as in heaven).

the rest of the Gospel must be read in its dazzling light, have what they must think of as a devastating rejoinder to my whole argument, clearly expressed by Bultmann in words I have already quoted: "Jesus . . . first came down from heaven with the message entrusted to him by the Father and then he ascended into heaven." This is probably the majority view nowadays, largely because of the extraordinary impact that narrative criticism has had upon Johannine scholarship;[45] but the suggestion that the prologue was composed quite late on in the history of the Johannine community is still a perfectly respectable opinion, and requires no further defense from me here. We may reasonably share the conviction of Klaus Berger and Jan-Adolf Bühner that the Johannine circle had come to believe in Jesus's preexistence *before* the prologue was grafted onto the Gospel to form a particularly strong introduction.

"For the law was given through Moses; grace and truth came through Jesus Christ" (John 1:17). What does not have to be determined here is whether the writer is looking at the Law positively (as, for instance, Raymond Brown contends), contrasting the enduring love shown in the Law with the supreme example of enduring love in Christ,[46] or negatively, suggesting that there was no truth and no love to be found in the Law. If the former reading is correct, the prologue will have been composed before the tension between the contending groups of disciples within the synagogue had reached breaking-point; if one prefers the latter interpretation, as I do myself, then the prologue must be seen as representing the view that the evangelist and his community eventually arrived at, according to which the revelation of Jesus completely superceded the Mosaic Law. If, as is conceivable, the evangelist was taking over the work of someone with a more positive view of the Law than his own he will no doubt even so have interpreted it negatively.

2. The Exaltation of the Son of Man

The next verse, John 3:14, is just as problematic as 3:13, though differently so. Here the word requiring explanation is not ascend, but exalt; and this verse focuses not on the ascent of Jesus into heaven but on his having

---

45. Bultmann, *Gospel of John*, 151. Besides Bultmann many major Johannine scholars, for a variety of reasons, adopt the same approach: Dodd, Barrett, Borgen, Culpepper, Moloney, Keener, Lincoln, and Frey.

46. Brown, *Gospel According to John*, 16.

being raised up on the cross: "And as Moses lifted up the serpent in the wilderness, so must the Son of Man be lifted up" (3:14). Although there is no mention here of cross or crucifixion, this is the first of what, somewhat inaccurately, we call John's passion predictions, all three of which, as in the synoptic gospels from which they are derived, are predicated of the Son of Man. For the quite ordinary verb ἱστάναι used in the Septuagint to tell the story of Moses and the bronze snake (Num 21:9) John has substituted a word meaning "exalt." This extraordinary conceit, also figuring in the other two predictions, is surely his own invention.[47] Those who attribute it rather to "tradition" are simply pushing the problem out of sight and evading the responsibility of considering how such a tradition might have arisen in the first place. (Many commentators believe that John is adopting and adapting the expression "exalted and greatly glorified" he found in LXX Isaiah 52:13. They may well be right, but authors borrow for a reason and the reason is never to be found in the text that is borrowed.)

Our familiarity with this well-known trope can blind us to the extraordinary transmutation of a barbaric punishment into a vision of exaltation. *Someone* must have been the first to have had this visionary gleam, and why should not that someone have been the evangelist himself? Meeks speaks of this saying as an "ironic pun" and a "jarring bit of gallows-humor,"[48] but it is surely more than that. We should ask ourselves then how John *imagined* the crucifixion. If he had ever actually witnessed a man dying in agony on the cross, one might suppose that a memory of this appalling torture would lead him to picture a scene something like, to take a well-known example, the terrifying portrayal of the crucifixion by Mathias Grünewald. If he had done so this tormented figure would surely have blocked out altogether any awareness of a man raised up, exalted, ascending up to heaven.[49] The deliberate choice of a word meaning "exalt" (reinforced by an avoidance of the words cross and crucifixion, suffering, death and dying) is surely something other than a clever verbal

47. Contra Borgen, who asserts that it is an independent traditional expression, since it occurs in different contexts in 8:34 and 12:23 (Borgen, "Exegetical Traditions," 247 and again, 252). But these contexts are not different: they too are predictions of the crucifixion.

48. Meeks, "Man from Heaven," 181 and 185.

49. Such in fact is the scene portrayed on the reverse side of the Isenheim altarpiece, a glorious Christ rising upwards out of the tomb: with modern technology the transformation might be conveyed by fading one side of Grunewald's painting into the other.

device. The third passion prediction exhibits an even more remarkable modulation, when Jesus declares that "the hour has come for the Son of Man to be *glorified*" (12:23). Although the predictions in all four Gospels refer to the same event, the contrast between John and, say, Mark, is striking. Where Mark's Jesus, in the first prediction (8:31), speaks of suffering and death, John's Jesus (3:14) speaks of lifting up or exaltation; and where in the third prediction Mark's Jesus (10:34) says that he is about to be mocked, spat upon, and scourged, John's Jesus talks of glorification! The crowd's response to this prediction is "How can you say that the Son of Man must be lifted up?" (12:34), interpreting what Jesus has just said about glorification as a reference to the exaltation (on the cross) of the Son of Man. Lifting up or exaltation on the one hand and glorification on the other are alternative ways of speaking of the same event.

Accordingly the evangelist is inviting his readers to *see past* their own memory or knowledge of Jesus's agonizing death to his triumph over the forces of evil: "Now is the judgment of this world, now shall the ruler of this world be cast out" (12:31), words spoken in the context of the third and last passion prediction.[50] This invitation can best be accounted for if we suppose that John himself had a vision overwhelming enough to eliminate the painful and humiliating aspects of Jesus's passion and to replace them with signs of exaltation and glory. Here if anywhere we may see some justification for C. H. Dodd's assertion that "the thought of this gospel is so original and creative that a search for its 'sources,' or even for the 'influences' by which it may have been affected, may easily lead us astray."[51] Yet this is no reason for thinking that the solution is to be found simply in what, in the same context, Dodd calls the evangelist's "powerful and independent mind." I no longer believe that John arrived at his insight from an especially brilliant collocation of two series of Jewish texts, one concerning the descent of angels to earth on a redemptive mission, the other concerning the ascent to heaven of apocalyptic visionaries. Religion has more to do with imagination than with logic. The explanation must lie rather in some sort of mystical experience that allowed the evangelist to see the hoisting-up of Jesus onto the cross as an exaltation.

Yet exaltation and glorification do not stop at the cross. In the preface to the farewell discourse, the last occurrence of the title in the Gospel, Jesus states: "Now is the Son of Man glorified, and in him God

50. Here is another indication of the association of the figure of the Son of Man with the theme of judgment. Cf. Kovacs, "Now Shall the Ruler of This World," 227–47.

51. Dodd, *Interpretation of the Fourth Gospel*, 6.

is glorified" (13:31). In the last of the three predictions, in the preceding chapter, it was clear from the context that the immediate reference of glorification, however surprisingly, was to the exaltation on the cross. But Jesus's announcement of his imminent glorification (εὐθύς, 13:32) in the supper room, as he is about to take leave of the disciples, must include some allusion to the resurrection—and possibly also to the ascension, which supplied the verb used by the risen Jesus to Mary Magdalene of his proximate and permanent departure (20:17).

But why, it may be asked (and here I would like to return briefly to the affirmation of the ascent of the Son of Man), was a belligerent challenge to the disciples of Moses placed in the immediate context of a response to a sympathetic enquirer, towards the beginning of the Gospel? It is not enough to say that in its finished state the Gospel provides no obvious slot for any reference to a visionary ascent during Jesus's lifetime, and that consequently it would look awkward wherever it was placed. The prologue, looming over the remainder of the Gospel with its portentous presentation of an incarnate divine being, ensures his uncontestable and uncontested dominance over all that follows. But quite apart from the prologue, which like many other scholars I assign to a second edition, the evangelist's decision to allow Jesus to manifest his glory as early as his first public appearance in the Gospel, at Cana (2:11)—equivalent to what the prologue itself says about the contemplation of the glory of the incarnate Logos—leaves no room anywhere else for an explicit statement concerning a reascent into heaven, so that even a hidden allusion looks intolerably obtrusive, presenting the same sort of disruption of the storyline that I have objected to in the standard explanation of John 3:13 as a reference to Jesus's ascension at the end of his life.

By another authorial decision, however, the evangelist had already placed the visit of Nicodemus, centered upon Jesus's instruction on the true meaning of the word ἄνωθεν, very early in his work. Here then was the obvious place to offer an explanation of all that this word implies, that is to say the true source of his authority to speak of heavenly things, which depended upon an actual ascent into heaven beforehand. The heavenly things are summarized in the next few verses: having descended from heaven, the Son of Man must now be exalted, and this exaltation (only later revealed to be the crucifixion) will fulfill what is now said to be a mission: that is to say the mission of the Son of *God*, God's loving gift to the world, which will be a source of life to all who believe in him. Nowhere else in the Gospel is there such a comprehensive summary of what the evangelist saw as God's salvific will. Of course it is hard to comprehend what he is saying here—that Jesus received a new revelation, so much more than a new Law, in the course of a visit to heaven as an apocalyptic seer—the original meaning, I think, of this lapidary text. Yet some may find it easier to believe than the prologue's mythical account of a divine being taking flesh.

3. Conclusion

The majority of commentators assume that the descent/ascent pattern associated with the title Son of Man in the Fourth Gospel was ready-made, an assumption that depends on a mostly unformulated belief that it was somehow borrowed from Gnosticism. Wayne Meeks is bolder. Towards the end of his famous article he comments that the legitimation of the Johannine sect's cultural distancing of itself from the world around it "would lead to the projection of some myth explaining that members of the group had an origin different from that of ordinary men. In Gnosticism it was the Sophia myth which provided the basic images for that projection—that same Sophia myth which provided important elements of the descent and ascent of the Son of Man in John."[52] But although this myth almost certainly lies behind the incarnation of the Logos, I have argued that the pattern of the ascending and descending Son of Man had nothing to do with any gnostic myth. Rather it must be seen as arising from the confluence of two originally distinct developments, first the tradition of Jesus as a visionary seer, and secondly the outcome of a long debate with "the disciples of Moses" that originated within the synagogue. The claim that the authority exercised by Jesus in healing and judging was truly divine, that he was not of this earth but had come down from heaven as the Son of Man was perceived as threatening and insulting by the parent community, and was no doubt one of the beliefs of the Jesus group that eventually led to a bitter and enduring break-up. Among the counterclaims of the Moses faction there were assertions that when the Law was revealed to him at Sinai, this was truly a heavenly ascent.[53]

52. Meeks, "Man from Heaven," 71–72.

53. "It is almost a commonplace in rabbinic traditions," remarks Meeks, "that when Moses 'went up to God' on Mt. Sinai, he ascended 'on high,' that is, to heaven" (Meeks, *Prophet-King*, 205). But in many other places too, where Moses is credited with having received special revelations over and above the law, it is assumed that this must have happened in heaven. See, for instance, 4 Ezra 14:4–5; 2 Apoc. Bar. 59:4. Both the book

No, said John, remembering the tradition of Jesus's ascent to heaven at the transfiguration: "no one has ascended into heaven except the one who came down, the Son of Man." The "heavenly things" that he was authorized and equipped to reveal superseded the revelation of Moses, so much so that the Scriptures, where the disciples of Moses sought for truth, really spoke of him.

This new proposal rests partly upon a particular exegesis of a few verses in John 9 that tell of a little exchange between Jesus and the blind man whom he has just cured, an exchange that reveals his real identity. This revelation, presented as sudden but almost certainly late, was of incalculable significance not just for the Johannine community but for the whole Christian church. Put simply, it meant that from being thought of as human, as he certainly was in the early days of the community, Jesus had come to be thought of as divine. We cannot say how long it took for this remarkable new idea to make its full impact. What we can say is that from the point of view of the development of Christian belief it was a truly momentous move, a change of mindset. With characteristically unobtrusive skill the evangelist has incorporated this change into the story of Jesus and integrated it into his Gospel. It is now the climax of a single episode in the book, but its message permeates the whole, radically affecting our understanding both of its time frame and of its space frame. Independently of the prologue it carries the idea of preexistence: "the glory which I had with thee before the world was made" (17:5). And it underlines as never before the enormity of the gap between above and below: "they are not of the world even as I am not of the world" (17:14). We have seen how awkwardly the message protrudes from 3:13. At the close of the same chapter the same message, its jagged challenge now planed down, is expressed reflectively, no doubt now with the prologue also in mind: "He who comes from above is above all; he who is of the earth belongs to the earth, and of the earth he speaks; he who comes from heaven is above all. He bears witness to what he has seen and heard" (3:31–32).

Before embarking on this essay I had in the penumbra of my consciousness a niggling, lingering dissatisfaction with the failure of scholarship to explain the Fourth Evangelist's use of the title "Son of Man." A long time ago I had advanced a clever but ultimately unsatisfactory explanation of my own, based on the juxtaposition of two Jewish traditions, to

of Jubilees and the Apocalypse of Moses present themselves as having been revealed in this way. See Stone, *Fourth Ezra*, 418–19.

which I had been directed by a short article of Peder Borgen and a rather longer one of Charles Talbert. The present essay has arisen from a careful rereading of the work of two other great scholars, both of whose books were the fruit of years of research into complex and challenging Jewish traditions. The first of these, the American Wayne Meeks, is one of the best-known and most influential biblical scholars of our age. The second, the German J. A. Bühner, is almost unknown. Inspired by the exceptionally high level of scholarship of their work, I reread the relevant passages of the Gospel itself, and went on to argue that the evangelist had a double source of inspiration for what we now think of as his descent/ascent motif, the first a recollection of two of Jesus's miracles and a fresh awareness of their significance, the second a contemplation of the crucifixion scene, accompanied by a memory of the triple prediction of the fate of the Son of Man. Towards the end of the Gospel the evangelist rounds off his story of descent and subsequent ascent in a scene in which Jesus announces to his friend Mary that "I am ascending to my father and your father, to my God and your God" (20:17): an alternative way of stating a message summarized in different words in the hymn prefacing his Gospel.

Readers with this great hymn before their eyes, perhaps picturing Jesus as watching and listening to God in some preexistent state, are likely to pay no heed to what was probably the apocalyptic, visionary source of the real Jesus's knowledge of God. "No one has ever seen God," concludes the prologue, except of course "the only Son—he has made him known." This conclusion, unquestionably, is in agreement with the general thrust of the Gospel as we have it. But as is true of any product of human art and ingenuity, John's Gospel is better understood if one's understanding also relates to the making of it.

7

Reflections on a Footnote

A Hidden Parable?

THE "FOOTNOTE" REFERRED TO in my title is to be found on page 386 of C. H. Dodd's second great book on the Fourth Gospel,[1] where he mentions an article of his first published in French in 1962 and subsequently in English under the title "A Hidden Parable in the Fourth Gospel" (1968). The second part of the book, devoted to the Sayings, is much shorter than the first ("the Narrative"), and only twenty-two of the 110 pages in this part are allotted to Parabolic Forms.[2] Dodd had earlier discovered "six passages which stand out from the rest by their unlikeness to the usual Johannine type, and their similarity to passages in the Synoptics"[3]; by the time his book was published he had come across a seventh, the "hidden parable," which he summarizes in a footnote. Since his own summary must be more reliable than anything I could manage myself I reproduce it here in its entirety:

> In John v. 19–20a (down to . . . αὐτὸς ποιεῖ) we have a perfectly realistic description of a son apprenticed to his father's trade. He does not act on his own initiative; he watches his father at work, and performs each operation as his father performs it. The affectionate father shows the boy all the secrets of his craft. So far there is no single expression which is not appropriate in

1. Dodd, *Historical Tradition in the Fourth Gospel.*
2. Dodd, *Historical Tradition in the Fourth Gospel*, 366–87.
3. Dodd, *Historical Tradition in the Fourth Gospel*, 386.

156

describing a situation in real life. The passage is a true parable. In the verses which follow (20b–30) it is interpreted and applied in allegorical fashion, in a classical exposition of basic Johannine Christology: the *métier* of the heavenly Father is κρίνειν καὶ ζῳοποιεῖν, and the incarnate Son dutifully carries out the work of the Father.[4]

In accordance with the primary purpose of his book, Dodd concludes his study of what he calls Parabolic Forms by stating as a high probability that for these John drew independently upon the common and primitive tradition, "and that he has preserved valuable elements in that tradition which the Synoptic evangelists have neglected."[5]

In fact the "Hidden Parable" article is largely devoted to a wide-ranging study of the phenomenon of trade apprenticeship in the ancient Near and Middle East, drawing first upon the Oxyrhynchus Papyri and secondly upon a much earlier essay by Lorenz Dürr.[6] Dodd's article concludes with the observation that there is slight but sufficient evidence to justify the assertion "that among the Jews of Palestine, as in the Hellenistic world, it was normal for an artisan father to teach the technique of his trade to his son."[7] In particular Dodd cites a passage from the Mishnah that refers to two Jewish families who ran traditional businesses for the temple, one, the Garmus, baking the shewbread, and the other, the Abtinas, preparing the incense.[8]

So "when the evangelist speaks of a father who, because he loves his son, shows him everything that he himself does, and of a son who, instead of acting on his own initiative, watches his father at work and does exactly as he does, he is describing in the simplest and most realistic terms a perfectly familiar situation in everyday life. It is a significant detail," adds Dodd, "that the apprentice *watches* his father at work. The picture is drawn from artisan life; the father is one who works with his hands, and the son learns by copying his actions." Thus this passage "conforms to all criteria for the true parable. It might be called the parable of the Son as Apprentice."[9]

4. Dodd, *Historical Tradition in the Fourth Gospel*, 386n2.

5. Dodd, *Historical Tradition in the Fourth Gospel*, 387.

6. Dürr, *Das Erziehungswesen im Alten Testament*.

7. Dodd, "Hidden Parable," 38.

8. See m. Yoma 3.11; Dodd, "Hidden Parable," 37n2.

9. Dodd, "Hidden Parable," 38–39.

Dodd already has enough material, one might think, to make his case, but whereas in *Historical Tradition* he habitually uses evidence drawn from the Synoptic Gospels simply to illustrate parallel forms, in this essay, to add extra color, he appeals directly to a verse in Mark in which Jesus is called a τέκτων (Mark 6:3) and a verse in Matthew where he is said to be the son of a τέκτων (Matt 13:55). For the *form* of the parable he points to a number of brief passages in Luke.

This is the final paragraph of the essay:

> There is thus good ground for believing that the parable of the Son as Apprentice was not originally composed by the author of the Fourth Gospel, but drawn by him from the general reservoir of primary tradition which also supplied parables to the other evangelists. Can we go further? If it is true that Jesus was himself both τέκτων and τέκτων υἱός, then it is hardly too bold a conjecture that we may have here an echo of his own words, recalling memories of the years of his youth when he learnt his trade in the family workshop at Nazareth.[10]

Knowing that the word τέκτων may be applied to any kind of artisan and is not necessarily restricted to practitioners of the craft of carpentry, Dodd prudently refrains from translating it. He seems, however, to have been thinking of Jesus as the humble carpenter's son depicted in the *Christ in the House of His Parents* of the pre-Raphaelite Sir John Everett Millais (a painting that attracted the scorn of Charles Dickens, who called it, in *Household Words*, "mean, odious, revolting and repulsive"[11]). Like Millais, and virtually all biographers of Jesus, Dodd was combining the evidence from Matthew and Mark concerning the job of Jesus's father with the Lucan tradition that places his childhood home in Nazareth.

Dodd remarks that Dürr takes Matthew's phrase, "son of a τέκτων," to be no more than a Semitic idiom for τέκτων (translated by Dürr, less cautious than Dodd, as *faber* or *Zimmermann*). Against this Dodd observes that "Matthew's expression is ὁ τοῦ τέκτονος υἱός (sic) and the two articles seem to rule out Dürr's interpretation. Besides," he adds, quite rightly, "the context, in Matthew as in Mark, requires a reference to family relationship."[12] In any case perhaps we should rather be thinking of a skilled craftsman of a superior kind (joiner, mason, cooper?), quite

10. Dodd, "Hidden Parable," 40.

11. Dickens, "Old Lamps," 13.

12. Dodd, "Hidden Parable," 37n3.

possibly working in neighboring Sepphoris, which was rebuilt and forti-
fied by Herod Antipas, as Josephus tells us (*AJ* 18.27) to make it "the
protection (πρόσχημα) of all Galilee."[13] Sepphoris, seemingly the center
of the rebellion against Rome that followed the death of Herod in 4 BCE,
was put to the flames by Varus, the Roman governor of Syria. Antipas,
Herod's successor (always called Herod in the Gospels), may have waited
until Varus's departure before beginning the work of rebuilding, because
to have started it sooner might well have been considered a serious af-
front by the governor. He is unlikely to have had to wait very long, because Roman legates were seldom in post for more than three years.[14] So
the rebuilding of Sepphoris may well have started soon enough to make
it necessary to call upon nearby craftsmen during Jesus's childhood and
early youth. And Sepphoris, after all, was only four miles distant from
Nazareth, a comfortable hour's walk for a fit young man, as Richard A.
Batey has reminded us.[15] Could Jesus, for instance, have participated, as
joiner or mason, in the construction of the fine theatre? Dodd will have
pictured Jesus working in a carpenter's shop in Nazareth rather than on
a building site in Sepphoris; in any case he was departing from his original brief by offering an image of Jesus in his youth or childhood that is
a world apart from anything that might have excited the interest of the
Fourth Evangelist.

Almost all later commentators who have read Dodd's essay make
some appreciative mention of it. Only a few, apparently, are aware of
the very short study by P. Gaechter.[16] Writing independently of Dodd,
Gaechter too focuses upon the widespread practice of family apprenticeship. He ignores Dodd's Hellenistic examples but, like Dodd, cites the
families that baked the shewbread and prepared the incense. He too
finds a parable in John 5:19; but whereas, as we shall see, Dodd bases his

13. The word πρόσχημα—something held in front of (προέχω)—commonly means
"ornament," which is how it is usually translated in this passage (Loeb, Schürer); but
walls are built round towns (τειχίζειν) not to beautify but to fortify. The walls of Sepphoris were rebuilt first to protect the city itself and secondly the whole of the region.
If Josephus had been thinking of architectural beauty he would surely have considered
the true jewel of Galilee to be the new capital, Tiberias, built much later.

14. Varus was certainly gone by 9 CE, because in that year he was commanding a
legion in Germany, where his shattering defeat by the forces of Arminius put an end
to the expansion of the Roman Empire eastwards beyond the Rhine, with momentous
consequences for the future of the whole of Europe.

15. Batey, *Jesus and the Forgotten City*.

16. Gaechter, "Zur Form von Joh. 5.19–30," 65–68.

argument entirely on the use of the definite article in parables or *Bild-worte*, Gaechter makes the additional observation that the Greek of John 5:19 is probably based upon a Semitism, the use of the definite form of the noun in sayings involving a type.[17] So, again like Dodd, he sees the use of the definite article in this passage as evidence that we have here a general statement concerning a father instructing his son in his own craft.

As well as emphasizing the parabolic nature of the first one-and-a-half verses (5:19–20a), Dodd contrasts this with the allegorical nature of what follows (vv. 20b–30), "the father and son of the parable becoming God the Father and Christ the Son. . . . But the allegorical interpretation," he insists, "is in no way necessary to the understanding of the picture drawn in the parable."[18] Then, towards the end of his essay, with reference to the picture of family apprenticeship in the parable, he adds: "This detail is not made use of in the theological exposition which follows; it is not a feature dictated by the requirements of the deeper meaning which is to be conveyed"[19]; and at this point he inserts an important footnote:

> Undoubtedly, when once the allegorical approach is established in the reader's mind he will discover symbolic meanings in all manner of details; and so here the words βλέπῃ τὸν πατέρα will remind him of the highly theological doctrine of vi. 46, ὁ ὢν παρὰ τοῦ θεοῦ οὗτος (sic) ἑώρακεν τὸν πατέρα, and this was probably intended by the evangelist; but it is not the theology that has produced the realistic detail of the parable.

Dodd's argument depends for its plausibility upon the truth of his assertion, right at the beginning of his essay, that "the article with πατήρ and υἱός is generic, indicating that the statement applies to *any* father and *any* son. (This is normal in parables or *Bildworte*.)"[20] But the opening assertion that "the Son can do nothing ἀφ' ἑαυτοῦ" is unquestionably a *self-reference*, clarified later in the discourse by a shift from the third to the first person: "*I* can do nothing ἀπ' ἐμαυτοῦ" (5:30). To translate it as "*a* son can do nothing of his own accord" would be wrong: the article here is not, *pace* both Dodd and Gaechter, generic, but specific. Dodd quite rightly points out that in parables or *Bildworte* the subject is regularly

17. Gaechter, "Zur Form von Joh. 5.19–30," 67.
18. Dodd, "Hidden Parable," 31–32.
19. Dodd, "Hidden Parable," 39.
20. Dodd, "Hidden Parable," 31.

definite.[21] Yet clearly the use of the definite article does not in itself prove the presence of a parable. Neither scholar has noticed that the parable, if there is one, comes *after* the opening statement; this concerns the Son's inability to act independently of his Father and has nothing to do with the parable, which is simply concerned with a boy watching, learning from, and imitating his father. Moreover, if there is indeed a parable lying behind the words "only what he sees the Father doing" it is, as the title of Dodd's essay indicates, a *hidden* parable. To insist, as he does, upon the difference between the parable in the first sentence and the allegory that follows,[22] is to shrug off any obligation to explain the *overt* significance of Jesus's claim that he "sees what the Father is doing."

We may observe too that neither in the section of Dodd's earlier book in which the whole discourse is discussed[23] nor in the occasional references to John 5:19-20 elsewhere in that book does he either quote or comment upon this claim. Yet in cutting off what he calls the parable from the allegory he is choosing to ignore the clear meaning of the text. In parabolic utterances the use of the definite article is to be accounted for by the convention, common to Semitic languages, including Akkadian, according to which the definite form of the noun is used in sayings involving a type. (This is a point well-made by both Dürr and Gaechter.) Yet "the Son can do nothing of his own accord" is *not* as it stands a parabolic statement. If it were, it would have to be translated "*a* son," like "*a* lamp" (Dodd), and "*a* sower" (Gaechter). Formally speaking it is no different from what Dodd calls "the theological exposition which follows," and it has many parallels elsewhere in the Gospel (cf. 6:38; 7:16; 8:28, 42; 12:49).

When other scholars, unwilling or unable to escape the commentator's tacit obligation to say something about every single verse in the Gospel, do reflect upon this passage, the result, almost without exception, is a limp paraphrase. Here, as a typical example, I quote from the commentary of Andrew Lincoln, not because it is any feebler than the rest,

21. In Mark 4:21, for instance, we have to translate, "is *a* lamp brought in to be put under a bushel . . . ?" But the Greek is ὁ λύχνος: cf. Matt 12:43; 23:24; Mark 3:27—all examples cited by Dodd ("Hidden Parable," 31n3). Gaechter ("Zur Form von Joh. 5.19-30," 67) cites the parable of the sower—ὁ σπείρων in all three Synoptics: Matt 13:3; Mark 4:3; Luke 8:5.

22. Dodd, "Hidden Parable," 39.

23. Dodd, *Interpretation of the Fourth Gospel*, 320-28.

62 DISCOVERING JOHN

but because it is the most recent commentary (in English) to which I have
ready access:

> *whatever the Father does, the Son likewise does.* This constitutes
> an elaboration of Jesus' earlier response in v. 17. He could say
> that his Father was working until now and that he was working,
> because as the Son he is simply doing what he sees his Father
> doing. The suggestion that behind this formulation lies a prov-
> erb about an apprentice son has some plausibility. Just as the
> apprentice son watches and then repeats the work of his father, a
> skilled artisan, so in this Christological adaptation Jesus claims
> that in his works, such as the healing on the sabbath, he is only
> imitating what he sees his Father doing.[24]

The Vision of God

It is a common experience of those who resort to commentaries on the
Bible in the hope of enlightenment to find that the most puzzling and
refractory passages elicit the fewest explanations. (The Johannine aporias
are a good example. Another is John 13:32.) Not that this particular passage, on the face of it, is especially complex. The syntax is simple, the
language limpid. But for Jesus to suggest that, as he was performing a
miraculous cure, he was watching and imitating his Father—what can
this mean? There is no problem about discerning the *purpose* of the assertion: not only is Jesus claiming divine authority for his actions, he is
associating his own action with the life-giving activity of God, and as
the discourse proceeds he also assumes the authority to judge. These are
extreme claims, but they are not hard to understand. The difficulty lies in
finding a context for the extraordinary idea that God deliberately demonstrated his working methods to the Son. When and where did he do
this? If, confronted with this question, we find ourselves at a loss how to
reply, we may relieve our sense of helplessness and disarray by answering
that the question itself is inappropriate. Why? Because Jesus is speaking
metaphorically. In speaking of himself as watching and imitating God, he
is simply affirming as graphically as possible that he has divine authority
for his actions. Dodd may be thought to provide part of the solution with
his suggestion of a hidden parable. Paradoxically, however, in revealing
the parable he is concealing the problem. We may simplify this somewhat

24. Schnackenburg, *Gospel According to St. John*, 202.

by altering it. Instead of asking *when*—for in this passage we find the present tense and elsewhere (6:46 and 8:38) the past—let us ask instead *what was the Fourth Evangelist's justification* in the first place for speaking of Jesus's direct vision of God?

There is nothing in Dodd's essay to tell us how he would answer this question, but, although in neither of his big books has he anything to say about John 5:19, he does comment briefly on 6:46, the verse mentioned in a note of "Hidden Parable" that alludes to its "highly theological doctrine"—a comment calculated less to clarify than to bemuse, for the theology, if this is a correct observation, is left unexplained. Following a remark concerning the Fourth Evangelist's presupposition that the Age to Come has arrived and that eternal life is already here, he continues:

> Nevertheless, the maxim holds good: θεὸν οὐδεὶς ἑώρακεν πώποτε (i. 18). Of one only can such direct vision of God be predicated: οὐχ ὅτι τὸν πατέρα ἑώρακέν τις εἰ μὴ ὁ ὢν παρὰ τοῦ θεοῦ, οὗτος ἑώρακέν τὸν πατέρα (vi. 46). The knowledge which Christ has of God, therefore, has that quality of direct vision . . . which for Jewish thinkers was reserved for the supernatural life of the Age to Come. This knowledge which is vision He mediates to men in the sense, ὁ ἑωρακὼς ἐμὲ ἑώρακεν τὸν πατέρα (xiv. 9), ὁ θεωρῶν ἐμὲ θεωρεῖ τὸν πέμψαντά με (xii. 45).[25]

I have two comments to make about this paragraph. In the first place it is to be observed that John 6:46 *contradicts* 1:18. Unlike 3:13, which specifically allows for a single exception (no one *except* the Son of Man), the last verse of the prologue, very forcibly expressed ("no one has ever seen God"), does not. The contradiction should first be acknowledged, and then explained. My own explanation is simply that in the second edition of the Gospel, which was the first to incorporate both the prologue and chapter 6, the evangelist, although broadly welcoming the insights of the prologue, feels that he must modify them slightly so as to allow for the truth, as he sees it, that ὁ ὢν παρὰ τοῦ θεοῦ, the one who is from God, *can* be said to have seen God, because it is from that very vision that he derives his authority to reveal to others what he knows. But it is surely in the highest degree unlikely that in formulating an explicit denial that *anyone* had seen God, the author of the prologue was making a mental

---

25. Dodd, *Interpretation of the Fourth Gospel*, 167.

exception for the one he calls μονογονὴς θεός/υἱός.[26] One of the great
mysteries of Johannine scholarship is the widespread assumption (which
I myself once shared) that whenever Jesus, in the body of the Gospel,
speaks of seeing or having seen God, he is referring to some strange vision in a preexistent past. The reason for this assumption is the extraordinary conceptual difficulty that arises when a heavenly being, the Logos,
is identified with a human being, Jesus Christ. Behind this identification
lies the remarkable leap of religious imagination performed by Ben Sira
and Greek Baruch when they identified wisdom with the law. When
wisdom tabernacled on earth in the form of the law, from being eternal
(בכל עת), Proverbs 8:30, she suddenly acquired a history. However, if the
law was ever thought of as dwelling alongside God it was not with the
human faculties of seeing and hearing. And it is a mistake, I believe, to
attribute to the human Jesus, when he speaks of seeing God, a power
that could only have been exercised *before* he came to be identified as the
incarnate Logos. The imaginative feat of the author of the prologue, in
identifying Jesus Christ as the eternal Logos, more than matched that of
Ben Sira and Greek Baruch. But could he possibly have thought of Jesus,
on the occasions when he speaks of seeing God, as reaching back in his
mind and memory to a time when he himself had not yet been born?

Like most commentators Dodd believes that the prologue should
govern our understanding of all that follows: "this pre-temporal (or more
properly, non-temporal) existence of the Son is affirmed with emphasis, and assumed all through the gospel."[27] But in the early history of the
members of the Johannine community, living alongside their Jewish
neighbors in the synagogue, there was no thought of Jesus as a mythical
divine being existing close to God before he took flesh and entered the
world. That conviction came later, though soon enough to influence the
composition of chapter 6, which itself belongs to the second edition of
the Gospel. For nowhere else in the Gospel does Jesus state so directly
and unequivocally, "I have come down from heaven" (6:38; cf. 6:42), in
the language of descent associated elsewhere with the Son of Man. This
statement, therefore, depends both upon the realization, quite late in the
history of the community, that Jesus had descended from heaven *as* the

26. The knowledge that *he* possesses comes not from vision but from propinquity,
exactly that propinquity claimed by Wisdom: "when he established the heavens I was
there. . . when he marked out the foundations of the earth, then I was beside him
[אצלו] like a master workman [?], rejoicing in his inhabited world" (Prov 8:27–31).

27. Dodd, *Interpretation of the Fourth Gospel*, 260.

angelic figure of the Son of Man[28] (and had also of course reascended there, as he foretells in 6:62) and upon the acceptance of the central tenets of the prologue. (Yet, as I have just remarked, the affirmation that he has seen the Father [6:46] conflicts with the categorical denial of the prologue that *anyone* has seen God.)

The prologue is anti-apocalyptic. God's plan for the world (the Logos) is not revealed by a visionary seer who has seen God and is consequently in a position to pass on his knowledge to others. Rather it takes the form of a theophany ("we have gazed on his glory"), a form of God's communication with the world found very often in the Bible. The revelation or "exposition" (ἐξήγησις) of God made by Jesus Christ is not, according to the prologue, the consequence of a vision. *That* form of revelation is what the supporters of Moses maintain (it is a constant theme in the Jewish tradition), but they are wrong to do so. Nor is it the case that the Jesus Christ of the prologue acts as an *angelus interpres*, expounding and explaining a new revelation. No: *he is the embodiment of that revelation*. "Grace and truth," states the prologue, "came about through Jesus Christ" (1:17). But for the Fourth Evangelist Jesus Christ *is* the truth. There are three distinct myths or metaphors in the Gospel used to indicate Jesus's entry into the world, all of them stemming from Jewish tradition. These should not be confused (although the last two are eventually blended together). The first is the wisdom tradition of the prologue, which corresponds to an equivalent tradition in the Hebrew Bible. Neither the word λόγος nor the tradition that it resumes and exemplifies is repeated or alluded to anywhere else in the Gospel. The second is the mission tradition, seen particularly clearly in 8:42: "I proceeded and came forth from God; I came not of my own accord, but he sent me." The third is the ascent/descent motif connected with the Son of Man, which closely parallels the biblical Moses tradition elaborated by the rabbis. According to this tradition the law was delivered to Israel by Moses after an ascent of Mount Sinai frequently thought of as an ascent as far as heaven.[29] This explains why the Gospel constantly emphasizes how the new revelation of Jesus has superseded the Mosaic law. The emphatic contrast between Moses and Christ with which the prologue concludes is no doubt one of the features that prompted the evangelist to accept it as a fitting preface to his work.

28. See Ashton, "Johannine Son of Man," 508–29.

29. Bühner, *Der Gesandte und sein Weg*, 271–315.

The point at which myth and history collide and fuse is in the very last sentence, indeed the very last word: [ὁ] μονογενὴς υἱὸς [θεὸς] ὁ ὢν εἰς τὸν κόλπον τοῦ πατρὸς ἐκεῖνος ἐξηγήσατο: "it is the only begotten Son, [now back] in the Father's bosom, who was his manifestation." There are different possible renderings of the verb ἐξηγεῖσθαι, which occurs nowhere else in the Gospel. It is especially problematic here because it apparently has no object, whereas in classical Greek, whenever it has the sense of interpret or explain, it is always transitive. Most translations *assume* an object for ἐξηγήσατο, namely αὐτόν, referring to the Father; but this makes it hard to find a rendering that does justice either to the general sense of the prologue itself or to the body of the Gospel, where Jesus conspicuously refrains from saying anything about God that could be construed as an interpretation or explanation. (This is what accounts for the plausibility of Bultmann's famous assertion that "the Jesus of the Fourth Gospel reveals nothing more than *that* he is the Revealer"). So it is up to the translator/exegete to decide upon the manner—and matter—of the revelation that is being proclaimed. There is no intentional allusion here to the many occasions in the Gospel in which Jesus uses the terms "Father" or "the one who sent me," for these are simply ways of stating his own identity. Rather, ἐξηγήσατο, in a proper use of the Greek Middle Voice whereby the results of the action are confined to the subject of the verb, surely alludes either to the divine theophany announced earlier in the phrase "we have gazed on his glory" (1:14)—or to the very person of Jesus—or to the Gospel itself (because the medium is the message). It is not just that the only-begotten Son manifested the Father: he *was* the manifestation, in his life and teaching on earth, and in his passion and resurrection. It was this extraordinary insight, no doubt, that persuaded the evangelist to embrace the prologue and adapt it as the preface to his own work. For he had already pictured Jesus proclaiming that "he who gazes upon me gazes upon him who sent me" (12:45) and as answering Philip's request to be shown the Father by informing him that "he who has seen me has seen the Father" (14:9).

The prologue opens in heaven, whereas the body of the Gospel begins (and continues) on earth. It starts (how else?) with a human Jesus. And at this point I must add my second comment on Dodd's observations about 6:46, which concerns his truly astonishing assertion that for Jewish thinkers any direct vision of God "was reserved for the life to come."[30] It is astonishing, both because of the absolute assurance with which it is made and also because it could not be further from the truth. I have no need myself to demonstrate the falsity of Dodd's position, for this has already been done by Christopher Rowland in his pioneering book, *The Open Heaven*. Rowland had no cause to refer to Dodd's *Interpretation* in this book —and he did not—but in the first three parts, where he discusses apocalyptic traditions before the common era, and in the fourth, "The Esoteric Tradition in Early Rabbinic Judaism," he produces an overwhelming amount of evidence that shows very clearly the importance of the visionary tradition in early and later Judaism.

In spite of this abundant evidence I know of only one scholar bold enough to suggest that underlying John's christology there is hidden an early apocalyptic tradition that Jesus ascended into heaven as a visionary seer, and was granted sight of God. In his masterly but totally neglected study, Jan-Adolf Bühner (1977) flies in the face of the virtually universal assumption that, wherever in the Gospel Jesus speaks of seeing God, he can only be referring to what is generally called his preexistence.

Yet before considering the possibility of an underlying visionary tradition, it is best to start by looking at the parable in context. The first charge that the Jews brought against Jesus was of performing his work of healing on the sabbath, a charge answered by Jesus with the words, "My father is working still, and I am working" (5:17), an answer which the Jews took to mean that he was making himself equal with God. In the long discourse that followed the evangelist expanded upon this answer, first with the saying we are now discussing, secondly by extending the idea of healing to that of giving life and judging ("for as the Father has life in himself, so he has granted the Son also to have life in himself, and has given him the authority to execute judgment, because he is the Son of Man" [5:26–27]), and thirdly with the statement that "I can do nothing on my own authority" (5:30), a rejection of the charge that he was making himself equal with God. The emphatic admission of total dependence in this final statement, whose full significance was brought out by Peder Borgen's work on the law of agency,[31] is simply a reassertion of Jesus's initial statement, "the Son can do nothing of his own accord" (5:19)—ἀφ' ἑαυτοῦ in the first instance, ἀπ' ἐμαυτοῦ in the second—and as I have pointed out, this involves much more than the simple idea (required by

30. Dodd, *Interpretation of the Fourth Gospel*, 167.
31. Borgen, "God's Agent in the Fourth Gospel," 137–48.

the parable) of a boy watching and imitating the actions of his father. But where did the evangelist derive his assurance that Jesus had actually seen God?

Added at a relatively late stage of the composition of the Gospel, chapter 6, as one might expect, also represents a late stage of the evangelist's christological thinking. I have already pointed out that it apparently includes a correction of the statement of the prologue that no one has ever seen God, because in 6:46 Jesus asserts on the contrary that "no one has ever seen the Father *except* the one who is from God." This affirmation, which conflicts with the generally anti-apocalyptic stance of the prologue, stems from an entirely different tradition, one best exhibited, as Bühner has shown, in the follow-up to the discussion with Nicodemus in chapter 3. It is here that we find the explicit justification of Jesus's statement that he is speaking of what he knows and bearing witness to what he has seen (3:11), namely that he had ascended into heaven (3:13), a claim that, as Hugo Odeberg argued long ago,[32] must be seen as a polemical denial of counter-claims made on behalf of other Jewish seers, notably Moses and Enoch.

The difficulty with this thesis, evidently, is that there is no room in the Fourth Gospel for an actual account of Jesus's ascent into heaven to receive special revelations. He manifested his glory as early as the marriage feast at Cana (2:11), and that glory never left him. Nevertheless it is by appealing to just such a tradition that we can best account for the references in the Gospel to Jesus's vision of God. It is no use objecting to this by waving a flag emblazoned with the word "theology" in our faces, for that is not an explanation but an attempt to dissuade us from asking for one.

Bühner distinguishes two strands in the tradition of an apocalyptic vision, the first a strand in which the emphasis is upon the correspondence between Jesus's earthly discourse and his heavenly vision, and the second a polemical strand that stresses the exclusive nature of his visionary experience.[33] If this is right, then the polemical strand must reflect and accompany the increasing hostility between two groups in the synagogue, the disciples of Moses on the one hand and the disciples of Jesus on the other, which is displayed in 3:13 and also in 6:46. Both strands can be seen quite clearly in the long discourse and debate in chapter 5. But

32. Odeberg, *Fourth Gospel.*
33. Bühner, *Der Gesandte und sein Weg,* 365.

the so-called "parabolic" statement in 5:19 (which is what we are discussing here) is such an appropriate defense of his miraculous intervention
earlier in the chapter that I am led to suspect it was composed *ad hoc*. Just
possibly Dodd is right to suppose that the evangelist is making use of a
little nugget of a parable that he found ready to hand in a store of traditional sayings. But would he have turned this into a statement concerning
Jesus's vision of the Father had he not already known of a tradition of
a heavenly ascent? There is nothing in the prologue to justify the common assumption that the evangelist here and elsewhere was thinking of
a preexistent vision; and in any case the prologue was almost certainly
added to the Gospel after chapter 5 was written. It is no doubt true that a
tradition of visionary ascent does not really tally with the suggestion that
"the Son" was watching what the Father was doing in heaven in order
to reproduce this activity in his own behavior on earth. In the visionary ascents that we find in the Jewish apocalypses, God is not seen to be
engaged in the work of giving life and passing judgment. So the hypothesis of an already-existing parable, modified so as to fit both the story of
the healing miracle and the discourse that followed, cannot be excluded.
Dodd points out that what he would like to call the parable of the Son as
Apprentice "is not a feature dictated by the requirements of the deeper
meaning which is to be conveyed."[34] But it could be said to be required, or
at least naturally elicited, by the evangelist's need to defend Jesus's actions
and to emphasize the precise significance of the miracle story that he had
inherited. Nevertheless it is hard to believe that he would have written of
Jesus watching and imitating the Father if he was not already aware of a
strong tradition of visionary ascent.[35]

---

34. Dodd, "Hidden Parable," 39.

35. This is fully discussed by Bühner (*Der Gesandte und sein Weg*) and commented
upon briefly in my 2011 article (Ashton, "Johannine Son of Man").

8

Browning on Feuerbach and Renan

A Death in the Desert

ROBERT CARROLL WAS INTERESTED throughout his career in what he called "the long history of the effects of the reception of the Bible in Western culture." In the nineteenth century that other Robert, the poet Browning, played a significant part in this history; and I hope therefore that this study of the one poem of Browning in which his response to the biblical criticism of his day is expressed most strongly will be thought an appropriate tribute to the work of a great twentieth-century scholar who would certainly have sympathized with Browning's attempts to come to grips with the new challenges offered by Strauss, Feuerbach, and Renan. In the essay that follows, rather than setting out in detail the challenges of Feuerbach and Renan to which Browning was replying in *A Death in the Desert*,[1] I simply want to consider his own response and to reflect on his arguments. After a few remarks concerning the structure of the poem certain key passages will be selected for further comment. In a conclud-ing section I will briefly consider the last poem of the volume (*Dramatis Personae*) in which *A Death in the Desert* first appeared.

A Death in the Desert is dominated by two central motifs: (1) *love* (forty occurrences as verb or noun in this 687-line poem); (2) *truth*

1. For Feuerbach, see Drew, *Poetry of Browning*, 200–227; for Renan, see Shaffer, "*Kubla Khan*," 191–224, and Culpepper, "Guessing Points and Knowing Stars," 53–65. Browning's *A Death in the Desert* may be found online at: https://rpo.library.utoronto. ca/poems/death-desert.

(twenty-five occurrences). In his reflections on love Browning is presumably thinking of Feuerbach; whereas the truth motif is readily related to his concerns for the work of Strauss and Renan, especially the latter, whose *Vie de Jésus* appeared in 1863, the year before the publication of *Dramatis Personae.*

The bulk of the poem consists of replies by the dying apostle to objections put in the mouths of imaginary interlocutors. Browning's Saint John had evidently read Feuerbach in George Eliot's translation (1854) as well as Renan's *Vie de Jésus* in the original French; so it is not surprising that he appears to be preoccupied with the nineteenth-century debate.

Like many of Browning's works *A Death in the Desert* is a masterpiece of indirection, starting hesitatingly, almost fumblingly, so that the reader has covered nearly a tenth of this long poem before the identity of the protagonist is made plain. This is disclosed in a quotation from the gospel read from an engraved tablet fetched "out of the secret chamber" by one of the dying man's attendants: "I am the Resurrection and the Life." It is another fifty lines before the speaker identifies himself without equivocation, declaring himself to be

> Trying to taste again the truth of things—
> (He smiled)—their very superficial truth;
> As that ye are my sons, that it is long
> Since James and Peter had release by death,
> And I am only he, your brother John,
> Who saw and heard, and could remember all. (112–17)

With typical economy, then, Browning closes his introductory section by announcing one of his most important themes: the message of the dying John, the last surviving eyewitness of what he calls "that Life and Death," is addressed to a generation that will no longer be able to appeal directly to the witness of the apostles: once his ashes are scattered there will be

> left on earth
> No one alive who knew (consider this!)
> —Saw with his eyes and handled with his hands
> That which was from the first, the Word of Life.
> How will it be when none more saith "I saw"? (129–33)

Browning proceeds partly by the use of inclusions, partly by the use of the leapfrogging or snail-shell technique familiar to students of Saint Paul. The whole poem is one vast inclusion, with an introductory section explaining the discovery of the manuscript and a concluding section commenting on the argument from the outside. Inside these there is another preface (to the manuscript itself) and another conclusion, explaining the circumstances of the apostle's last discourse and telling of his death and burial. This is a Chinese doll of a poem. One of its minor inclusions comes early on, where the apostle' s first uncertain words of explanation are balanced by a more definite assertion some forty lines later. Between these lies a curious twenty-three-line parenthesis, containing a little essay in rational psychology that sketches a doctrine of three souls after the manner of Plotinus. This concludes: "What Does, what Knows, what Is, three souls, one man" (103).

Towards the beginning of the poem the speaker betrays some confusion regarding his own identity, thus heralding the leading motif, namely, the tension between fact and faith and the movement from "a very superficial truth" to a more profound one. Even the physical description of the cave in which the dying man is lying touches on this motif:

> But in the midmost grotto: since noon's light
> Reached there a little, and we would not lose
> The last of what might happen on his face. (26–28)

Characteristically, Browning's noon, which introduces the important motif of the sun, only "reaches there a little" and the "noon and burning blue" are outside the cave, not inside. The setting, which is repeated halfway through the poem in a passage reminiscent of the cave in Plato's *Republic*, contributes to its argument.

Browning's winding style makes it hard to lay out the poem's structure precisely. Yet he succeeds in marking off certain sections quite clearly. In line 133 the question "How will it be when none more saith 'I saw'?" anticipates the conclusion of the section that follows:

> Was John at all, and did he say he saw?
> Assure us, ere we ask *what* he might see! (196–97)

This particular section (134–97) brilliantly summarizes all the works ascribed to the apostle John commencing with his oral teaching:

> Since I, whom Christ's mouth taught, was bidden teach,
> I went, for many years, about the world,
> Saying "it was so; so I heard and saw,"
> Speaking as the case asked: and men believed. (135–38)

But this seemingly clear, matter-of-fact statement is a starting-point, not a conclusion.

It suits Browning's purpose to treat the book of Revelation, which records an open disclosure of heavenly truth, as the first of John's written works; then come the letters, and finally, most important of all, the Gospel:

> Since much that at the first, in deed and word,
>
> Lay simply and sufficiently exposed,
>
> Had grown (or else my soul was grown to match,
>
> Fed through such years, familiar with such light,
>
> Guarded and guided still to see and speak)
>
> Of new significance and fresh result;
>
> What first were guessed as points, I now knew stars
>
> And named them in the Gospel I have writ. (168–75)

"What first were guessed as points, I now knew stars." This one verse concisely sums up Browning's central paradox: the points, hard little nuggets of historical fact, are just guessed at: the stars, enlargements or expansions of the points, and consequently less clearly defined, are *known*, but the knowledge is not that of the historian but of the believer.

In the following section this little metaphor is taken up again (another example of Browning's leapfrogging technique), and expanded into the remarkable simile of the optic glass that reverses the movement, creating a distancing effect through being

> turned on objects brought too close,
>
> Lying confusedly insubordinate
>
> For the unassisted eye to master once.
>
> Look through his tube, at distance now they lay,
>
> Become succinct, distinct, so small, so clear!
>
> Just thus, ye needs must apprehend what truth
>
> I see, reduced to plain historic fact,
>
> Diminished into clearness, proved a point
>
> And far away: ye would withdraw your sense
>
> From out eternity, strain it upon time. (230–39)

But having performed this operation, John's imaginary audience is immediately told to

> stand before that fact, that Life and Death,
> Stay there at gaze, till it dispart, dispread,
> As though a star should open out, all sides,
> Grow the world on you, as it is my world. (240–43)

John had already declared that

> that Life and Death
> Of which I wrote "it was"—to me, it is;
> —Is, here and now: I apprehend nought else. (208–10)

The journey he traveled between the "was" and the "is" is one he expects other people to make too: Browning, like Kierkegaard in *The Philosophical Fragments*, comes very close here to the perspective of the evangelist himself, whose concern is for what Kierkegaard calls "the contemporary Christian"; though both of these writers of course are attempting to answer questions that belong to their own century. These questions demand just as big a leap from one time to another, from sight to inference, from superficial knowledge to profound faith as was required by the evangelist: "Blessed are those who have not seen and yet believe."

The following section is the clearest *inclusio* in the whole poem, for the question that concluded the preceding section is repeated verbatim at the end of this one:

> What do I hear say, or conceive men say,
> "Was John at all, and did he say he saw?
> Assure us, ere we ask what he might see!" (334–36)

In the meantime the poet has treated us to a meditation on truth: the word itself occurs eight times within 100 lines. It is compared to Prometheus's fire, so much more precious than material goods of gold or purple. But then the speaker asks whether, if the worth of Christ were as plain as that of fire, it would be possible to give him up:

> Therefore, I say, to test man, the proofs shift,
> Nor may he grasp that fact like other fact,
> And straightway in his life acknowledge it,
> As, say, the indubitable bliss of fire. (295–98)

To make this point Browning adopts a curious stratagem. In the Fourth Gospel's version of the Passion, John himself, alone among the disciples, remains present right up to the crucifixion. But now the poet turns instead to the synoptic account, according to which John, along with all the others, forsook Jesus at the moment of his arrest—an account that turns him into a liar. Shaffer thinks that Browning borrowed this suggestion from Renan.[2] However that may be, Browning's John finds a value in his act of cowardice: if, having witnessed the life, he was, despite what he says in his Gospel, absent from the death, then he could claim precisely that lack of sight which is given the character of a beatitude at the end of the Gospel. Accordingly, "my soul had gained its truth, could grow" (312). This is his answer to the objection of those who sigh, "It had been easier once than now" (299).

Next Browning introduces his second important motif, which has received only a brief mention up until now but is anticipated in an earlier remark about the First Epistle, in which John, "reasoning from my knowledge," had taught that "men should, for love's sake, in love's strength believe" (147–48). "Was truth safe for ever, then?" he asks (318). "Not so," he replies, sustaining the comparison with fire:

> Already had begun the silent work
> Whereby truth, deadened of its absolute blaze,
> Might need's love's eye to pierce the o'erstretched doubt. (319–21)

How love can pierce the integument of doubt the poet nowhere makes clear. Here, perhaps, is the clearest example of the fideism he shares with Kierkegaard.

The difficulty is not shirked but rather voiced by one of the speaker's imaginary interlocutors in one of the longest sections of the poem, in which the integrity of the Gospel is called into question:

> Here is a tale of things done ages since;
> What truth was ever told the second day?
> Wonders, that would prove doctrine, go for nought,
> Remains the doctrine, love; well, we must love,
> And what we love most, power and love in one,
> Let us acknowledge on the record here,
> Accepting these in Christ: must Christ then be?
> Has He been? Did not we ourselves make Him? (370–77)

The allusions to Feuerbach is reinforced:

---

2. Shaffer, "Kubla Khan," 196.

'Tis mere projection from man's inmost mind,
And, what he loves, thus falls reflected back.
Becomes accounted somewhat out of him. (383–85)

Before any answer is given to this challenge the poem swerves off course to deal with a completely different problem, which concerns the cessation of miracles. This is a favorite topic of Browning's, one that he can deal with quite confidently: an assent that cannot be withheld, because the evidence is compelling, simply is not faith. Before man has reached maturity, says John, he requires adventitious aids to belief: fully grown he needs them no longer, no more than a gardener, once his seeds have come to fruition, needs the tickets he used to remind him where he first planted them. Similarly

This book's fruit is plain,
Nor miracles need prove it any more. (443–44)

The miracle that was originally required comes as a surprise: it has been invented for the occasion, for John claims to have performed it himself:

I cried once, "That ye may believe in Christ,
Behold this blind man shall receive his sight!" (459–60)

Shaffer interprets this claim as a self-aggrandizing gesture on the part of John, intended to underline his position as Christ's favourite disciple; but it may rather be an adaptation of the story of the healing of the cripple by Peter and John (Acts 3:1–10), shifting the restoration of the power to walk to the restoration of sight that fits in better with Browning's purpose. The poet's defense of the miracle, at any rate, is straightforward:

I say, that miracle was duly wrought
When, save for it, no faith was possible. (464–65)

True faith, however, does not need miracles—after the childhood years during which immature minds had to be, as John puts it, "spoon-fed with truth":

So faith grew, making void more miracles
Because too much: they would compel, not help. (472–73)

Browning now returns to tackle the Feuerbachian challenge he had raised earlier. In yet another turn of his spiraling argument he states the objection more clearly:

> Since such love is everywhere,
> And since ourselves can love and would be loved,
> We ourselves make the love, and Christ was not. (505–7)

Here is a claim to self-sufficiency that John cannot tolerate:

> How shall ye help this man who knows himself,
> That he must love and would be loved again,
> Yet, owning his own love that proveth Christ,
> Rejecteth Christ though very need of Him?
> The lamp o'erswims with oil, the stomach flags
> Loaded with nurture, and that man's soul dies. (508–13)

If you overcharge a stomach with food or a lamp with oil, then

> This is death and the sole death,
> When a man's loss comes to him from his gain
> Darkness from light, from knowledge ignorance,
> And lack of love from love made manifest. (483–86)

This is scarcely an effective refutation of Feuerbach, who is allowed only the briefest of answers:

> But this was all the while
> A trick; the fault was, first of all, in thee,
> Thy story of the places, names and dates,
> Where, when and how the ultimate truth had rise,
> —Thy prior truth, at last discovered none,
> Whence now the second suffers detriment. (514–19)

Short as it is, this, one might think, is already an effective refutation of a very specious argument. Feuerbach might have added that if the Christ of Christian belief (his real target) was simply a projection of human aspirations, then he had no further need of him, either for love or for true knowledge. But this further riposte is not allowed, and the poem swings back without further ado to the seemingly irrelevant question concerning miracles which, as we have seen, caused Browning no discomfort:

> And why refuse what modicum of help
> Had stopped the after-doubt, impossible
> "I" the face of truth—truth absolute, uniform? (522–24)

After this question (which has already been answered) the interlocutor switches to a different line of attack, ironically comparing John's approach with the old mythological account of Prometheus's discovery of fire:

> "The fact is in the fable," cry the wise,
> "Mortals obtained the boon, so much is fact,
> Though fire is spirit and produced on earth." (534–36)

Then follows the challenge:

> As with the Titan's, so now with thy tale:
> Why breed in us perplexity, mistake,
> Nor tell the whole truth in the proper words? (537–39)

If, then, the story of Christ is no more than a mythological rendering of a truth (human love?) that can be stated more directly, cannot we dispense with it altogether? Perhaps not. The story may nevertheless retain its hold on the human imagination. But the dying man shows no interest in this argument, turning instead to another of Browning's most cherished ideas, the man's place in the world and his fundamental difference from God: man is

> A thing nor God nor beast,
> Made to know that he can know and not more:
> Lower than God who knows all and can all,
> Higher than beasts which know and can so far
> At each beast's limit. (576–80)

From here Browning moves to the final brilliant simile, that of the sculptor or statuary. Here he comes close to Plato's καλὸν ψεῦδος or Wallace Stevens's supreme fiction:

> God's gift was that man should conceive of truth
> And yearn to gain it, catching at mistake,
> As midway help till he reach fact indeed.
> The statuary ere he mould a shape
> Boasts a like gift, the shape's idea, and next
> The aspiration to produce the same;
> So, taking clay, he calls his shape thereout,
> Cries ever "Now I have the thing I see":
> Yet all the while goes changing what was wrought
> From falsehood like the truth, to truth itself.

How were it had he cried "I see no face,
No breast, no feet i' the ineffectual clay"?
Rather commend him that he clapped his hands,
And laughed, "It is my shape and lives again!"
Enjoyed the falsehood, touched it on to truth,
Until yourselves applaud the flesh indeed
In what is still flesh-imitating clay.
Right in you, right in him, such way be man's!
God only makes the live shape at a jet. (605–23)

Is this a satisfactory answer? Opinions will differ. There is little doubt that Browning found it so, provoking thereby Thomas Hardy's exasperated comment that his smug optimism was "worthy of a dissenting grocer." For those, like Hardy, unprepared to make the leap of faith into "truth itself," *A Death in the Desert* is unlikely to seem anything more than "a falsehood like the truth."

Epilogue

Browning was good at getting inside other people's skins; in fact, it was what he was best at. His most famous poem, *My Last Duchess*, was an early illustration of this chameleon-like skill; and many of his very greatest works figure in two collections, *Men and Women* (1855) *and Dramatis Personae* (1864) in which a remarkable series of vividly portrayed characters appear upon the stage he has constructed for them, all exhibiting the strange *introspection d'autrui* that Charles du Bos rightly perceived to be Browning's special talent.

Among these the Saint John of *A Death in the Desert* occupies a particular place. No one is likely to appeal directly to, say, Bishop Blougram (= Cardinal Wiseman) or Mr Sludge (= E. E. Home, the American medium) for insight into the poet's deepest beliefs, although no doubt some of these have slipped into the interstices. But *A Death in the Desert* is a different story. Having read, like his creator, the best-known works of Ludwig Feuerbach (*Das Wesen des Christentums*) and Ernest Renan (*Vie de Jésus*), the dying apostle attempts to confront their arguments and find a satisfactory answer to them.

It might be objected that this in itself does not entitle us to treat Saint John's words as a direct expression of his creator's opinions. But at the end of the collection in which this poem appears, *Dramatis Personae*, there is an epilogue for three speakers, the first unmistakably King David, the second later identified (by Browning) as Renan, and the third the poet himself, speaking for once *in propria persona*: "Friends, I have seen through your eyes: now use mine!" (68).

The first speaker, King David, whose voice represents a time and a culture without doubts, concludes triumphantly:

> For the presence of the Lord,
> In the glory of His cloud,
> Had filled the House of the Lord. (19–21)

At this point he is interrupted by the second speaker, Renan, who resoundingly interjects:

> Gone now! All gone across the dark so far,
> Sharpening fast, shuddering ever, shutting still,
> Dwindling into the distance, dies that star
> Which came, stood, opened once! We gazed our fill
> With upturned faces on as real a Face
> That, stooping from grave music and mild fire,
> Took in our homage, made a visible place
> Through many a depth of glory, gyre on gyre,
> For the dim human tribute. Was this true? (22–30)

Not, certainly, for Renan: contemplating the vast expanse of the sky, he asks despairingly,

> How shall the sage detect in yon expanse
> The star which chose to stoop and stay for us? (50–51)

All that he himself can see in the vault of heaven is "a mist of multitudinous points." Unlike Saint John, whose greatest work (the Gospel) depended upon his ability to use points in order to construct stars, Renan renounces any attempt to do the same, and gloomily reflects on the disappearance of a face that is as much the face of God himself as it is the face of Christ, God's human representative.

In the thirty-six lines that conclude the poem, Browning reflects upon the diversity of humankind, each person fleetingly the center of the universe, "king of the current for a minute," until "the flock of waves" moves on to circle around another momentary king. Since the poet himself, throughout *Dramatis Personae*, has been acting in the manner of the waves, focusing briefly and tellingly upon one character after another, we cannot doubt his sincerity in celebrating the real if evanescent significance of each individual human being. This celebration, he reflects, is the work of the world as a whole, whose walls "divide us, each from another, me from you."

If the world can do this, he concludes, "Where's the need of Temple?" He confidently dismisses all that King David, the first of his three speakers, had lauded:

> What use of swells and falls
> From Levites' choirs, Priests' cries, and trumpet-calls?

Not for him, then, the pomp and circumstance of organized religion. In the final triplet, however, he summons back a being whose definitive disappearance the second speaker, Renan, had just been lamenting:

> That one Face, far from vanish, rather grows,
> Or decomposes but to recompose,
> Become my universe that feels and knows.

This, then, is Browning's response to Renan, not an argument but a strongly-felt refusal to accept the latter's colorfully worded banishment of Christ from the universe. For Browning, as for John, there was evidently enough material in the historical points that (despite the efforts of David Strauss) were still visible, to construct (or recompose) a star.

The disagreement persists into the twenty-first century.

John Ashton
13 June 1931 – 3 February 2016

Christopher Rowland

John was my friend and colleague, dialogue partner, and companion for forty years. The collection of essays, which he organized and presented to me to mark my retirement, remains a tangible token of our friendship. A mutual friend told me recently how excited John was about this initiative, how keen he was to keep it secret from me, and how he had almost told me on many occasions. That was so endearing—and so typical of him and his friendship, which so many of us enjoyed.

Close bonds of friendship were particularly evident in the last months of John's life, as his friends responded so readily to his needs, when his ability to cope with everyday life diminished. As someone who now lives a distance away from Oxford, I was struck by the way in which his Oxford friends, especially those from Wolfson College, rallied round and responded, to one who himself was a dear friend to them.

I have a vivid memory of my first meeting with John as he sat in the armchair in my tiny study in the University of Newcastle. Quite independently, John and I had been thinking along similar lines about the apocalyptic dimension of the Gospel of John. I remember our conversation that day about issues, which would eventually come to see the light of day in his two great books on the Gospel of John (*Understanding the Fourth Gospel*, 1991) and on the religion of Paul (*The Religion of Paul the Apostle*, 2000). I am thankful that John used his great literary gifts and wide reading to publish his original insights on the subject, preeminently in *Understanding the Fourth Gospel* published in his sixtieth year.

The Gospel of John stood at the center of John's research and writing through much of his adult life. Some years ago John shared with me a reflection, in which he narrated his developing understanding of the Gospel of John in relation to the story of his life. Although the reflection has until now remained unpublished, I have used it as my inspiration and guide for this valedictory tribute, because John himself was very keen to see it published as an introduction to his last essays on the Gospel of John. John gave his autobiographical reflection the title "Discovering the Gospel of John: A Fifty-Year Journey of Exploration." Reading the account of his journey of exploration of the Gospel told me almost as much about John himself as it did about what he had discovered about the Gospel and how his thinking had evolved. The section "Emerging from Depression" is relatively brief, but there is a stark clarity in his writing that is sad and very moving. It is testimony to John's extraordinary ability to survive what were clearly straitened, precarious circumstances, whilst still living with courage and integrity, even hope, however often hopes were dashed.

What came across to me as I read the narrative was a deep affinity between what he had written about his life and the subject matter of the Gospel of John. From my limited experience of the Spiritual Exercises of Ignatius of Loyola, I was struck by how much of the Exercises had stayed with John. After reading "Discovering the Gospel of John" when John sent it to me eighteen months before his death, I suggested to him that what I read was an account of the long and, at times, difficult exploration of his vocation, in which the Gospel Of John had been a *vademecum*; gospel text and life came together in an Ignatian way.

John's "Fifty-Year Journey of Exploration" of the Gospel of John began in 1964, the third year out of the four that John spent studying theology at a seminary in France. From those lectures he attended, John picked up two themes: firstly, that the opening verses of the Gospel are about God's plan for humankind; and secondly, there is a distinction between two moments of understanding, a partial one told within the story in the Gospel of John and a fuller understanding to be expected later (John 16:12–13). This is typical of apocalyptic literature, where often there is a distinction between two types of revelation, one shadowy and the other clear and explicit, and two *times* of revelation. The first is reserved for a few visionaries; only later will the apocalyptic mystery be made manifest to all. Such insights were complemented by John's discovery of the poetry of Wallace Stevens and the latter's insistence on the role of imagination in transforming into poetry the world around us. This is what John found in the Gospel as (and I quote John's words) "the visionary glow of the Johannine prophet has welded tradition and belief into the shining affirmation of the finished Gospel."[1] The Johannine Jesus speaks of the Spirit-Paraclete "bringing to remembrance" (John 14:26). As John put it elsewhere in a book published nearly twenty years before *Understanding the Fourth Gospel,* "remembrance is not simply a question of flashing a recorded image on to an inner screen. Suddenly, one remembers, and in remembering, grasps the full significance of the event or remark for the first time: 'Ah, now I understand what he meant when he said such and such.'"[2] There were many such moments in John's own intellectual journey when he recalled, understood, and grasped the full significance of comment or event for the first time and bequeathed that insight to us in what he has written in a string of books and articles over the last thirty years.

It is no surprise that it was John who first introduced me to Robert Browning's "A Death in the Desert," and some lines by Browning about John the seer and evangelist capture so well John's developing understanding of the Gospel of John:

> Since much that at the first, in deed and word,
>
> Lay simply and sufficiently exposed,
>
> Had grown (or else my soul was grown to match,
>
> Fed through such years, familiar with such light,
>
> Guarded and guided still to see and speak)
>
> Of new significance and fresh result;
>
> What first were guessed as points, I now knew stars,
>
> And named them in the Gospel I have writ.

I conclude with some more words from the Gospel of John that take me back to where I started. "You are my friends," Jesus tells those with whom he sat down to eat on the eve of his death. The language about friendship in these verses is distinctive and has few parallels elsewhere in the other gospels (Luke 12:4 is an exception). It links the biblical text, to which John devoted so much of his intellectual energy and creativity, with how he lived, loving and being loved by his friends, to the very end. John remained true to his vocation, intellectually and personally. It worked out

---

1. Ashton, *Understanding the Fourth Gospel,* 1st edition, 434.

2. Ashton, *Why Were the Gospels Written?,* 80–82.

so providentially in Oxford, where friendship was the key—in the humane and friendly environment of Wolfson College, which was literally his home for many years, but home in more ways than one; with friends, colleagues, and former students, especially those in Oxford's Faculty of Theology, which was so blessed to have such a distinguished exegete in its midst; with his own family; and also, particularly in the last thirty years, with the worldwide biblical studies community.

John, friend and gifted student of the gospel which bears your name, we shall miss you greatly.

Bibliography

Ashe, Geoffrey. *King Arthur's Avalon: The Story of Glastonbury.* London: Collins, 1957.

Ashton, John. "Bridging Ambiguities." In *Studying John: Approaches to the Fourth Gospel,* 71–89. Oxford: Clarendon, 1994.

———. "Browning on Feuerbach and Renan." In *Sense and Sensitivity: Essays on Reading the Bible in Memory of Robert Carroll,* edited by Alastair G. Hunter and Phillip R. Davies, 374–94. JSOTSup 348. Sheffield: Sheffield Academic Press, 2002.

———. *The Gospel of John and Christian Origins.* Minneapolis: Fortress, 2014.

———. *The Interpretation of John.* London: SPCK, 1986.

———. "The Johannine Son of Man: A Proposal." *New Testament Studies* 57 (2011) 508–29.

———. "John and the Johannine Literature: The Woman at the Well." In *The Cambridge Companion to Biblical Interpretation,* edited by John Barton, 259–75. Cambridge: Cambridge University Press, 1998.

———. "'Mystery' in the Dead Sea Scrolls and the Fourth Gospel." In *John, Qumran, and the Dead Sea Scrolls: Sixty Years of Discovery and Debate,* edited by Mary L. Coloe and Tom Thatcher, 53–68. Early Judaism and Its Literature 32. Atlanta: Society of Biblical Literature, 2011.

———. *The Religion of Paul the Apostle.* New Haven: Yale University Press, 2000.

———. "Riddles and Mysteries: The Way, the Truth, and the Life." In *Jesus in Johannine Tradition,* edited by Robert T. Fortna and Tom Thatcher, 333–42. Louisville: Westminster John Knox, 2001.

———. "Second Thoughts on the Fourth Gospel." In *What We Have Heard from the Beginning: The Past, Present, and Future of Johannine Studies,* edited by Tom Thatcher, 1–18. Waco: Baylor University Press, 2007.

———. *Studying John: Approaches to the Fourth Gospel.* Oxford: Clarendon, 1994.

———. "The Transformation of Wisdom: A Study of the Prologue of John's Gospel." *NTS* 32 (1986) 161–86.

———. *Understanding the Fourth Gospel.* 1st ed. Oxford: Clarendon, 1991; 2nd ed. Oxford: Clarendon, 2007.

———. *Why Were the Gospels Written?* Cork: Mercier, 1973.

Ashton, John, ed. *Revealed Wisdom: Studies in Apocalyptic in Honour of Christopher Rowland.* Ancient Judaism and Early Christianity 88. Leiden: Brill, 2014.

Ashton, John, and Tom Whyte. *The Quest for Paradise: Visions of Heaven and Eternity in the World's Myths and Religions.* New York: HarperCollins, 2001.

Aune, David E. *The Cultic Setting of Realized Eschatology in Early Christianity.* Supplements to Novum Testamentum 28. Leiden: Brill, 1972.

Barrett, C. K. *The Gospel According to St. John.* 2nd ed. London: SPCK, 1978.

——. *The Gospel of John and Judaism: The Franz Delitzsch Lectures, University of Münster, 1967.* Translated from the German by D. M. Smith. London: SPCK, 1975.

——. *The Prologue of St. John's Gospel.* London: Athlone, 1971.

Batey, Richard A. *Jesus and the Forgotten City: New Light on Sepphoris and the Urban World of Jesus.* Grand Rapids: Baker, 1991.

Bauckham, Richard. "The Beloved Disciple as Ideal Author." *Journal for the Study of the New Testament* 15 (1993) 21–44.

——. *Jesus and the Eyewitnesses: The Gospels as Eyewitness Testimony.* Grand Rapids: Eerdmans, 2006.

——. "Papias and Polycrates on the Origin of the Fourth Gospel." *The Journal of Theological Studies* 44 (1993) 24–69.

——. *The Testimony of the Beloved Disciple: Narrative, History, and Theology in the Gospel of John.* Grand Rapids: Baker Academic, 2007.

Bauckham, Richard, ed. *The Gospel for All Christians: Rethinking the Gospel Audiences.* Edinburgh: T. & T. Clark, 1998.

Beasley-Murray, George R. *John.* Word Biblical Commentary 36. Waco: Word Books, 1987.

Becker, Jürgen. *Das Evangelium des Johannes.* Ökumenischer Taschenbuch-Kommentar zum Neuen Testament 4/1–2. Gütersloh: Gerd Mohn, 1979, 1981.

——. "Das Verhältnis des johanneischen Kreises zum Paulinismus. Anregung zur Belebung einer Diskussion." In *Paulus und Johannes. Exegetische Studien zur paulinischen und johanneischen Theologie und Literatur,* edited by Dieter Sänger and Ulrich Mell, 473–95. WUNT 198. Tübingen: Mohr Siebeck, 2006.

Bennett, Zoë, and David B. Gowler, eds. *Radical Christian Voices and Practice: Essays in Honour of Christopher Rowland.* Oxford: Oxford University Press, 2012.

Blass, Friedrich, and Albert Debrunner. *A Greek Grammar of the New Testament and other Early Christian Literature.* Translated and edited by Robert W. Funk. Chicago: University of Chicago Press, 1961.

Bligh, John. "Jesus in Samaria." *The Heythrop Journal* 3 (1962) 329–46.

Boers, Hendrikus. *Neither on This Mountain Nor in Jerusalem: A Study of John 4.* SBL Monograph Series 35. Atlanta: Scholars, 1988.

Borgen, Peder. "God's Agent in the Fourth Gospel." In *Religions in Antiquity: Essays in Memory of Erwin Ramsdell Goodenough,* edited by Jacob Neusner, 137–48. Leiden: Brill, 1968.

——. "Some Jewish Exegetical Traditions as Background for Son of Man Sayings in John's Gospel (John 3,13–14 and Context)." In *L'Évangile de Jean: Sources, rédaction, théologie,* edited by Marinus de Jonge, 243–58. BETL 44. Leuven: Louvain University Press, 1977.

Botha, J. Eugene. *Jesus and the Samaritan Woman: A Speech Act Reading of John 4.1–42.* Supplements to Novum Testamentum 65. Leiden: Brill, 1991.

——. "John 4:16a: A Difficult Text Speech Act Theoretically Revisited." In *The Gospel of John as Literature: An Anthology of Twentieth-Century Perspectives,* edited by Mark W. G. Stibbe, 183–92. New Testament Tools and Studies 17. Leiden: Brill, 1993.

Bretschneider, Karl Gottlieb. *Probabilia de evangelii et epistularum Joannis apostoli, indole et origine eruditorum judiciis modeste subjecit.* Leipzig: Barth, 1820.

Brown, Raymond E. *The Community of the Beloved Disciple: The Life, Loves and Hates of an Individual Church in New Testament Times.* London: Geoffrey Chapman, 1979.

———. *The Gospel According to John*. 2 vols. Anchor Bible 29 and 29A. New York: Doubleday, 1966, 1970.

———. *New Testament Essays*. New York: Paulist, 1965.

Bühner, Jan-Adolf. *Der Gesandte und sein Weg im 4. Evangelium: Die kultur- und religionsgeschichtlichen Grundlagen der johanneischen Sendungschristologie sowie ihre traditionsgeschichtliche Entwicklung*. WUNT 2/2. Tübingen: Mohr Siebeck, 1977.

Bultmann, Rudolf. "Der religionsgeschichtliche Hintergrund des Prologs zum Johannes-evangelium." In *Eucharisterion: Studien zur Religion und Literatur des Alten und Neuen Testaments: Hermann Gunkel zum 60. Geburtstag*, edited by Hans Schmidt, 2:3–26. Göttingen: Vandenhoeck & Ruprecht, 1923.

———. "Die Bedeutung der neuerschlossenen mandäischen und manichäischen Quellen für das Verständnis des Johanesevangeliums." *ZNW* 24 (1925) 100–46.

———. "Die Eschatologie des Johannesevangeliums," *Zwischen den Zeiten* 6 (1928) 4–22 (translated into English as "The Eschatology of the Gospel of John." In *Faith and Understanding I: Collected Essays*, edited by Robert W. Funk and translated by Louise Pettibone Smith, 165–83. London: SCM, 1969).

———. *Die Geschichte der synoptischen Tradition*. FRLANT 29. 7th ed. Göttingen: Vandenhoeck & Ruprecht, 1967.

———. *The Gospel of John: A Commentary*. Translated by G. R. Beasley-Murray et al. Philadelphia: Westminster, 1971 (= *Das Evangelium des Johannes*. Göttingen: Vandenhoeck & Ruprecht, 1941).

———. "Johannesevangelium." In *Religion in Geschichte und Gegenwart*, cols. 840–50. 3rd ed. Tübingen: Mohr Siebeck, 1959.

———. *Theology of the New Testament*. Translated by Kendrick Grobel. 2 vols. London: SCM, 1955 (= *Theologie des Neuen Testaments*. 2 vols. Tübingen: Mohr Siebeck, 1948, 1953).

Burkitt, F. Crawford. *Evangelion da-Mepharreshe: The Curetonian Version of the Four Gospels*. 2 vols. Cambridge: Cambridge University Press, 1904.

Carmichael, Calum M. "Marriage and the Samaritan Woman." *NTS* 26 (1980) 332–46.

Charlesworth, James H., ed. *The Dead Sea Scrolls: Hebrew, Aramaic, and Greek Texts with English Translations*. Vol. 1, *Rule of the Community and Related Documents*. PTSDSSP. Louisville: Westminster John Knox, 1994.

———. *The Old Testament Pseudepigrapha*. 2 vols. London: Darton, Longman & Todd, 1983, 1985.

Chilton, Bruce D. "The Transfiguration: Dominical Appearance and Apostolic Vision." *NTS* 27 (1980–81) 115–24.

Collins, John J. "Apocalyptic Eschatology as the Transcendence of Death." *CBQ* 36 (1974) 21–43.

———. "The Eschatologizing of Wisdom in the Dead Sea Scrolls." In *Sapiential Perspectives: Wisdom Literature in Light of the Dead Sea Scrolls: Proceedings of the Sixth International Symposium of the Orion Center for the Study of the Dead Sea Scrolls and Associated Literature, 20–22 May, 2001*, edited by John J. Collins et al., 49–65. STDJ 51. Leiden: Brill, 2004.

———. "The Mysteries of God: Creation and Eschatology in 4QInstruction and the Wisdom of Solomon." In *Wisdom and Apocalypticism in the Dead Sea Scrolls and in the Biblical Tradition*, edited by Florentino García Martínez, 287–305. BETL 168. Leuven: Leuven University, 2003.

———. "Qumran, Apocalypticism, and the New Testament." In *The Dead Sea Scrolls Fifty Years After Their Discovery: Proceedings of the Jerusalem Congress, July 20-25, 1997*, edited by Lawrence H. Schiffman et al., 133–38. Jerusalem: Israel Exploration Society and the Shrine of the Book, 2000.

Coloe, Mary L., and Tom Thatcher, eds. *John, Qumran, and the Dead Sea Scrolls: Sixty Years of Discovery and Debate*. Early Judaism and Its Literature 32. Atlanta: Society of Biblical Literature, 2011.

Colpe, Carsten. "ὁ υἱὸς τοῦ ἀνθρώπου." *TDNT* 8 (1972) 400–77.

Conzelmann, Hans. "Present and Future in the Synoptic Tradition." *Journal for Theology and the Church* 5 (1968) 26–44.

Cross, Frank M. *The Ancient Library of Qumran and Modern Biblical Studies*. Garden City, New York: Doubleday, 1958.

Culpepper, R. Alan. "C. H. Dodd as a Precursor to Narrative Criticism." In *Engaging with C.H. Dodd on the Gospel of John*, edited by Tom Thatcher and Catrin H. Williams, 31–65. Cambridge: Cambridge University Press, 2013.

———. *The Gospel and Letters of John*. IBT. Nashville: Abingdon, 1998.

———. "Guessing Points and Knowing Stars: History and Higher Criticism in Robert Browning's 'A Death in the Desert.'" In *The Future of Christology: Essays in Honor of Leander E. Keck*, edited by Abraham J. Malherbe and Wayne A. Meeks, 53–65. Minneapolis: Fortress, 1993.

———. *John, the Son of Zebedee: The Life of a Legend*. Edinburgh: T. & T. Clark, 2000.

———. "The Pivot of John's Prologue." *NTS* 27 (1980–81) 1–31.

Daube, David. "Jesus and the Samaritan Woman: The Meaning of συγχράομαι." *JBL* 69 (1950) 137–47.

Davies, Philip R. "Death, Resurrection, and Life after Death in the Qumran Scrolls." In *Judaism in Late Antiquity, Part Four: Death, Life-after-Death, Resurrection and the World-to-Come in the Judaisms of Antiquity*, edited by Alan J. Avery-Peck and Jacob Neusner, 189–211. Leiden: Brill, 2000.

de Jonge, Marinus. *Jesus: Stranger from Heaven and Son of God: Jesus Christ and the Christians in Johannine Perspective*, edited and translated by John E. Steely. SBL Sources for Biblical Study 11. Missoula: Scholars, 1977.

de la Potterie, Ignace. "De sensu vocis 'emet in Vetere Testamento." *Verbum Domini* 27 (1949) 336–54.

———. "L'arrière-fond du thème johannique de vérité dans saint Jean." In *Studia Evangelica I*, edited by Kurt Aland et al., 277–94. Texte und Untersuchungen 73. Berlin: Akademie-Verlag, 1959.

———. *La vérité dans saint Jean*. 2 vols. Analecta Biblica 73–74. Rome: Biblical Institute, 1977.

Dickens, Charles. "Old Lamps for New Ones." *Household Words* 1 (15 June, 1850) 12–14.

Dodd, C. H. "A Hidden Parable in the Fourth Gospel." In *More New Testament Essays*, 30–40. Manchester: Manchester University Press, 1968.

———. *Historical Tradition in the Fourth Gospel*. Cambridge: Cambridge University Press, 1963.

———. *The Interpretation of the Fourth Gospel*. Cambridge: Cambridge University Press, 1953.

Drew, Philip. *The Poetry of Browning: A Critical Introduction*. London: Methuen, 1970.

Drewermann, Eugen. *Tiefenpsychologie und Exegese: Die Wahrheit der Formen / Die Warhheit der Werke und der Worte*. 2 vols. 2nd ed. Olten: Walter, 1991.

Dürr, Lorenz. *Das Erziehungswesen im Alten Testament und im Antiken Orient*. Leipzig: Hinrichs, 1932.

Dunn, James D. G. "Let John Be John: A Gospel for its Time." In *The Gospel and the Gospels*, edited by Peter Stuhlmacher, 293–322. Grand Rapids: Eerdmans, 1991.

Elgvin, Torleif. "The Mystery to Come: Early Essene Theology of Revelation." In *Qumran Between the Old and New Testaments*, edited by Frederick H. Cryer and Thomas L. Thompson, 113–50. JSOT Supplement Series 290. Sheffield: Sheffield Academic, 1998.

———. "Wisdom and Apocalypticism in the Early Second Century BCE." In *The Dead Sea Scrolls Fifty Years after their Discovery: Proceedings of the Jerusalem Congress, July 20–25, 1997*, edited by Lawrence H. Schiffman et al., 226–47. Jerusalem: Israel Exploration Society and the Shrine of the Book, 2000.

———. "Wisdom at Qumran." In *Judaism in Late Antiquity, Part Five: The Judaism of Qumran: A Systemic Reading of the Dead Sea Scrolls*, edited by Alan J. Avery-Peck et al., 2:147–69. Leiden: Brill, 2001.

Emerton, John A. "Melchizedek and the Gods: Fresh Evidence for the Jewish Background of John 10:34–36." *The Journal of Theological Studies* 17 (1966) 399–401.

Eslinger, Lyle. "The Wooing of the Woman at the Well: Jesus, the Reader and Reader-Response Criticism." *Literature and Theology* 1 (1987) 167–83.

Feuerbach, Ludwig. *The Essence of Christianity*. Translated by Marian Evans. London: Chapman, 1854.

Fitzmyer, Joseph A. *Sapiential Texts, Part 1*. DJD 15. Oxford: Clarendon, 1997.

———. *Qumran Cave 4*. DJD 20. Oxford: Clarendon, 2000.

———. "Qumran Literature and the Johannine Writings." In *Life in Abundance: Studies of John's Gospel in Tribute to Raymond E. Brown*, edited by John R. Donahue, 117–33. Collegeville: Liturgical, 2005.

Fletcher-Louis, Crispin H. T. *All the Glory of Adam: Liturgical Anthropology in the Dead Sea Scrolls*. STDJ 42. Leiden: Brill, 2002.

Fortna, Robert T. *The Gospel of Signs: A Reconstruction of the Narrative Source Underlying the Fourth Gospel*. SNTS Monograph Series 11. Cambridge: Cambridge University Press, 1970.

Fossum, Jarl E. "Ascensio, Metamorphosis: The 'Transfiguration' of Jesus in the Synoptic Gospels." In *The Image of the Invisible God: Essays on the Influence of Jewish Mysticism on Early Christology*, 71–94. Freiburg: Universitätsverlag, 1995.

Frey, Jörg. *Die johanneische Eschatologie. Band 2: Das johanneische Zeitverständnis*. WUNT 110. Tübingen: Mohr Siebeck, 1998.

Gaechter, Paul. "Zur Form von Joh. 5.19–30." In *Neutestamentliche Aufsätze: Festschrift für Professor Josef Schmid zum 70. Geburtstag*, edited by Josef Blinzler et al., 65–68. Regensburg: Pustet, 1963.

García Martínez, Florentino. *The Dead Sea Scrolls Translated: The Qumran Texts in English*. Leiden: Brill, 1997.

García Martínez, Florentino, and Eibert J. C. Tigchelaar, eds. *The Dead Sea Scrolls Study Edition*. 2 vols. Leiden: Brill, 1997.

Genette, Gérard. *Figures III*. Paris: Seuil, 1972.

Goetz, Joseph. "Mythe." In *Dictionnaire de spiritualité ascétique et mystique, doctrine et histoire*, edited by Marcel Viller et al., 10:1985–86. Paris: Beauchesne, 1980.

Gunkel, Hermann. "Ziele und Methoden der Erklärung des Alten Testaments." In *Reden und Aufsätze*, 11–29. Göttingen: Vandenhoeck & Ruprecht, 1913.

Haacker, Klaus. "Gottesdienst ohne Gotteserkenntnis. Joh 4,22 vor dem Hintergrund der jüdisch-samaritanischen Auseinandersetzung." In *Wort und Wirklichkeit. Studien zur Afrikanistik und Orientalistik. Teil 1: Geschichte und Religionswissenschaft - Bibliographie. Festschrift für Eugen Ludwig Rapp*, edited by Brigitta Benzing, et al., 1:110–26. Meisenheim am Glan: Hain, 1976.

Haenchen, Ernst. *John 1*. Translated Robert W. Funk. Hermeneia: Philadelphia: Fortress, 1984.

Harnack, Adolf von. *Geschichte der altchristlichen Litteratur bis Eusebius*. Volume II.1. Leipzig: Hinrichs, 1887.

———. *Lehrbuch der Dogmengeschichte*. Tübingen: Mohr Siebeck, 1931.

———. "Über das Verhältniß des Prologs des vierten Evangeliums zum ganzen Werk." *Zeitschrift für Theologie und Kirche* 2 (1892) 189–231.

Harrington, Daniel J. "Two Early Jewish Approaches to Wisdom: Sirach and Qumran Sapiential Work A." In *The Wisdom Texts from Qumran and the Development of Sapiential Thought*, edited by Charlotte Hempel et al., 263–76. BETL 159. Leuven: Leuven University, 2002.

———. *Wisdom Texts from Qumran*. London: Routledge, 1996.

Harrington, Daniel J., and John Strugnell. "Qumran Cave 4 Texts: A New Publication." *JBL* 112 (1993) 491–99.

Harris, J. Rendel. "The Origin of the Prologue to John's Gospel." *Expositor* 12 (1916) 147–70; 314–20; 388–400; 415–26.

Hengel, Martin. *Die johanneische Frage. Ein Lösungsversuch. Mit einem Beitrag zur Apokalypse von Jörg Frey*. WUNT 67. Tübingen: Mohr Siebeck, 1993.

———. *The Johannine Question*. London: SCM, 1989.

———. "The Prologue of the Gospel of John as the Gateway to Christological Truth." In *The Gospel of John and Christian Theology*, edited by Richard Bauckham and Carl Mosser, 265–94. Grand Rapids: Eerdmans, 2008.

Hill, Charles E. *The Johannine Corpus in the Early Church*. Oxford: Oxford University Press, 2004.

Holmes, Michael W. *The Apostolic Fathers: Greek Texts and English Translations*. 3rd ed. Grand Rapids: Baker Academic, 2007.

Hooker, Morna D. *Beginnings: Keys that Open the Gospels*. London: SCM, 1997.

Jolles, André. *Einfache Formen: Legende, Sage, Mythe, Rätsel, Spruch, Kasus, Memorabile, Märchen, Witz*. Tübingen: Niemayer, 1982.

Jones, Maurice. *The New Testament in the Twentieth Century*. London: Macmillan, 1914.

Käsemann, Ernst. *Jesu Letzer Wille nach Johannes 17*. 3rd ed. Tübingen: Mohr Siebeck, 1980.

Kelso, James A. "Riddle." In *Encyclopaedia of Religion and Ethics*, edited by James Hastings, 10:765–70. Edinburgh: T. & T. Clark, 1918.

Kenny, Anthony. *Christianity in Review: A History of the Faith in 50 Books*. London: Darton, Longman & Todd, 2015.

Kierkegaard, Søren. *The Philosophical Fragments, or, A Fragment of Philosophy*. Translated and edited by David F. Swenson et al. Princeton: Princeton University Press, 1962.

Kister, Menahem. "Wisdom Literature and Its Relation to Other Genres: From Ben Sira to *Mysteries*." In *Sapiential Perspectives: Wisdom Literature in Light of the Dead Sea*

Scrolls: Proceedings of the Sixth International Symposium of the Orion Center for the Study of the Dead Sea Scrolls and Associated Literature, 20–22 May, 2001, edited by John J. Collins et al., 13–47. STDJ 51. Leiden: Brill, 2004.

Koester, Craig R. Review of *Understanding the Fourth Gospel*, by John Ashton. *Review of Biblical Literature* (2009).

————. *Symbolism in the Fourth Gospel: Meaning, Mystery, Community*. Minneapolis: Fortress, 1995.

Kovacs, Judith. "'Now Shall the Ruler of This World be Driven Out': Jesus' Death as Cosmic Battle in John 12:20–36." *JBL* 114 (1995) 227–47.

Kuhn, Karl Georg. "Die in Palästina gefundenen hebräischen Texte und das neue Testament." *Zeitschrift für Theologie und Kirche* 47 (1950) 192–211.

Kümmel, Werner Georg. *Introduction to the New Testament*. Rev. ed., London: SCM, 1975.

Lagrange, Marie-Joseph. *Évangile selon saint Jean*. 7th ed. Paris: Gabalda, 1948.

Lamarche, Paul. "Le Prologue de Jean." *Recherches de science religieuse* 52 (1964) 529–32.

Lange, Armin. *Weisheit und Prädestination: Weisheitliche Urordnung und Prädestination in den Textfunden von Qumran*. STDJ 18. Leiden: Brill, 1995.

Lausberg, Heinrich. *Der Johannes-Prolog. Rhetorische Befunde zu Form und Sinn des Textes*. NAWG 5. Göttingen: Vandenhoeck & Ruprecht, 1984.

Lee, Dorothy A. *The Symbolic Narratives of the Fourth Gospel: The Interplay of Form and Meaning*. JSNT Supplement Series 95. Sheffield: JSOT, 1994.

Leroy, Herbert. *Rätsel und Missverständnis: Ein Beitrag zur Formgeschichte des Johannesevangeliums*. Bonner Biblische Beiträge 30. Bonn: Hannstein, 1968.

Léon-Dufour, Xavier. *Lecture de l'Évangile selon Jean, Vol. 1*. Paris: Seuil, 1988.

————. "Le signe du Temple selon saint Jean." *Recherches de science religieuse* 39 (1951–52) 155–75.

Lieu, Judith M. *The Theology of the Johannine Epistles*. Cambridge: Cambridge University, 1991.

Lightfoot, Joseph Barber. *The Apostolic Fathers*. London: Macmillan, 1889.

Lincoln, Andrew T. *The Gospel According to Saint John*. BNTC. London: Continuum, 2005.

Lindars, Barnabas. *Behind the Fourth Gospel*. London: SPCK, 1971.

————. *The Gospel of John*. NCB Commentary. London: Marshall, Morgan & Scott, 1972.

Link, Andrea. *Was redest du mit ihr? Eine Studie zur Exegese-, Redaktions- und Theologiegeschichte von Joh 4,1–42*. Biblische Untersuchungen 24. Regensburg: Pustet, 1992.

Lohfink, Norbert. "Die deuteronomistische Darstellung des Übergangs der Führung Israels von Moses auf Josue: Ein Beitrag zur alttestamentlichen Theologie des Amtes." *Scholastik* 37 (1962) 32–44.

Lohse, Eduard. *Die Texte aus Qumran: Hebräisch und Deutsch mit masoretischer Punktation. Übersetzung, Einführung und Anmerkungen*. München: Kösel, 1971.

Loisy, Alfred. *Le quatrième évangile*. Paris: Picard, 1903.

Macdonald, John, trans. *Memar Marqah: The Teaching of Marqah*. 2 vols. BZAW 84. Berlin: Töpelmann, 1963.

Malina, Bruce J., and Richard L. Rohrbaugh. *Social-Science Commentary on the Gospel of John*. Minneapolis: Fortress, 1998.

Martyn, J. Louis. "Glimpses into the History of the Johannine Community." In *L'Évangile de Jean: Sources, rédaction, théologie*, edited by Marinus de Jonge, 149–75. BETL 44. Leuven: Leuven University Press, 1977.

———. *The Gospel of John in Christian History: Essays for Interpreters*. New York: Paulist, 1978.

———. *History and Theology in the Fourth Gospel*. 1st ed. Louisville: Westminster John Knox, 1968; 3rd ed. Louisville: Westminster John Knox, 2003.

———. "Source Criticism and *Religionsgeschichte* in the Fourth Gospel." In *Jesus and Man's Hope*, edited by Donald G. Millar, 1:247–73. Pittsburgh: Pittsburgh Theological Seminary, 1970.

Meeks, Wayne A. "'Equal to God.'" In *The Conversation Continues: Studies in Paul and John in Honor of J. Louis Martyn*, edited by Robert T. Fortna and Beverly R. Gaventa, 309–22. Nashville: Abingdon, 1990.

———. "The Man from Heaven in Johannine Sectarianism." *JBL* 91 (1972) 44–72.

———. *The Prophet King: Moses Traditions and the Johannine Christology*. NovTSupp 14. Leiden: Brill, 1967.

Merenlahti, Petri. *Poetics for the Gospels? Rethinking Narrative Criticism*. Studies of the New Testament and its World. London: T. & T. Clark, 2002.

Milik, J. T., and Dominique Barthélemy. *Qumran Cave 1*. DJD. Oxford: Clarendon, 1955.

Moore, Stephen D. "Are There Impurities in the Living Water that the Johannine Jesus Dispenses? Deconstruction, Feminism, and the Samaritan Woman." *Biblical Interpretation* 1 (1993) 207–27.

Newsom, Carol A. *The Self as Symbolic Space: Constructing Identity and Community at Qumran*. Atlanta: Society of Biblical Literature, 2004.

Neyrey, Jerome H. *The Gospel of John*. New Cambridge Bible Commentary. Cambridge: Cambridge University Press, 2007.

———. "Jacob Traditions and the Interpretation of John 4:10–26." *CBQ* 41 (1979) 419–37.

Nickelsburg, George W. E. *1 Enoch 1: A Commentary on the Book of 1 Enoch*. Hermeneia: Minneapolis: Fortress, 2001.

———. *Resurrection, Immortality and Eternal Life in Intertestamental Judaism*. Harvard Theological Studies 26. Cambridge: Harvard University Press, 1972.

O'Day, Gail R. *Revelation in the Fourth Gospel: Narrative Mode and Theological Claim*. Philadelphia: Fortress, 1986.

Odeberg, Hugo. *The Fourth Gospel Interpreted in its Relation to Contemporaneous Religious Currents in Palestine and the Hellenistic-Oriental World*. Uppsala: Almquist & Wiksell, 1929.

Okure, Teresa. *The Johannine Approach to Mission. A Contextual Study of John 4:1–42*. WUNT 2/31. Tübingen: Mohr Siebeck, 1988.

Olsson, Birger. *Structure and Meaning in the Fourth Gospel: A Text-Linguistic Analysis of John 2:1–11 and 4:1–42*. Coniectanea Biblica 6. Lund: Gleerup, 1974.

Pollard, T. Evan. "Cosmology and the Prologue of the Fourth Gospel." *Vigiliae Christianae* 12 (1958) 147–53.

Porzig, Walter. "Das Rätsel im Rigveda: Ein Beitrag zum Kapitel 'Sondersprache.'" In *GERMANICA: Festschrift für Eduard Sievers zum 75. Geburtstage*, 646–60. Halle an der Saale: Niemayer, 1925.

Renan, Ernest. *Vie de Jésus*. Paris: Gallimard, 1974.

Reynolds, Benjamin E. *The Apocalyptic Son of Man in the Gospel of John.* WUNT 2/249. Tübingen: Mohr Siebeck, 2008.

Richter, Georg. *Studien zum Johannesevangelium.* Biblische Untersuchungen 13. Regensburg: Pustet, 1977.

Ridderbos, Herman N. *The Gospel of John: A Theological Commentary.* Grand Rapids: Eerdmans, 1997.

Rofé, Alexander. "Revealed Wisdom: From the Bible to Qumran." In *Sapiential Perspectives: Wisdom Literature in Light of the Dead Sea Scrolls: Proceedings of the Sixth International Symposium of the Orion Center for the Study of the Dead Sea Scrolls and Associated Literature, 20–22 May, 2001,* edited by John J. Collins et al., 1–11. STDJ 51. Leiden: Brill, 2004.

Roustang, François. "Les moments de l'acte de foi et ses conditions de possibilité. Essai d'interprétation du dialogue avec la Samaritaine." *Recherches de science religieuse* 46 (1958) 344–78.

Rowland, Christopher. *The Open Heaven: A Study of Apocalyptic in Judaism and Early Christianity.* London: SPCK, 1982.

———. "'Open thy Mouth for the Dumb': A Task for the Exegete of Holy Scripture." *Biblical Interpretation* 1 (1993) 228–45.

Rowland, Christopher, and Christopher R. A. Morray-Jones. *The Mystery of God: Early Jewish Mysticism and the New Testament.* Compendia Rerum Iudaicarum ad Novum Testamentum 12. Leiden: Brill, 2009.

Rowland, Christopher, and Crispin H. T. Fletcher-Louis. *Understanding, Studying and Reading: New Testament Essays in Honour of John Ashton.* JSNT Supplement Series 153. Sheffield: Academic Press, 1998.

Sanders, E. P. *The Historical Figure of Jesus.* London: Penguin, 1993.

Sanders, J. N. *The Fourth Gospel in the Early Church: Its Origin and Influence on Christian Theology up to Irenaeus.* Cambridge: Cambridge University Press, 1943.

Schlatter, Adolf. *Der Evangelist Johannes. Wie er spricht, denkt und glaubt: Ein Kommentar zum vierten Evangelium.* 1st ed. Stuttgart: Calwer, 1930.

Schnackenburg, Rudolf. *The Gospel According to St. John.* Vol. 1. London: Burns & Oates, 1968.

Schneiders, Sandra M. "A Case Study: A Feminist Interpretation of John 4:1–42." In *The Revelatory Text: Interpreting the New Testament as Sacred Scripture,* 180–99. San Francisco: HarperCollins, 1991.

Schnelle, Udo. *Das Evangelium nach Johannes.* ThKNT 4. Leipzig: Evangelische Verlagsanstalt, 1998.

Schottroff, Luise. "Johannes 4,5–15 und die Konsequenzen des johanneischen Dualismus." *ZNW* 60 (1969) 199–214.

Schürer, Emil. "Über den gegenwärtigen Stand der johanneischen Frage." In *Johannes und sein Evangelium,* edited by Karl Heinrich Rengstorf, 1–27. Wege der Forschung 82. Darmstadt: Wissenschaftliche Buchgesellschaft, 1973.

Schüssler Fiorenza, Elisabeth. *In Memory of Her: A Feminist Theological Reconstruction of Christian Origins.* New York: Crossroads, 1983.

Schwartz, Eduard. "Aporien im vierten Evangelium." *Nachrichten vor der Königlichen Gesellschaft der Wissenschaft zu Göttingen: Philologisch-historische Klasse* (1907) 243–72; (1908) 115–48, 149–88, 497–650.

Shaffer, E. S. *"Kubla Khan" and the Fall of Jerusalem: The Mythological School in Biblical Criticism and Secular Literature 1770–1880.* Cambridge: Cambridge University Press, 1975.

Smith, D. Moody. *The Composition and Order of the Fourth Gospel: Bultmann's Literary Theory.* New Haven: Yale University Press, 1965.

———. "The Contribution of J. Louis Martyn to the Understanding of the Gospel of John." In *The Conversation Continues: Studies in Paul and John In Honor of J. Louis Martyn*, edited by Robert T. Fortna and Beverly R. Gaventa, 275–94. Nashville: Abingdon, 1990.

Smith, D. Morton. "The Origin and History of the Transfiguration Story." *Union Seminary Quarterly Review* 36 (1980) 39–44.

Stanton, Graham. "The Fourfold Gospel." *NTS* 43 (1997) 317–46.

Stevens, Wallace. *The Necessary Angel: Essays on Reality and the Imagination.* New York: Vintage, 1965.

———. *Opus Posthumous.* London: Faber & Faber, 1959.

Stibbe, Mark W. G. "Introduction." In *The Gospel of John as Literature: An Anthology of Twentieth-Century Perspectives*, 1–13. New Testament Tools and Studies 17. Leiden: Brill, 1993.

———. *John as Storyteller: Narrative Criticism and the Fourth Gospel.* SNTS Monograph Series 73. Cambridge: Cambridge University Press, 1994.

Stone, Michael E. *Fourth Ezra: A Commentary on the Book of Fourth Ezra.* Hermeneia: Minneapolis: Fortress, 1990.

———. "Lists of Revealed Things in the Apocalyptic Literature." In *Magnalia Dei: The Mighty Acts of God: Essays on the Bible and Archaeology in Memory of G. Ernest Wright*, edited by Frank Moore Cross et al., 414–52. Garden City: Doubleday, 1976.

Streeter, B. H. *The Four Gospels: A Study of Origins.* London: Macmillan, 1924.

Strugnell, John, et al., eds. *Qumran Cave 4.* DJD 34. Oxford: Clarendon, 1999.

———. *4QInstruction (Sapiential Texts) Part 2.* DJD 24. Oxford: Clarendon, 2000.

Stuckenbruck, Loren T. "4QInstruction and the Possible Influence of Early Enochic Traditions: An Evaluation." In *The Wisdom Texts from Qumran and the Development of Sapiential Thought*, edited by Charlotte Hempel et al., 245–61. BETL 159. Leuven: Leuven University, 2002.

Talbert, Charles H. "The Myth of a Descending-Ascending Redeemer in Mediterranean Antiquity." *NTS* 22 (1975–76) 418–43.

Thatcher, Tom, ed. *What We Have Heard from the Beginning: The Past, Present, and Future of Johannine Studies.* Waco: Baylor University Press, 2007.

Thatcher, Tom, and Catrin H. Williams, eds. *Engaging with C. H. Dodd on the Gospel of John: Sixty Years of Tradition and Interpretation.* Cambridge: Cambridge University Press, 2013.

Theobald, Michael. *Das Evangelium nach Johannes: Kapitel 1–12.* RNT. Regensburg: Pustet, 2009.

———. *Die Fleischwerdung des Logos: Studien zum Verhältnis des Johannesprologs zum Corpus des Evangeliums und zu 1 Joh.* Neutestamentliche Abhandlungen NF 20. Münster: Aschendorff, 1988.

———. *Herrenworte im Johannesevangelium.* Herders Biblische Studien 34. Freiburg: Herder, 2002.

Thyen, Hartwig. *Das Johannesevangelium.* HNT 6. Tübingen: Mohr Siebeck, 2005.

Turner, E. G. *Greek Manuscripts of the Ancient World*. 2nd ed. London: Institute of Classical Studies, 1987.

Van Belle, Gilbert, ed. *The Death of Jesus in the Fourth Gospel*. BETL 200. Leuven: Leuven University Press, 2007.

van Unnik, W. C. "The Purpose of St. John's Gospel." In *Studia Evangelica I*, edited by Kurt Aland et al., 382–411. Texte und Untersuchungen 73. Berlin: Akademie-Verlag, 1959.

Vermes, Geza. *The Complete Dead Sea Scrolls in English*. London: Penguin, 1997.

von Aberle, Moritz. "Über den Zweck des Johannesevangeliums." *Theologische Quartalschrift* 42 (1861) 37–94.

Wacholder, Ben-Zion, and Martin Abegg Jr. *A Preliminary Edition of the Unpublished Dead Sea Scrolls: The Hebrew and Aramaic Texts from Cave Four*. Washington, DC: Biblical Archaeology Society, 1991.

Wellhausen, Julius. *Das Evangelium Johannis*. Berlin: Reimer, 1908.

Wilkens, Wilhelm. *Die Entstehungsgeschichte des vierten Evangeliums*. Zollikon: Evangelischer Verlag, 1958.

Williams, Catrin H. *I Am He: The Interpretation of 'Anî Hû' in Jewish and Early Christian Literature*. WUNT 2/113. Tübingen: Mohr Siebeck, 2000.

———. "'I Am' or 'I Am He'? Self-Declaratory Pronouncements in the Fourth Gospel and Rabbinic Tradition." In *Jesus in Johannine Tradition*, edited by Robert T. Fortna and Tom Thatcher, 343–52. Louisville: Westminster John Knox, 2001.

Williams, Catrin H., and Christopher Rowland, eds. *John's Gospel and Intimations of Apocalyptic*. London: Bloomsbury, 2013.

Windisch, Hans. "Jesus und der Geist im Johannes-Evangelium." In *Amicitiae Corolla: Essays Presented to James Rendel Harris on the Occasion of his Eightieth Birthday*, edited by H. G. Wood, 303–18. London: University of London, 1933.

Witherington, Ben, III. *John's Wisdom: A Commentary on the Fourth Gospel*. Cambridge: Lutterworth, 1995.

Wittengenstein, Ludwig. *Culture and Value*. Edited by Georg Henrik von Wright. Oxford: Blackwell, 1970.

Wrede, William. *Charakter und Tendenz des Johannesevangelium*. Tübingen: Mohr Siebeck, 1903.

———. *Das Messiasgehemnis in den Evangelien: Zugleich ein Beitrag zum Verständnis des Markusevangeliums*. Göttingen: Vandenhoeck & Ruprecht, 1901.

Zumstein, Jean. *Kreative Erinnerung. Relecture und Auslegung im Johannesevangelium*. 2nd ed. Zürich: Theologischer Verlag, 2004.

———. "Le prologue, seuil du quatrième évangile." *Recherches de science religieuse* 83 (1995) 217–59.

Index of Names and Subjects

Index of Sources

∽   ∽

∽

CPSIA information can be obtained
at www.ICGtesting.com
Printed in the USA
BVHW072025260720
584563BV00002B/245